TRADERS IN A BRAV

Ranga Kay
28th May 96.

TRADERS IN A
BRAVE NEW WORLD

The Uruguay Round and the Future of
The International Trading System

Ernest H. Preeg

THE UNIVERSITY OF CHICAGO PRESS
Chicago and London

ERNEST H. PREEG holds the William M. Scholl Chair in International Business at the Center for Strategic and International Studies in Washington, D.C. He has served as ambassador to Haiti, as chief economist at the Agency for International Development, and as a delegate to the Kennedy and Uruguay rounds of GATT.

THE UNIVERSITY OF CHICAGO PRESS, CHICAGO 60637
THE UNIVERSITY OF CHICAGO PRESS, LTD., LONDON
©1995 by The University of Chicago
All rights reserved. Published 1995
Printed in the United States of America
04 03 02 01 00 99 98 97 96 95   1 2 3 4 5
ISBN: 0-226-67959-4 (cloth)

Library of Congress Cataloging-in-Publication Data

Preeg, Ernest H.
    Traders in a brave new world : the Uruguay Round and the future of the international trading system / Ernest H. Preeg.
        p. cm.
    Includes bibliographical references and index.
    1. Uruguay Round (1987–)   2. General Agreement on Tariffs and Trade (Organization)   3. International trade.   I. Title.
HF1721.P7324   1995
382'.92—dc20
                                                                    95-18585
                                                                         CIP

⊗The paper used in this publication meets the minimum requirements of the American National Standard for Information Sciences—Permanence of Paper for Printed Library Materials, ANSI Z39.48-1984.

MIRANDA: O, wonder!

How many goodly creatures are there here!

How beauteous mankind is! O brave new world,

That has such people in 't!

PROSPERO: 'Tis new to thee.

Shakespeare, *The Tempest*

Contents

....

Appendixes

Preface

This work is akin to a biography of the Uruguay Round of multilateral trade negotiations. The round had a lengthy, thirteen-year life from the initial call to action by U.S. Trade Representative William Brock in May 1981 until the final signing ceremony in Marrakesh, Morocco, on April 15, 1994. It was without question the grandest event in commercial diplomatic history, with 117 participants and a wide-ranging agenda. It also produced the most important trade agreement ever, which not only provides a major stimulus to world income and trade but will have a decisive impact on the changing structure of global economic relationships as well.

As in most lives, time and circumstance tempered early aspirations. The original goals were less than fully achieved, and new issues rose to prominence during the negotiations. The Canadian proposal to create a new World Trade Organization (WTO), for example, came relatively late in the game, in 1990, but this institutional upgrading of trade and related policies will have far-reaching effects on the extent to which governments accept multilateral rules for the conduct of trade policy. The Uruguay Round also had a complex life, whose meaning transcends the legal language of the final agreement. In important respects, the agreement reflects compromise derived from competing national trade interests, and numerous markers were laid down for moving forward later on less than definitive Uruguay Round results. This study attempts to shed analytic light and to provide political perspective on the heavily negotiated 424-page final text.

The art of biography, moreover, is to place the protagonist in a broader historic setting and to assess the interaction. The Uruguay Round, in this sense, was both a cause and an effect of a fundamental transformation of the world trading system that took place during the decade of the 1980s. That transformation occurred within an even more momentous political context that led to the abrupt end of the cold war. It was not a sudden or dramatic reordering as was the case, for example, for the Smoot-Hawley tariff in 1930, which unleashed a worldwide protectionist binge, or for the creation of the postwar Bretton Woods system, including the General Agreement on Tariffs and Trade (GATT). The transformation of the 1980s, in contrast, was evolutionary in character, with various interacting forces influencing the outcome. The Uruguay Round was at the center of this process of change as an attempt to reassert the primacy of the GATT multilateral system over strong tendencies toward inward-directed economic nationalism and regional trading blocs. The round was only intermittently the dominant factor, however, and at times proceeded tentatively, buffeted by events elsewhere. As for the broader political setting, the astonishing collapse of the Soviet Union influenced the final phase of the Uruguay Round, to both positive and negative effect.

Finally, there is the task of evaluating the impact of the oeuvre for the future. The international trade agenda for the remainder of the 1990s will be determined to a large extent by what was accomplished and not accomplished in the Uruguay Round. The agreement provides a strengthened foundation of multilateral commitments, but further steps to open markets and broaden the competence of the WTO will be forthcoming. The overall agenda for the new trade order, in any event, has become essentially three-track in concept, consisting of further multilateral commitments, expanded regional free trade agreements, and selective bilateral accords. The three tracks will continue to evolve during the 1990s, and the primacy of the multilateral WTO track is by no means assured. The overarching question, which is left for the final chapter, is toward what longer-term order of economic relationships should these three tracks be converging.

The structure of the presentation is relatively straightforward. Chapter 1 introduces four principal developments that worked to transform the trading system during the 1980s, establishing the broader global setting noted above. The prologue and chapters 2–7 present the historical account of the Uruguay Round, generally in chronological form but with "topical addenda" inserted at appropriate points, which provide more unified, in-depth discussions of five key issues, namely trade in services, protection of intellectual property, agriculture, GATT institutional reform, and trade and the environment. Chapter 8 contains a summary and critique of the final agreement, and chapter 9, building on the results of the Uruguay Round, lays out a trade agenda for the remainder of the 1990s. The final chapter is a more speculative commentary on the political underpinnings and longer-term prospects for the brave new world economic order.

One note on nomenclature regards the name change of the European Community (EC) to the European Union in November 1993. This book retains the EC appellation up to the time of change, in keeping with the contemporary usage.

My personal relationship with the course of events recounted has been long and varied. While on sabbatical from government service in 1983–1984, I edited and contributed to a volume of papers entitled *Hard Bargaining Ahead: U.S. Trade Relations with Developing Countries*, which was a critique of the frustrated U.S. attempt to launch a new round at the GATT ministerial meeting of November 1982. Back in government, I was a member of the U.S. delegation to the Punta del Este meeting that launched the Uruguay Round in September 1986, and I participated in support of the round over the ensuing two years, principally with respect to U.S. negotiating objectives vis-à-vis developing countries. I joined the Center for Strategic & International Studies (CSIS) in the summer of 1988 to conduct an evaluation of U.S. interests in the GATT as the Uruguay Round reached its mid-point, which resulted in *The American Challenge in World Trade*. As an accredited journalist writing commentary on the round, I attended the ministerial meetings in Montreal in November 1988 and in Brussels in December 1990, then continued, with Ahabian determination, to track events as the negotiations—as well as this book—extended three years beyond their scheduled conclusions.

I also note a longer perspective on the GATT trading system dating back to the Kennedy Round of 1963–1967, during which time I was a member of the U.S. delegation, and after which I wrote an analytic history of that round entitled *Traders and Diplomats*. This current work has some similarities of structure with the earlier effort, and the prolonged U.S.-EC struggle over trade in agriculture during the Uruguay Round had a nostalgic, *déjà vu* character. But inferences of a sequel relationship should not be overdrawn. The brave old world order of the 1960s was greatly different, contained—if not quaint—in comparison to the tumultuous panoply of trade interests engaged today. And the current author is "an older, other person," distinct from the more ideologically committed earlier chronicler. Indeed, the contrast between old and new orders in world trade has much to do with a generational change of outlook with respect to the ideal of a universal, nondiscriminatory trading system of equally participating sovereign states, the ultimate GATT system. From the perspective of this older person, the prospect for achieving such an ideal order, at this time, appears far more clouded. Perhaps it is being overtaken by the rapid pace of events, and certainly it is more contingent on deliberate choices yet to be confronted. The Uruguay Round experience, in broadest terms, provides much of the foundation for defining such future contingencies for world trade.

I want to acknowledge the generous financial support provided for this project by the Ford and Dr. Scholl Foundations. The many individuals who assisted during the several years of preparation—from providing background materials and reading manuscripts to extended brain-picking—are too numerous to list, and I simply wish to extend my deepest thanks to all. I do note the special courtesy afforded me at the GATT archives, an invaluable source of documentation for the round. I also owe special thanks to those senior negotiators and members of the GATT secretariat who read through and commented on the lengthy draft manuscript during the busy spring of 1994. I was able to interview about twenty-five such participants, almost all non-Americans, during a trip to Europe in April and a similar number of Americans in Washington, including participants in a rousing day-long group session at CSIS in May, which brought back memories for Uruguay Round veterans covering the entire period 1981–94. Dedicated support was provided by successive research assistants Sam Armstrong, Jonathan Levine, and Chris Chivvis, and equally dedicated secretarial support came from Constance Kaczka, Maya Rao, and Bobbi Kahlow. Last and most, my wife, Sally, who was more directly engaged in the earlier Kennedy Round book, again contributed the needed ingredients of encouragement, understanding, and love.

Prologue: Rendezvous at Punta

Saturday, September 13, 1986. Andrews Air Force Base was still dark when cars began depositing their passengers at the VIP lounge next to an idling U.S. Air Force executive jet. The travelers included three U.S. cabinet members— Trade Representative Clayton Yeutter, Secretary of Commerce Malcolm Baldrige, and Secretary of Agriculture Richard Lyng—two dozen senior officials from various agencies, and a few journalists who had paid the premium fare for enhanced access to the official party. The plane departed at 7:00 A.M. for Punta del Este, Uruguay, carrying the leaders of the U.S. delegation to a ministerial level meeting of the General Agreement on Tariffs and Trade (GATT) that would launch the most ambitious undertaking ever to broaden and strengthen the world trading system.

The agenda for the Punta meeting was laden with contentious issues, and the outcome was uncertain. On the eve of the conference, President Ronald Reagan warned that "the mutually destructive practice of subsidizing agricultural exports" had created an "intolerable" situation: "We expect to have it corrected."[1] The commissioner for external relations of the European Community (EC), Willy de Clercq, wryly commented that the American approach "over-concentrates on the issue of subsidies."[2] The transatlantic discord on farm trade was a twenty-five-year-old stalemate about to be reengaged.

Distinguishing this eighth "round" of GATT multilateral trade negotiations, however, was the critical role of developing countries. Past rounds had resulted in agreements predominantly among the industrialized countries of North America, Western Europe, and Japan, with the many poorer countries left to a passive role. Now the structure of world trade was changing fundamentally. The more advanced, or newly industrializing, countries of Asia and Latin America had become highly competitive exporters of manufactured goods, but they were not generally bound by GATT rules. Developing countries, in turn, faced a growing maze of quota restrictions in industrialized-country markets. The GATT was thus becoming less and less relevant to rapidly growing trade between industrialized and developing countries, and the new round of negotiations would be the decisive test to restore its credibility.

The U.S. plane landed at Manaus, Brazil, for refueling. The lush Amazon

1

jungle setting symbolized the immense untapped resources of the developing world, and the modern military facilities were a reminder of the past special relationship between Brazil and the United States. But as the official party lingered in the passenger lounge, word got back that takeoff was delayed because hard currency payment for the fuel had not been fully confirmed. The plane finally resumed its flight, but the prolonged stop was a harbinger of the coming years of U.S.-Brazilian haggling over almost every issue of substance in the GATT negotiations—the new special relationship.

)(

Punta del Este is a beach resort of elegant homes where the wealthy of Buenos Aires spend summer weekends. September, however, is still late winter in Punta, and chilling winds greeted the two thousand delegates from seventy-two countries. The conference convened in the cramped facilities of the Victorian-style San Rafael hotel. Several hundred representatives of the media occupied a makeshift tent that almost blew away on the second day of the conference. Hotels opened early to receive delegates, but some rooms were without heat. Service, while uniformly friendly, was less than full.

No passing inconveniences, however, detracted from the warm, almost euphoric atmosphere of the opening session on September 15. Foreign Minister Tadashi Kuranari of Japan, representing the host country of the preceding Tokyo Round, proposed that this one be called the Uruguay Round. He then introduced the Uruguayan hosts, President Julio Maria Sanguinetti and Foreign Minister Enrique Iglesias, the conference chair. Iglesias set the tone for the conference: "A gathering of this kind does not occur often. . . . It constitutes . . . a recognition of the historical importance of the task before us. An attempt is being made to confront at the same time—and possibly for the first time in GATT's history—the shortcomings of the past with the challenges of the future."[3]

The 1980s were indeed turbulent for world trade, and at this midpoint the outlook was mixed. The decade opened with the world economy in the throes of the second oil shock. The United States tightened monetary policy to stifle inflation, which induced a severe recession with global repercussions. Many developing countries, especially in Latin America, had accumulated large external debts, which could not be serviced with the high interest rates prevailing in the early 1980s. World trade declined in 1982 for the first time since the 1930s.

The decade of the 1980s, however, was also a period of economic restructuring, with increased emphasis on private-sector-driven growth and open trade. The U.S. recovery, beginning in 1982, led the way to a burgeoning Asia-

Pacific economy and phenomenal export-led growth in East Asia. Developing countries elsewhere were reevaluating the traditional economic strategy of high protection and a predominant state role in the economy. A market-oriented development strategy was more compatible with the principles underlying the GATT trading system. Barber Conable, president of the World Bank, elaborated in his plenary statement on September 15: "Countries that have been highly active in international trade, adopting outward-oriented development strategies, have had a much better economic performance than those that have tried to develop behind protectionist barriers. In other words, economic inefficiency is the price of protection, and in this sense trade liberalization is the handmaiden of efficient development."[4]

The changing attitudes of developing countries within the GATT had become apparent in the months leading up to the Punta del Este meeting. The longstanding developing-country bloc had split. The Preparatory Committee, after ten laborious sessions, ended by forwarding two draft ministerial declarations to the Punta conference. The first was supported by a coalition of forty-eight industrialized and developing countries led by Switzerland and Colombia, the G-48, which proposed an ambitious agenda to liberalize trade and broaden the mandate of the GATT. The second draft declaration—proposed by ten hard-line developing countries, the G-10, led by India and Brazil—contained a far more restrictive scope for the negotiations.

The split in the solidarity of developing countries was fundamental not only for the ensuing Uruguay Round negotiations but as a signal of the shift in economic philosophy taking place in the world, which would gain dramatic momentum by the end of the decade. The country divisions between the G-48 and the G-10 were revealing. Latin America was split down the middle with Chile, Colombia, Jamaica, Mexico, Trinidad and Tobago, and Uruguay in the G-48, while Argentina, Brazil, Cuba, Nicaragua, and Peru were among the hard-liners. Among Asian nations, India was alone in the G-10, while ten East and South Asian countries were among the strongest supporters of the G-48 draft.

)(

By the second day of the conference, while ministerial statements continued in plenary session, serious negotiations began in smaller group meetings. Some peripheral issues were dealt with quickly, although they would reemerge before the round ended. In late August the Soviet Union had requested observer status in the GATT, including a presence in the Uruguay Round, but its bid was shunted aside, based on the categoric U.S. assessment that the Soviet economy was incompatible with the GATT trading system.

The U.S. initiative to include international labor standards on the Uruguay Round agenda was also dropped in the face of near unanimous opposition.

A more sensitive issue was the EC "balance of benefits" proposal (BOB) to withhold Uruguay Round benefits to trade surplus countries whose markets were not sufficiently open. It was clearly directed at Japan and other competitive Asian exporters, and EC representatives joked that a better rendering of BOB was "bash the oriental bastards." The response of the Japanese representative was uncharacteristically sharp, lamenting "Japan bashing" with "racial undertones" and commenting that bilateral trade restrictions against Japan may have caused World War II.[5] The United States sided with Japan on the grounds that the ministerial statement should not be directed at individual countries, which was decisive in defeating the EC proposal. This trans-Pacific solidarity raised concerns among Europeans of an emerging Asia-Pacific alliance against Europe, but in fact the BOB concept later became an even more contentious U.S.-Japanese bilateral issue outside the GATT.

The major issues of the Punta meeting were agriculture and the three "new issues," namely trade in services, protection of intellectual property, and trade-related investment measures. The United States was determined to achieve a major reduction in trade-distorting farm-support programs, and the principal target was the European Community. The specific objectives were increased access to the European market for farm products and, even more important, the phasing out of export subsidies, which went to the heart of the European Common Agricultural Policy (CAP).

The U.S. assault on the EC farm policy was strongly supported by a group of fourteen agricultural exporting countries, the Cairns group, which had first met in Cairns, Australia, a month earlier. U.S. secretary of agriculture Lyng and Australian minister John Dawkins alternated demands on EC commissioner de Clercq and his European colleagues that explicit objectives for agricultural negotiations be inscribed in the ministerial declaration. Lengthy sessions of the agricultural group dragged on from Tuesday through Thursday, which both sides viewed as initial skirmishes.

The three new issues were aimed at broadening the GATT mandate to include the increasingly integrated relationships between trade in goods, services, investment, and technology. They reflected the changing realities of the international economy and the consequent declining relevance of the existing GATT, given its limited mandate to trade in goods. They were also issues principally between industrialized and developing countries, since the latter had long resisted international commitments in these politically sensitive policy areas.

The specific objectives of Punta del Este were distinct among the three issues. Delegates broadly agreed that trade in services needed to be brought within some international framework, but the G-10 opposed linking services to the GATT. Protection of intellectual property was more controversial in concept. Some developing countries viewed patent rights for multinational companies as unjustifiable monopoly profits, and India led the opposition to any international commitments for intellectual property. Investment issues, in turn, became more narrowly targeted on developing-country practices of placing performance requirements on foreign investment, such as minimum domestic content and export targets.

Initial small group negotiations on these three issues were more dispersed and less coordinated than talks on agriculture. Indian finance minister V. P. Singh, who would come and go as prime minister during the course of the Uruguay Round, declared the proposal to hold negotiations on services in the GATT as "untenable" and related it to the "long struggle against colonial rule," but he was little engaged in the detailed talks.[6] The seasoned Brazilian negotiator Paulo Batista firmly opposed the G-48 positions on all three fronts. Shortly before the Punta meeting, the EC had violated G-48 solidarity by formulating compromises with the G-10, which infuriated the Americans, but officially returned to the fold as the ministerial deliberations got under way. There were, in fact, differences of view within the EC. France was most eager to accommodate the hard-line developing countries, with support from the Commission, which, at times, exceeded its mandate from member states. This led to an unusual public rebuke of a commission negotiator by a member state minister during the opening formal reception by President Sanguinetti.

Reconciling the G-48 text, which had broadened support to about sixty participants by the start of the conference, and the G-10 text required a tactical choice. Conference leaders from both sides could negotiate compromise language throughout, or the majority of G-48 members could hold firm, ceding only minimum changes to the minority group. GATT Director-General Arthur Dunkel attempted the former course in quiet talks with members of the G-10 away from the conference site, but he was deluged with over a hundred amendments to the G-48 text and quickly abandoned his initiative. Most of the G-48 group, in fact, arrived at Punta confident that they had the numbers and the momentum to prevail. As the conference proceeded, however, some Asian and Latin American developing countries among the G-48 became concerned that the United States was secretly making substantial concessions to Brazil and India to save the conference, leaving them isolated and embarrassed. At one point, General Lee Hsien Loong, head of the Singapore delegation, angrily stalked out of a G-48 caucus meeting. The decisive participant, as in past GATT negotiations, was the United States, and by Thursday conflicting signals were circulating in the corridors of the San Rafael hotel.

)(

There were seventy-five members of the U.S. delegation: the three cabinet members, fifty-eight others from the executive branch, nine corporate leaders, two labor representatives, two farm organization officials, and one member of the Congress. Private sector leaders, such as James Robinson, chairman of the American Express Company, and Edmund Pratt, chairman of Pfizer Corporation, highlighted U.S. priority interests in trade in services and protection of intellectual property. Director Rudolph Oswald of the AFL-CIO commented that the labor representatives were there "as the heavies to complain about the $150 billion trade deficit and the two million jobs lost."[7]

Concern about the unprecedented U.S. trade deficit was not limited to labor, however, and was a major driving force at the Punta conference. A front-page story in the September 19 New York Times predicted a deficit approaching $200 billion for 1986. It quoted Federal Reserve Board chairman Paul Volcker, describing "deep fissures in the world economy," and investment banker Robert Hormats, warning that trade imbalances "are threatening economic disaster." Congress was busily drafting protectionist legislation in Washington, while its lone member at Punta, free trader William Frenzel, commented that while Congress did not have high expectations for the conference, success could help cool protectionist sentiment.[8] Political frustration over the trade deficit and waning confidence that GATT could maintain open markets constituted a central challenge for all trading nations at Punta del Este.

Clayton Yeutter had articulated in detail U.S. objectives for the conference the previous week in a speech before the U.S. Chamber of Commerce in Washington: "As currently constituted, GATT does not address many of the realities of modern trade. . . . Many Americans look at our $150 billion trade deficit and at the growing use of subsidies, non-tariff barriers and other GATT illegal practices throughout the world and wonder why we are still a signatory of the GATT." As for specifics, "the escalating pattern of protectionism in agriculture must be reversed." The three new issues were similarly highlighted. In a warning to India and Brazil, Yeutter stated that "nations that engaged in three or four percent of the world's trade cannot be allowed to jeopardize the future of the world trade system."[9]

During the first three days of the conference, members of the large U.S.

delegation received specific functional or country assignments to develop support for U.S. positions. Secretary Lyng led effort in agriculture and Secretary Baldrige in intellectual property. Private-sector representatives and Congressman Frenzel worked full time in small meetings and over meals to emphasize that the conference outcome would significantly affect attitudes about trade policy in the United States. Yeutter and his deputy, Michael Smith, orchestrated the overall U.S. effort while participating in the almost continuous meetings of a core group of senior representatives chaired by Iglesias.

Despite the intense diplomatic activity, delegates made little progress in resolving principal differences through Friday morning, and the conference was scheduled to conclude Saturday morning. Clayton Yeutter appeared determined to reach a mutually satisfactory agreement with India and Brazil, even if that involved significant compromise, which was a growing concern not only of other G-48 delegates but of some U.S. delegates as well. Toward midnight Friday, Yeutter convened senior members of his delegation to discuss tactics for the final all-night negotiating session. The consistent advice was to hold firm on all key issues since Brazil appeared inclined to be helpful while India was more and more isolated. Smith, the acerbic veteran trade negotiator, later commented: "I would not have been as genteel as Clayton. I would have rooted the Brazilians out and read Batista the riot act. . . . I thought we had a chance to stomp on India and Brazil and took issue with Clayton on that."[10]

)(

The all-night negotiation of September 19–20 in fact was a more or less complete stomp on the hard-line group, and the final ministerial declaration was close to the original G-48 draft.

Early in the evening, the U.S.-EC impasse on agriculture had been resolved. The arrival of French agriculture minister François Guillaume on Thursday opened a more definitive stage of the discussions. Within the EC, German minister for economy Martin Bangemann and United Kingdom trade minister Paul Channon, who also represented the EC presidency, pressed for a more forthcoming response. The EC position was vulnerable in that there was no concrete counterproposal, but simply a negation of the U.S. and Cairns group proposals. The categoric warnings of President Reagan and Trade Representative Yeutter, as well as protectionist sentiment in the U.S. Congress, constituted a real threat to a continental economy diagnosed as suffering from "Euro-sclerosis." The final agreed language called for "the reduction of import barriers" and "increasing discipline on the use of all direct and indirect subsidies . . . including the phased reduction of their negative effects." The Americans had originally proposed explicit reference to export subsidies, but there was no doubt that "all direct and indirect subsidies" included export subsidies. The three new issues were resolved seriatim. Talks on trade-in-services had narrowed down to organization of the negotiations. Brazil and India wanted services kept entirely separate from other parts of the Uruguay Round and indeed from any linkage with the GATT, while the G-48 position sought an integrated negotiation that would tie the final results for trade in goods to those for services. In short, talks focused on single- versus dual-track negotiations, and Friday morning discussions broke off over this issue. By evening, however, the EC had offered a compromise proposing two separate negotiations, one for trade in goods and the other for services, with both tracks coming together at the end of the day. The Americans tightened the linkage by proposing that both negotiating groups report to the senior-level Trade Negotiations Committee (TNC), chaired by Iglesias and GATT director-general Arthur Dunkel. The whole process would be supported by the GATT secretariat.

This compromise proposal amounted to little more than a procedural face saving for the G-10, but when Clayton Yeutter accepted it late into the night Friday, he claimed it as a show of flexibility by the United States and then proceeded to take an adamant stand on trade-related investment measures, asking for corresponding flexibility from others. There had been widespread talk, which included U.S. delegates, that investment issues would be relegated to further study, the kiss of death for the duration of the Uruguay Round. Now, however, Yeutter held firm, insisting that such measures be subject to negotiation to avoid "adverse affects on trade." Brazil and India acquiesced, flexibility reciprocated.

Yeutter, having expended his political capital, then left the room, leaving the last issue, protection of intellectual property, to Secretary Baldrige. The taciturn, former businessman was a formidable interlocutor at 4 A.M., and delegates finally agreed to negotiate new rules and disciplines for intellectual property rights as they affected trade, including a multilateral framework for international trade in counterfeit goods.

The major elements of an ambitious mandate for the Uruguay Round were thus in place as dawn broke September 20 over the eastern point, Punta del Este.

)(

The ministerial declaration had other important provisions, principally concerning what developing countries wanted from the industrialized countries: liberalization of trade in textiles and apparel, stringent limitations on the use

of quota restrictions in other sectors, and reduced barriers for tropical products. All were included within the Uruguay Round mandate.

A particularly contentious issue was "standstill and rollback," which was an
immediate commitment not to undertake new trade restrictions inconsistent
with the GATT and to phase out such existing restrictions during the course
of the Uruguay Round. The target was the growing use of informal import
quotas and "voluntary" export restraints against developing-country exports.
The industrialized countries accepted explicit language on standstill and rollback in the ministerial declaration but later interpreted the language as having little relevance to existing practices, which injected an initial note of discord across the weakening yet still potent North-South divide.

Still other provisions of the declaration included reductions in tariff and
nontariff measures, subsidies and countervailing duty measures, a strengthening of the GATT dispute-settlement mechanism, and improvements in previously negotiated GATT codes and agreements. It added up to the most comprehensive agenda ever adopted and included all of the key issues contained
in the G-48 proposals. Members of the U.S. delegation indulged themselves in
a round of self-congratulation. Secretary Baldrige commented at the final
press conference: "We came down here knowing what we wanted. Our opponents knew what they did not want. Any time you have this situation in a
negotiation, you have an advantage."[11]

The Press also commented favorably concerning the ministerial declaration of intent but remained cautious about the ultimate outcome. The *Financial Times*, in an editorial entitled "Kiss of Life for Gatt," praised the outcome:
"By overcoming deeply felt differences, especially between north and south,
ministers in Punta del Este this week have sent a signal to the world that the
open trading system can be revitalized in such a way as to reinforce, not drag
down, growth and stability in the world economy." Yet it then went on to warn:
"Setting an agenda is one thing: repairing the worn fabric of the Gatt by rewriting the rules and negotiating mutual concessions that will liberalize trade is
another." The *New York Times* was more blunt: "This wholesome start won't
lead to anything, however, unless Congress grants America's delegation the
latitude they need to negotiate. . . . The disposition on Capitol Hill in an election year is blatantly protectionist."[12]

)(

The Punta del Este declaration was indeed a watershed for the world trading
system. Delegates reached a consensus to reinvigorate and broaden its structure to deal with the rapidly changing economic realities of the 1980s and

1990s. The pace of change, however, would continue to challenge the fore-sight of trade negotiators during the ensuing eight years. Economic dichotomy between North and South would fade, between East and West disintegrate. Amazing new technologies applied by multinational companies would pose a fundamental threat to the concept of national economic sovereignty. *Global-ization* would be the catchword for a brave new world of traders and diplomats. A popular anecdote from the Punta meeting recounted the surprise of Chair-man Robinson when the San Rafael hotel did not accept his American Express card, or any other credit card, off season. The incident was nevertheless the passing vestige of a bygone era.

Much credit for the success of the Punta meeting was attributed to its chair-man, Enrique Iglesias, and in many respects he epitomized the groundswell of change that was transforming the world trading system. His patience and diplomatic skills in bringing together key delegates in informal sessions brought him unanimous praise. Clayton Yeutter commented that he "led the conference masterfully."[13] Iglesias summarized his role as "fighting not so much for words but a climate of understanding," and fostering "the need for reality."[14] The forty-six-year-old economist and banker, however, had not al-ways been the liberal trade advocate he was at Punta. He had been best known as the longtime executive director of the U. N. Economic Commission for Latin American, the citadel of the protectionist import substitution model for economic development. At Punta, in contrast, he championed a greatly strengthened GATT trading system, and he would go on to become president of the Inter-American Development Bank, dedicated to market-oriented pol-icy reform. It was the new economic man Iglesias who presided at Punta.

The struggle between rapidly changing economic realities and the legacy of protracted legalistic negotiating procedures within the GATT would also be a continuing challenge for the political leadership of Uruguay Round partici-pants. GATT negotiating tradition prevailed at the close of the Punta confer-ence on Saturday morning, September 20. Brazil, with the support of the EC, insisted that the chairman close the meeting with two gavels, one for goods and one for services, a final attempt to revive the dual-track approach. The Americans argued strenuously for one gavel for the entire ministerial declara-tion. Discussion became heated, and sleepy delegates were beginning to leave to catch flights home when a sensible adviser asked, "Why not have three?" And so the Punta del Este meeting ended with three resounding blows of Enrique Iglesias's gavel.[15]

The Decade That Transformed World Trade

The 1980s was a decade of transformation for the world trading system. The experience can be summarized as an apparent paradox: Just as international trade relationships were becoming truly global, the liberal trading system of multilateral rules and commitments—the GATT—was losing relevance and credibility. In fact, the process of change was less a paradox than an irony of historic circumstance. Markets were integrating throughout the world, but at an uneven pace by region and by sector. The GATT system, in parallel, lacked the flexibility and political support to respond fully to the new circumstances. Initiative was shifting to regional free trade agreements, bilateral negotiations, and unilateral trade liberalization.

In this context, the Uruguay Round was intended to bolster waning credibility in the GATT structure through renewed multilateral trade liberalization and a broadened institutional mandate. The GATT had been established in 1948 as an interim set of commitments by twenty-three nations, pending adoption of a broadly based, permanent International Trade Organization. When the ITO failed ratification, the thirty-five articles of the GATT became the only multilateral basis for governing world trading practices. Article I establishes the principle of most-favored-nation (MFN) treatment, or nondiscrimination among trading partners. Other articles call for the use of tariffs rather than quotas where import protection is necessary and for the avoidance of export subsidies. GATT members negotiated progressive liberalization of trade during a series of "rounds," whereby tariffs were reduced on a reciprocal basis and were "bound" against future increase. In the seven GATT rounds that preceded the Uruguay Round, tariffs on manufactured products in the industrialized countries were reduced dramatically from an average of 40 percent in 1948 to about 6 percent in 1980.

The GATT commitments, however, had always been limited principally to trade restrictions at the border, while other policies affecting trade increased in relative importance as tariffs were reduced. Trade in basic agricultural commodities and in services were not generally covered by GATT rules. Developing countries, which came to constitute a majority of GATT membership, were exempted from binding GATT commitments, while trade with centrally planned communist countries was irrelevant to GATT market-oriented principles. Unless the GATT mandate could be broadened to encompass these various trade relationships, they would be addressed outside the GATT, which was precisely what was happening in the early 1980s.

The transformation of world trade relationships that took place during the 1980s—and continues to evolve in the 1990s—was a complex process, consisting of numerous developments, some emanating from the private sector and others from governments. Four central developments of particular consequence for the Uruguay Round are introduced here and developed more fully in subsequent chapters as they interacted with the course of the negotiations.

Global Market Integration

During the 1980s two underlying and related forces greatly deepened the integration of markets across national borders. The first was a surge in technological innovation centered on the information technology sector. The application of microelectronics-based technologies—which dates from the introduction of the transistor in the 1950s—gathered momentum during the 1980s, with sweeping impact on various sectors of economic activity, national and international. The second force was increasing private-sector initiative to operate on an international if not global scale. Corporations adjusted strategies to ever-wider market horizons. The reduced cost of communication and transportation resulting from applied new technologies facilitated the process. Broader markets were required to support large investments for new technology development and state-of-the-art production facilities. Economic gains from vertical integration between high-wage industrialized countries and the low-wage "newly industrialized" nations of Asia and Latin America created pressures to internationalize. Those that failed to do so risked losing competitiveness. As a consequence, international trade, investment, and technology transfer, in terms of corporate strategies and government policies, became more deeply interrelated, and the term *trading system* took on a correspondingly broader meaning as well.

This process of market integration is most readily apparent in the growth of trade relative to world income. Table 1.1 illustrates that trade in goods grew twice as fast as world income from 1983 to 1993, the decade following the global recession of 1981–82. Comparable figures are not available for growth of trade in services, but since the mid-1980s, services trade in value grew faster than trade in goods, thereby increasing the trade dependency of na-

12

TABLE 1.1: Growth in the Volume of World Merchandise (percent increase)

	Exports	Output
1983	2.5	2.0
1984	8.5	7.0
1985	3.5	3.0
1986	4.5	2.5
1987	5.5	3.0
1988	8.5	4.5
1989	7.0	3.3
1990	4.9	2.0
1991	3.1	0.0
1992	4.0	1.0
1993	2.9	2.0
Cumulative	70.5	34.6

Source: International Trade: Statistics (Geneva: GATT) 1989–93.

tional economies at an even faster pace. In 1993 world exports of goods and services together amounted to 21 percent of world income.

International direct investment also grew faster than income. From 1980 to 1993, investment grew by over 11 percent per year globally, in current dollars, to a total stock of $2.1 trillion in 1993. Yet another dimension of the integration process has been a rapid increase in various forms of corporate alliances, from joint ventures to technology sharing to marketing arrangements, particularly for technology-intensive industries. For example, the number of technology cooperation agreements worldwide in the biotechnology, information technology, and new materials sectors increased from 317 in 1975–79 to 2,629 in 1985–89.[1]

As a consequence of this trade/investment/technology-driven market integration, trade in the manufacturing and service sectors has become preponderant, reinforcing a longer-term trend. Table 1.2 shows that exports of agricultural products and nonagricultural raw materials have been in secular decline since the 1960s. By 1992 they accounted for only 13 percent and 3 percent of world exports of goods, respectively. Mineral fuels—principally petroleum—fluctuated, reflecting swings in petroleum prices, and have settled in the 10 percent range since the late 1980s. In contrast, exports of manufactures reached new highs of over 70 percent by the early 1990s and 75 percent in 1992. Statistics for exports of services are not available for the earlier years, but the GATT Secretariat estimated world exports of commercial services at

13

TABLE 1.2 Sectoral Share of World Exports of Goods
(percent)

	1963	1970	1980	1985	1990	1992
Manufactures	54	62	55	63	72	75
Mineral fuels	10	10	25	19	11	9
Agricultural products	29	21	15	14	13	13
Nonagricultural raw materials	7	7	5	4	4	3

Sources: Monthly Bulletin of Statistics (New York: United Nations, 1963–85); International Trade: Statistics (Geneva: GATT, 1990, 1992).

$1 trillion in 1992, compared with $3.7 trillion for trade in goods. Combining goods and services for 1992, the sectoral shares were manufactures 58 percent, services 22 percent, agriculture 10 percent, mineral fuels 7 percent, and nonagricultural raw materials 3 percent.

Policy responses to this deepening market integration have been wide ranging and for the most part accommodating. Some involve steps toward comprehensive regional free trade, and others have been more selective at the bilateral level or have been unilateral in terms of structural reform programs. The multilateral policy response came through the Uruguay Round, the subject of most of what follows, but one important example at the outset of the challenge facing the GATT is that of the telecommunications sector.

Telecommunications constitute the economic infrastructure of an emerging information-based society. The sector brings together trade in goods and services, absorbs large amounts of international investment, and relies on the application of rapidly evolving new technologies. GATT commitments in the telecommunications sector in the mid 1980s, however, were very limited. Trade in telecommunications equipment had been included in GATT negotiations to lower tariffs, but such equipment was purchased principally by government monopolies through public procurement practices that often precluded or greatly restricted imported products. The Tokyo round included a GATT procurement code, but industrialized participants to the code mostly excluded the telecommunications sector while developing countries refused even to adopt the code. The most rapid growth in the telecommunications sector occurred in applied services, which were not part of the GATT mandate. The same exclusion prevailed for increasingly complex intellectual-property rights. Wide-ranging government subsidies, trade-related performance requirements for foreign investment, and technical standards fell within the GATT mandate, but the existing provisions and codes were too general to have significance.

This uneasy yet quiescent situation—a not very relevant GATT for the telecommunications sector—was jolted in 1984, when the United States dramatically broke up and privatized AT&T. This action immediately produced asymmetry in market access between a U.S. market very open to imports, which promptly began to flow in, and publicly controlled foreign markets not generally accessible to U.S. exports of telecommunications goods and services. In terms of the conceptual underpinnings of the GATT trading system, the new situation involved the relationship between the explicit provision of most-favored-nation treatment and the implicit assumption of reasonably comparable market access among major trading partners—"reciprocity" for short. The MFN/reciprocity relationship in the telecommunications sector would become a major issue of contention in the Uruguay Round and in related negotiations outside the GATT, and continues following the round. It also cuts across all of the dimensions of the global market-integration process—trade, investment, and technology issues—for an industry that is itself central to generating such integration.

The Tripolarization of Industrial Development

The globalization of world markets under way during the 1980s was uneven geographically and tended to accelerate a tripolarization of industrial development in Western Europe, North America, and East Asia. A dominant tripolar relationship in the world economy has been the subject of extensive analysis at least since the early 1970s. The Trilateral Commission of distinguished leaders and scholars was formed in 1973 to foster cooperative approaches to economic issues within the three-cornered industrialized grouping. Books and articles proliferated.[2] During the 1980s, however, the tripolar relationship deepened considerably and took on more distinctive regional characteristics in terms of both market organization and policy orientation.

The deepening tripolar character of would trade is shown in table 1.3. Between 1980 and 1990, the share of world imports "within the poles"—that is within Western Europe, North America, and East Asia—increased from 40 to 49 percent; imports among the poles also increased in market share, from 19 to 27 percent. All other trade, between the three industrialized centers and other parts of the world—including Central and South America, South Asia, Africa, the Middle East, the former Soviet Union and Eastern Europe—as well as among these other parts of the world, dropped sharply as a share of world

TABLE 1.3: The Tripolarization of World Trade
(percent of world imports of goods)

	1980	1990	1993
Within the three poles			
OECD Europe	28.0	33.2	31.0
North America	5.9	6.5	7.5
East Asia[a]	6.1	9.5	11.2
Subtotal (within)	40.0	49.2	49.7
Among the three poles			
Europe–North America	7.7	8.0	7.2
East Asia–North America	7.1	10.5	11.1
Europe–East Asia	4.6	8.0	7.5
Subtotal (among)	19.4	26.5	25.8
All other	40.6	24.3	24.5

Source: Direction of Trade Statistics Yearbook (Washington, D.C.: IMF, 1981, 1991, June 1994); Foreign Trade Development of the Republic of China (Taiwan: Board of Foreign Trade, 1994).
[a]Japan, South Korea, China, Taiwan, Hong Kong, ASEAN.

trade, from 41 to 25 percent. In other words, by decade's end about half of world trade occurred within the three industrial poles, another quarter took place among the three, and only the remaining quarter accounted for all other countries.

The deepening tripolarization of world trade reflected to some extent the regional orientation of corporate strategies. Trade growth was concentrated in the manufacturing and service sectors, often related to new investment projects and intra-firm shipments of components. Multinational companies increasingly pursued investment-led market strategies both within the three regions, to establish market presence and circumvent protectionist policies, and across the regions, to rationalize production and capture economies of scale.

In broadest terms and evident in all three regions, the tripolarization process involved two interacting dimensions—a market-driven deepening of trade and investment dependencies based on existing policy frameworks and the adoption of more integrated regional policies by governments. The two dimensions were mutually reinforcing. Deepening private sector dependencies created pressures for a more integrated policy relationship among regional trading partners, while most regional policy initiatives, by definition, encouraged still deeper dependencies. The form of this market-force–policy-initiative interaction, however, was distinctive in each of the three regions.

The West European grouping is the most deeply integrated of the three in both trade dependencies and policy framework. The share of exports to other West European countries has risen steadily, exceeding 70 percent by 1992. The European Community was a customs union for three decades and has had free trade agreements with members of the European Free Trade Association (EFTA). Bold EC initiatives of the late 1980s to create a unified internal market by 1992—the EC-92 program—and to establish a single currency will ultimately bring the now European Union members into almost complete economic and monetary union. A broadening of the regional grouping toward a "common European space" gathered momentum that has led to full Union membership for most EFTA countries and association or free trade arrangements with East European and other neighboring countries. Further deepening and broadening of the European trading bloc during the 1990s seems likely, with the ratio of internal to external trade rising to 3:1 or higher.[3]

A North American trade bloc took definitive shape during the 1980s and is distinctive in its asymmetric trade dependencies. Canada and Mexico are highly dependent on the U.S. market, in each case for more than 70 percent of total exports by decade's end, while less than 30 percent of corresponding U.S. exports go to its two contiguous neighbors. All three countries, however, recorded an increase in the North American share of total exports during the latter 1980s. The most striking policy development was the change in U.S. policy, long opposed to preferential trading arrangements, to favor regional free trade. The United States negotiated one-way free trade for imports from Caribbean Basin countries in 1982 and bilateral free trade with Canada in an agreement concluded in 1988. The trilateral U.S.-Canada-Mexico, North American Free Trade Agreement (NAFTA) entered into force in 1994, and similar pacts with other hemispheric countries are anticipated. It is noteworthy that a principal motivation for Canada and Mexico to seek free-trade agreements with the United States was the assessment that export potential in the other two industrialized regions was unpromising. There was a tripolar reinforcement effect in the formation of regional policy frameworks.

The East Asian grouping is the least clearly defined of the three, but it has acquired greater cohesion since the mid-1980s based on extraordinary export-led growth. Currency realignments in 1985–86 to reduce the huge U.S. trade deficit with Asia induced a major shift by Asian exporters toward regional trading partners. From 1985 to 1993, the share of Japanese exports going to the United States declined from 39 percent to 30 percent, while the share to

East Asia increased from 24 percent to 36 percent. Similar shifts took place in South Korea and Taiwan. East Asian regional growth, initially driven by Japanese technological and financial resources, has broadened. By decade's end, South Korea had a net outflow of direct investment, and Greater China—China, Taiwan, Hong Kong, and overseas ethnic Chinese—is progressively challenging Japanese primacy in investment and trade throughout the region. A regional policy framework is far more limited in East Asia, however, than in Western Europe and North America. Free trade agreements exist only between Australia and New Zealand and, in the early stages, among the six-member Association of South East Asian Nations (ASEAN). In addition, Japan has substantial regionally oriented financial programs for investment guarantees, export credit, and economic aid for technical assistance and infrastructure projects, which have the effect of giving a strong preferential stimulus to Japanese investment and exports in East Asia. General discussion of a broader East Asian trade grouping has focused on a possible defensive reaction to deepening preferential blocs in Europe and North America, but the lack of political cohesion has inhibited such action.

The outlook for the remainder of the 1990s is for a further deepening and broadening of the tripolar orientation of industrial development in the world economy. New technology development and investment remains overwhelmingly concentrated in these regions. Each is also extending in geographic scope, Europe to the east, North America to the south, and East Asia to all contiguous areas. Whether the three poles drift apart in terms of relative economic dependencies or become more integrated within one large grouping of advanced industrialized countries is a central question that will be determined, to some extent, by policies pursued in the years ahead. There has been a leveling off of tripolar shares of trade from 1990 to 1993 (see table 1.3), but this trend's effect could be largely cyclical. A growing interest in deeper economic ties across the Pacific is embodied in the Asia-Pacific Economic Cooperation (APEC) intergovernmental framework, established in 1989, and in 1994 APEC established a long-term goal of trans-Pacific free trade by 2020. This poses the prospect of an evolving bipolar world economy, with the Asia-Pacific grouping distinct from a European group stretching from the Atlantic to the Urals.

The Triumph of Economic Liberalism

During the 1980s, the ideological dimension to global market integration and various initiatives to reduce trade barriers was the decisive and unexpected triumph of economic liberalism over the two competing ideologies of previous decades, competitions characterized as North/South and East/West. Market-based and private-sector–driven national economies became the undisputed model for economic organization, which, in turn, entailed decentralization of economic power and a more promising basis for political pluralism and democratic government.

In October 1981 President Ronald Reagan attended a summit meeting with twenty-one leaders of industrialized and developing countries in Cancun, Mexico. They intended to launch "global negotiations" within the United Nations on a statist Third World program, including increased official aid, cartels to raise prices of raw materials, and greater power for developing countries in international organizations. The conference cochairman, President José Lopez Portillo of Mexico, deprecated the GATT, IMF, and World Bank, claiming they caused developing countries "deepened resentment and frustration" and tended to be "mere sounding boards" of the industrialized countries.[4] The *New York Times* referred to Reagan's alternative free-market approach for development as "wishful thinking,"[5] but the U.S. president resisted pressures to begin UN controlled global negotiations and stuck with the GATT and other existing institutions as the appropriate negotiating forums. The Cancun meeting turned out to be the last hurrah for the high-profile North/South meetings so prominent during the 1960s and 1970s.

In December 1989 the Berlin wall fell, and within a year the Soviet Union and almost all of the communist countries of Eastern Europe had jettisoned an economic strategy based on central planning for some form of market-oriented approach with emphasis on private-sector initiative.

These two events at the beginning and the end of the decade crystallized the dramatic changes in ideological orientation that took place, but the real story of the 1980s was the demonstration of which economic strategy worked and which didn't. It became increasingly evident that the so-called import substitution model for economic development—whereby dependence on imports is reduced through high levels of protection and public sector control—didn't work. The experience of Argentina, Brazil, Egypt, Peru, the Philippines, and Zambia, among others, displayed a familiar pattern of noncompetitive state controlled industry, growing public sector deficits, inflation, and balance-of-payments crises. The failure of centrally planned economies was even more devastating. Economic infrastructure crumbled, environmental degradation damaged public health, production stagnated or fell, and corruption and black markets undermined state distribution systems.

The positive example of the 1980s began with the sustained economic expansion of the U.S. economy, beginning in 1982. A strong West European recovery followed later in the decade. In both cases, the policy prescription called for lower marginal tax rates, privatization of public enterprises, and deregulation. The most remarkable experience in private sector and export-driven growth, however, was in East Asia. Japan became the role model, followed first by the "Four Tigers"—South Korea, Taiwan, Hong Kong, and Singapore—and later by the more populous Southeast Asian nations. China, too, demonstrated extraordinary growth performance through market-oriented reforms, first in agriculture and then in industry. By decade's end, market-oriented reforms produced remarkable results in Latin America as well, first in Chile, Costa Rica and Mexico, later in Venezuela, Argentina, and elsewhere.

The triumph of economic liberalism as the underlying concept for economic development and growth did not mean, however, that national economic policies had become laissez-faire free trade. Government policies remained pervasive in their economic effects. Among industrialized countries, policies affecting investment and trade in high technology industries were becoming more complex and subject to protectionist abuse. Economic strategy in many poorer and formerly communist countries was at the early stages of transition toward a market economy. Enormous restructuring problems and limited political cohesion threatened implementation.

In this radically changed political context, the GATT multilateral trading system became the bellwether for an evolving world economic order, although the bell more often than not rang faintly. The groundswell of applied economic liberalism moved the GATT steadily from an institution viewed with "resentment and frustration" to a bastion of successful and fashionable economic reform. GATT norms for market-oriented, open trade were fundamental to such reform, and multilateral GATT commitments provided assurance that new export industries would have stable if not expanded market access abroad. Mexico finally joined the GATT in 1987 and became a firm, unfrustrated supporter. A series of other membership applications followed, including one for readmission of China, and membership passed the hundred mark by decade's end. The Soviet Union changed from a longstanding critic, claiming that GATT served capitalist imperialism, to an ardent suitor seeking at least observer status as a support for internal reforms.

On August 23, 1990, President Bush's national security adviser, Brent Scowcroft, commented: "We believe we are creating the beginning of a new world order coming out of the collapse of the U.S.-Soviet antagonisms."[6] The immediate context was the Iraqi invasion of Kuwait, and *new world order* became the catchphrase for numerous but never fully defined U.S. foreign policy goals addressed in presidential statements. The problem was that new-world-order thinking focused on political-security relationships in the context of military actions through the United Nations. The more fundamental transformation in the world order during the 1980s, rather, was more political/economic than political/security in character, summed up as the triumph of economic liberalism. The underlying challenge was to broaden and deepen the grouping of industrialized democracies in the world and to convert the historic order of nation-state conflict into one of economic competition and cooperation.

The Changing U.S. Leadership Role

The critical role of leadership within the international trading system has been studied extensively. The United Kingdom's role from mid-nineteenth century to 1914 is widely recognized. Lack of leadership during the great depression of the 1930s, when world trade collapsed, is more controversial. In his classic study, Professor Charles Kindleberger concluded that the depression was "so wide, so deep, and so long because the international economic system was rendered unstable by British inability and U.S. unwillingness to assume responsibility for stabilizing it." Even more pointed is his "main lesson of the interwar years . . . that for the world economy to be stabilized, there has to be a stabilizer—one stabilizer." For the trading system, the stabilizer had, inter alia, "to keep the import market open in periods of stress."[7]

Such leadership needs to be based on national self-interest or an altruistic calling, and since World War II a dominant U.S. trade-leadership role has been based on both. Global export interests and a commanding technological lead enabled the United States, more or less, to keep its market open during periods of stress, while the GATT multilateral system based on nondiscrimination ensured equal access to all markets. The market-oriented GATT rules also reinforced U.S.-led political cohesion of the West during the cold war. As for the altruistic calling, a habit of active trade leadership became embedded in the "foreign policy establishment" and was a source of public pride. The cultural roots ran even deeper, described by Winston Churchill as "the processes whereby English-speaking peoples throughout the world have achieved their distinctive position and character."[8]

U.S. trade leadership during the 1980s, however, changed in important respects, which raised questions about its future direction and staying power. The United States remained the dominant driving force during the Uruguay Round, albeit with some lapses in the final phase, but at the same time a reappraisal of traditional trade strategy gathered momentum within the country. A sharply reduced technological lead, especially vis-à-vis Japan, and a burgeoning trade deficit beginning in mid-decade elicited calls for a more

forceful response than was possible through GATT commitments and procedures. Various bilateral trade-balancing proposals, the antithesis of the GATT
approach, were considered, and a presidential mandate for unilateral market-
opening through an extension of the now famous Section 301 became law. The
United States pursued a more active government role to support "strategic"
industries. The broadest criticism of the GATT approach held that it preserved
an "uneven playing field" with U.S. markets more open than foreign markets.
Proposed alternatives or additions to the GATT status quo included regional
free trade and other bilateral or plurilateral agreements.

On numerous occasions during the Uruguay Round, U.S. presidents and
cabinet members stated that if the Uruguay Round did not succeed the United
States would pursue bilateral and regional alternatives. At times, U.S. trade
policy was described as pure pragmatism. Whatever worked best for U.S. trade
interests would be U.S. trade policy. Even though such statements were usually made in a tactical context—pressing others to be more forthcoming in the
Uruguay Round—they would have been simply unthinkable in earlier decades
when the GATT multilateral system was the warp and woof of U.S. trade
policy.

The Uruguay Round also reaffirmed the lack of alternatives to a dominant
U.S. leadership. The EC, except at the very end, was inhibited from strong
trade liberalizing initiatives by protectionist forces within the Community,
particularly French intransigence on farm sector liberalization, and a cumbersome decision-making process that tended toward lowest common denominator results. Japan, the only other contender for principal leadership, remained
on the defensive about lack of access to its market and was culturally adverse
to assertive participation in the rough and tumble of multilateral trade negotiations.

At the conclusion of his book, Professor Kindleberger posed as the most
attractive, though most difficult, alternative to the "one stabilizer," U.S. leadership role—the cession of economic sovereignty to an international body. In
the international financial field, the IMF and the World Bank have moved
substantially in that direction in organizational terms. A strong and independent secretariat with respected leadership receives direction from a governing
board based on weighted majority voting which, in effect, constitutes a colle-
gial leadership by the major economic powers. The creation of a new World
Trade Organization in the Uruguay Round will enable some strengthening
of the leadership role of the corresponding international trade body, but as
explained in the concluding chapters here, the new WTO will still fall far short
of a decisive cession of sovereignty.

><

These four principal developments brought about a transformation in world trade during the 1980s: Global market integration, tripolarization of industrial development, the triumph of economic liberalism, and a changed U.S. leadership role. The international economic order, moreover, will continue to evolve through the 1990s and beyond, and an understanding of what lies ahead begins with a detailed account of what occurred during the Uruguay Round.

T W O

The Wobbly Bicycle, 1979–1982

The Uruguay Round agenda began to take shape at the time the previous Tokyo Round concluded. On April 12, 1979, after almost six years of negotiations, GATT Director-General Olivier Long announced that the Tokyo Round had ended "with a broad measure of agreement on the issues negotiated," but he hastily added: "There is, however, one uncompleted sector of negotiations. This is the examination of the adequacy of the present multilateral safeguard system."[1] He further explained that while negotiations would continue on the safeguards issue, approval of the other elements of the Tokyo Round agreement would not be held up to await the outcome. Greatly disappointed, developing countries who had participated in the round boycotted the ceremony to initial the agreement. They rallied the following month at the United Nations Conference on Trade and Development (UNCTAD) in Manila, where the obliging UNCTAD secretariat concluded that the Tokyo Round agreements "do little to help poor nations, and only serve to perpetuate a trading system that works more and more against them."[2]

The GATT Article XIX safeguards clause permits temporary import restrictions when increased imports "cause or threaten serious injury to domestic producers." In practice, however, Article XIX was ignored because its conditions were too stringent, requiring formal consultations in GATT to justify the restrictions, nondiscriminatory application, and compensatory import liberalization on other products. During the 1970s bilateral import quotas or "voluntary" export restraints were increasingly imposed outside the GATT, principally against Japan and the more advanced developing countries. In addition, trade in textiles and apparel was subject to a broad network of bilateral quotas under the GATT-sanctioned Multifiber Arrangement (MFA).

Tokyo Round negotiators attempted to make the Article XIX safeguards clause somewhat more flexible on the condition that industrialized countries would then commit themselves to its provisions for any temporary restrictions. The negotiations foundered on whether import quotas could be applied selectively—that is, against one or a few countries rather than indiscriminately against all. The European Community insisted on the right of selectivity while developing countries resisted, knowing they were most likely to be

24

"selected" for import restrictions. The safeguards issue got nowhere during follow-on negotiations in 1979 and would reemerge as a major objective for developing countries in the Uruguay Round. Bilateral quotas are fundamentally at odds with the GATT multilateral tariff-based system and, even more during the 1980s, posed a central challenge for an open trade relationship between the industrialized countries and the newly industrialized nations of Asia and Latin America.

In 1979, however, the GATT was still viewed primarily as an undertaking among the industrialized nations. Despite the developing-country boycott, the public reaction was generally favorable, albeit with varying qualifications. The *New York Times* declared the round "A Remarkable Step Forward on Trade." The *Journal de Genève* labeled it "a victory with a bitter taste" (une victoire au goût amèr) in view of the grave status of the world economy. The *Economist* aptly summed it up as "a step toward freer trade and away from the protectionism which, for the first time in 30 years, is today reacquiring not just political attractions but, in some quarters, intellectual respectability." Perhaps most prescient, a commentary in the *Frankfurter Allgemeine* concluded that "The Tokyo Round is not an end but a springboard for venturing into new territory in terms of trade policy."[3]

An immediate concern was that the Tokyo Round agreement was hostage to the U.S. Congress. While virtually all other governments were assured that an agreement signed in Geneva would be ratified by parliaments back home, this was not the case for the United States. After the preceding Kennedy Round, concluded in 1967, the U.S. Congress did not ratify two parts of the final agreement, an antidumping code and a special arrangement for the chemicals sector. For the Tokyo Round, U.S. negotiating credibility recovered somewhat through a creative provision of the 1974 Trade Act referred to as the "fast track." It provided that the president would submit the final agreement to the Congress for a simple yes or no vote within sixty legislative days, no amendments permitted. This would preclude the unacceptable situation of Congress revising the agreement for further negotiation within the GATT. Nevertheless, congressional approval of the Tokyo Round remained uncertain. A spokesman for organized labor stated that the agreement could do "an immense amount of damage" to the American economy and called for a renegotiation of the agreement.[4]

Concern about congressional ratification was ill-founded, however, largely because of the political skills of U.S. trade representative Robert Strauss. He carefully prepared the congressional leadership, developed bipartisan consensus for the agreement in private committee sessions during the three months prior to the formal signing in April, and moved the final agreement quickly through public hearings with strong bipartisan support. The agreement passed the House 395–7, the Senate 90–4, and President Carter signed it into law on July 26, 1979. Many members of the Congress probably didn't examine closely the agreement and were brought along by the momentum created by the affable Texan. They would not be so seduced again at the end of the Uruguay Round.

In any event, few if any expected the Tokyo Round to have major impact on trade. The first of two principal achievements reduced by about one-third tariffs on manufactured products by industrialized countries and was phased in over eight years. It continued the pattern of earlier rounds, and the one-third reduction was later adopted as the target for the Uruguay Round. The second achievement was the negotiation of six codes to deal with nontariff measures, namely subsidies, technical barriers, import licenses, government procurement, customs valuation, and antidumping procedures. The codes broadened and clarified the scope of GATT competence, but they had limited effect in actual trade practice. Most were very general and allowed wide-ranging exceptions. They were also open-ended, with membership optional. Developing countries by and large opted not to join. None of the codes was ever adopted by a majority of GATT members.

The most important code by far involved subsidies. The problem of export subsidies, in particular, had been a principal ground for launching the Tokyo Round and would emerge again as the most intractable issue in the agricultural sector of the Uruguay Round. Export subsidies are proscribed under GATT Article XVI, but the definition of subsidies and the procedure for dealing with them are not spelled out. Most countries have countervailing duty authorities to apply import duties to offset foreign subsidies, and the U.S. countervailing duty law in the 1970s was the most severe. It had no injury test—that is, the need to demonstrate potential harm to domestic industry—and the countervailing duty was applied automatically once a foreign subsidy was judged to exist in response to a domestic complaint. This is precisely what happened when U.S. dairy producers filed a complaint against EC export subsidies as provided by the Community's Common Agricultural Policy. A showdown between the irresistible U.S. countervailing duty law and the immutable EC farm policy was only avoided by the Tokyo Round, whereby President Ford, under the 1974 Trade Act, was permitted to waive the automatic imposition of countervailing duties for up to four years, pending a satisfactorily negotiated resolution of the issue in the new GATT Round.

The subsidies code that emerged from the Tokyo Round had an ironic twist.

A more precise definition of unacceptable subsidies and a commitment to phase them out were agreed, and in return the United States accepted an injury test for application of countervailing duties. The code, however, applied principally to trade in manufactured goods. Agricultural subsidies for primary products were subject to only minor restraints. The EC farm policy as potential *causus belli* of a transatlantic trade war in 1973 was thus finessed in the 1970s and left to reemerge in more virulent form in the 1980s.

Tokyo Round negotiators tried hard but failed to resolve another important issue, a strengthening of the GATT dispute settlement mechanism. The existing mechanism lacked credibility because it provided that any one party to a dispute, even the accused party, could veto the formation of a dispute panel or later consideration of a dispute-panel report by the GATT Council. It also was vulnerable to long delays that put the overall process in disrepute and encouraged members to deal with trade disputes outside the GATT. The Tokyo Round negotiations pitted the United States against the EC, with the former pressing for a formula to end one-country veto power and the EC firmly resisting. The Tokyo Round was useful in putting existing procedures in writing, but it did not resolve the central problems of delay and veto power. These issues would be reengaged in the Uruguay Round, this time with pressures building in the other direction—to constrain U.S. unilateral actions.

Precipitating Causes

These were some of the origins of the Uruguay Round emanating from the Tokyo Round. They did not in themselves, however, constitute anything approaching an agenda for a new round. After six years of vexatious negotiations, trade policy officials in all major capitals were suffering from a severe case of GATT fatigue. A prevalent view was that the Tokyo Round was the last in the series of lengthy, comprehensive negotiations that would lead to a single "package deal" at the conclusion. Officials wondered if a continuous process of single-issue negotiations within the GATT would be preferable. The safeguards issue, for example, was remanded to a GATT committee in November 1979 in the hope of reaching the negotiated solution that had eluded Tokyo Round negotiators.

The continuous-negotiation approach for progressive trade liberalization, however, was seriously flawed. Individual policy initiatives to liberalize trade usually involve one group of countries whose exporters benefit from the result and another group whose import-competing industries are adversely affected. Governments of the latter group confront sharply focused political opposition that can best be neutralized by counterbalancing gains for particular export

27

industries in other sectors. The overall "gains from trade" for consumers unfortunately lack political force. A balance of specific "benefits" and "concessions" thus constitutes the political basis for the comprehensive approach for trade negotiations. It would nevertheless take several years after the completion of the Tokyo Round for this simple lesson of trade negotiation politics to regain consensus within the GATT.

Whether to begin a new comprehensive round would not, in any event, become an issue of abstract deliberation. Rather, two more concrete dimensions of negotiating strategy would be determinant—the agenda of pressing issues that would emerge in the early 1980s, and the impact of world economic conditions on the GATT trading system.

GATT rounds of multilateral negotiations had always been agenda driven, with a predominant U.S.-West European orientation. From 1947 to 1955, the first four rounds remained relatively low-key affairs to reduce the extraordinarily high postwar tariffs on a mutual basis. The Dillon Round of 1958–60 had the more pointed objective of adjusting the balance of market access after the formation of a customs union by the six initial members of the European Community. A customs union is permitted by GATT Article XXIV, provided that the harmonized level of external trade barriers is no higher than the previously existing national levels. With respect to the formation of the EC, however, there was disagreement within the GATT as to whether this condition had been met. The United States and some others felt that the overall level of EC protection was higher than preexisting national levels. The Dillon Round circumvented a potential impasse by allowing the EC to reduce its industrial tariffs an additional 20 percent—a reduction considerably more than those of the United States and others—and to claim the differential as an indirect offset to complaints about the Community's overall level of protection. One result was that the GATT never formally judged the compatibility of the European Community customs union with GATT Article XXIV.

The Kennedy Round of 1963–67 represented an even more forceful, explicitly political response to the formation of the European Community and a desire to prevent the Atlantic Alliance from drifting apart into two regional trading blocs. President Kennedy took the initiative for across-the-board tariff cuts of 50 percent principally for this political objective, and the round centered on protracted U.S.-EC negotiations to this end. The Tokyo Round had a broader agenda, but the pending trade dispute between the United States and the European Community over export subsidies for farm products provided critical political pressure for the United States to seek negotiating authority from the Congress and to reach a final overall agreement.

At the outset of the 1980s, an action-forcing agenda for a new GATT round was less apparent. The U.S.-EC trade relationship faced some problems, such as steel import quotas. Developing-country participation in the GATT became strained, particularly over the safeguards issue. The United States had expressed interest in bringing "new issues" of trade policy into the international trading system, most notably trade in services. There was growing apprehension within Western Europe about rising imports from Japan and the newly industrialized Asian countries. But a sense of urgency to initiate serious negotiations within the GATT in these areas, individually or jointly, was lacking.

World economic developments became a more serious and growing concern. The oil shocks of 1973 and 1979 had created large trade deficits for numerous oil importing countries. Beginning in the late 1970s, higher interest rates to curb inflation in the United States exacerbated debt service problems in Latin America. By 1981 the U.S. monetary squeeze in conjunction with soaring fiscal deficits triggered a recession in the United States with repercussions throughout the world economy. Higher unemployment, in turn, bred protectionist pressures to shelter faltering domestic industries.

A lackluster GATT program and growing protectionist pressures gave new impetus, especially within the United States, to a trade policy strategy based on the "bicycle theory." A liberal trade policy, according to this theory, must have forward momentum toward a still-more-open trading system or it will fall prey to ever-present protectionist forces. A bicycle must stay in motion or it will fall down. Thus protracted GATT rounds to liberalize trade kept the protectionist wolves at bay. The Kennedy Round had done this for more than four years in the 1960s, the Tokyo Round for almost six years in the 1970s, and the best defense against growing protectionism in the early 1980s was the offense of yet another GATT round. The bicycle theory would be sorely tested during the 1980s. The new trade liberalization initiative, ultimately the Uruguay Round, would drag on for thirteen years while the GATT as vehicle for sustaining liberal trade would lose momentum. The bicycle would wobble, at times barely keeping its equilibrium.

U.S. Call to Action

The initiative for a new GATT round, as in the past, came from the United States, but with somewhat mixed signals from a new president. Ronald Reagan assumed the presidency in January 1981 as a confirmed free trader, but during the election campaign he had evoked the vision of a North American accord to invigorate trade, investment, and growth among the United States, Canada, and Mexico.[5] In the spring of 1981, Secretary of State Alexander Haig

29

directed his assistant secretary for inter-American affairs, Thomas Enders, to develop a positive economic dimension to the hard-line anticommunist political strategy for Central America. The forceful, creative Enders came up with the Caribbean Basin Initiative, which integrated one-way free trade into the United States with a doubling of economic aid and support for private investment for Central America and Caribbean countries. These regional concepts were alien to traditional U.S. trade policy based on the GATT multilateral system.

The new U.S. trade representative, William Brock, like his predecessor Robert Strauss, was a politician with little experience in trade policy. He had been congressman and senator from Tennessee and later chairman of the Republican Party. His proven capability for dealing with the Congress was rightly considered an asset for trade policy implementation, but his skills in trade diplomacy had to be learned on the job, at some cost. Professional staff presented the new trade representative with a strategy directed ultimately to a new round of GATT negotiations that would concentrate on new issues not covered by the existing GATT system: trade in services, trade-distorting investment measures, trade in high technology industry, counterfeit goods, and the transition of the more advanced developing countries into fuller compliance with GATT obligations. The strategy would begin with an initiative at the Organization for Economic Cooperation and Development (OECD), which Brock undertook in his statement at the June 1981 OECD ministerial meeting. He opened bluntly: "Today we are experiencing inflation and economic stagnation. These subject us to protectionist pressures which we must resist." He called on the OECD to develop an action program "to address the trade issues of the future," emphasizing the new issues as well as the longstanding problems of subsidies for agriculture and the unresolved safeguards code. He made no explicit mention of a new GATT round. The OECD ministerial resolution responded by inviting the OECD secretary general to establish a work program and report its conclusions at the subsequent ministerial meeting in May 1982.

The first step toward forming an agenda for the new round thus was taken in the OECD, not the GATT. The GATT did not meet regularly at ministerial level, leaving no opportunity for ministers to act together as they did in the OECD. The GATT also lacked effective support mechanisms for policy deliberations at lower levels. The secretariat was under tight wraps to limit its work to existing GATT commitments and was not disposed toward forward-looking policy analysis. These various institutional weaknesses of the GATT would later be addressed in the Uruguay Round negotiating group with the infelicitous acronym FOGS, for functioning of the GATT system.

The GATT would nevertheless have to play the central role in formal preparations for a new round, and one member of the U.S. delegation to the 1981 OECD ministerial meeting traveled on to Geneva to meet with the new GATT director-general, Arthur Dunkel, and U.S. resident representative to the GATT Michael Smith. The Americans outlined a scenario for holding a GATT ministerial meeting in 1982 that could establish a work program leading to a new GATT round. Dunkel was receptive. The U.S. initiative for a GATT ministerial meeting was pursued with other members, and in November 1981 the GATT Council decided to convene its next session the following year at ministerial level.

The announcement of a GATT ministerial meeting made no mention of a possible new round of negotiations. Developing countries in particular were not interested in a protracted new round, preferring early action on outstanding issues affecting their exports. The press, however, quickly noted that the last time the GATT Council had met at ministerial level, in 1973, was to launch the Tokyo Round, and that GATT ministerial meetings had traditionally been utilized either to begin or conclude a round of negotiations.

A GATT Preparatory Committee began work on an agenda for the ministerial meeting, initially expected to consist of three parts. The first would be a political commitment by ministers to resist protectionist pressures and to respond to special problems of developing countries. The second part related to substantive matters to be submitted to ministers either for immediate agreement or for directives toward solutions within a specified time. The familiar issues of the safeguards code, a framework for agricultural trade, and a mechanism for dispute settlement fell into this category. The third part would deal with issues requiring further study before policy recommendations could be developed. This could include trade in services, trade-related investment measures, the textile sector, and special trade aspects of high-technology products.

The structure of the agenda was flexible—or, perhaps, ambiguous—with respect to a possible new round. The second part of the agenda would deal with issues for immediate decision while the third part could begin preparatory work for a later round centered on the new issues. Ultimately, both parts would be merged into the Uruguay Round agenda, but this was not yet the stated intent of any government.

A U.S. strategy to lay the groundwork for a new round was thus successfully initiated in 1981. It would almost founder in 1982, however, in part from inept execution. One problem was lack of consensus among OECD countries as to what, precisely, the GATT ministerial meeting ought to accomplish. The European Community supported an eventual new round, including negotia-

31

tion of such new issues as trade in services, but it did not press for an early decision. Certainly, a renewed assault on the EC agricultural policy was not welcome. The Americans had difficulty explaining their objectives for some of the new issues, especially trade in high-technology industries, which aroused European and Japanese suspicions.

U.S. intentions about a new round were further clouded at the May 1982 OECD ministerial meeting when Trade Representative Brock made his first public proposal: "One idea I would like you to consider is a new round of trade negotiations within the GATT involving an exchange of preferential tariff concessions by developed countries for developing countries whose products have been graduated out of GSP [i.e., the general system of tariff preferences]—or are soon to be—in return for increased commitments by these developing countries on the reduction of tariff and non-tariff barriers to their markets."[6] This proposal emanated from a conversation between Brock and World Bank President A. W. Tom Clausen. Clausen felt industrialized countries should do something to compensate unilateral trade liberalization by some developing countries in the context of World Bank–supported policy reform programs. However, the Brock proposal implied commitments by developing countries to bind the lower trade barriers against future increase within the GATT in return for GSP concessions of limited trade interest. This nonstarter drew no support from other OECD ministers.

The biggest roadblock to the U.S. strategy for a new round in any event would be the developing countries. They were disappointed with the Tokyo Round outcome and wanted immediate action on the safeguards issue as well as a freeze on any new quotas or other protectionist measures against their exports. They were wary of being drawn into an action program for the new issues and viewed the U.S. objective of trade liberalization for the service sector as a plot by the industrialized countries to gain one-sided benefits. Leadership of a unified developing-country bloc centered on Brazil and India, the principal trading nations of South America and South Asia. In the past, developing countries had been peripheral to the GATT negotiating process, but the emerging agenda of trade issues for the 1980s brought them into a more central position. The United States did not take this change fully into account, nor did it undertake the major diplomatic effort that would have been necessary to gain support for its GATT ministerial objective of a comprehensive work program linked, however conditionally, to a new GATT round.

In May the OECD ministers pledged "the determination of their governments to participate fully and constructively . . . in the upcoming GATT ministerial meeting," but there was no meeting of the minds as to the content of such constructive participation. The lack of agreement became more clear during the summer and early autumn sessions of the GATT Preparatory Committee. The developing countries, with the support of the European Community, turned down flatly Brock's proposal for a new North/South round. They pressed instead for a one-year deadline to agree on a safeguards code, which was resisted by the EC. U.S. efforts to obtain a commitment to liberalize trade in agriculture likewise fell on deaf Community ears. Developing countries refused even to study the issue of trade in services within the GATT framework. On November 3 the GATT Preparatory Committee suspended its work, confronted with impasse on almost all key issues.

Meanwhile, the world economy had deteriorated steadily since the end of the Tokyo Round in 1979, and was in deep recession at the time of the GATT

TABLE 2.1: Growth in World Production and Exports
(volume, in percent)

	1979	1980	1981	1982
World Production	4	1	1	−2
World Exports	6	1.5	0	−2

Source: International Trade 1981/1982 (Geneva: GATT, 1983). p. 1.

ministerial meeting. As shown in table 2.1, world exports were flat in 1981 and declined by 2 percent in 1982, the first absolute decline since the 1930s. The protectionist backlash in the United States crystallized in the Fair Practices in Automotive Products Act, supported by more than half of the members of the House of Representatives, which provided for a sharp increase in the domestic content of automobiles produced in the United States and for related import quotas. A congressional trade expert characterized the bill as "outrageous," but "it's the only game in town."[7] U.S. Deputy Trade Representative David MacDonald summed up his frustration: "If someone had told you a couple of years ago that unemployment would be 10 percent, that the steel industry would be running at 45 percent capacity, that farm income would have dropped 40 percent in three years, that automobile sales would be running at half the 1979 rate, and that similar developments would occur (elsewhere), what would you have anticipated the state of our trade relations would be?"[8]

GATT Ministerial, 1982

The GATT ministerial meeting of November 24–29, 1982, has generally been considered something between a failure and a fiasco. From the press: "the mad Gatters' tea party," "a bitter defeat for the devotees of an open trading system," and "avoiding fiasco was a kind of success."[9] French Foreign Minister Michel Jobert provided the most widely quoted one liner: "une reunion inutile et inopportune."[10] The head of the EC delegation concluded that the conference had been "badly prepared, badly organized and should never had been held at this time."[11] A somewhat more upbeat U.S. Trade Representative Brock gave the results "a grade of C that could stretch to C+ depending on future actions."[12]

A GATT ministerial meeting had never before convened during deep global recession, which was why some considered the event inopportune. Protectionist pressures emanating from the recession, however, were a major reason that the United States wanted to activate the GATT liberal trade mechanism. The U.S. strategy, however flawed in execution, was applied bicycle theory under increasingly ominous circumstances, and in this context Brock's hope for retrospective upgrading would be borne out, at least to C+ if not to low-honors B.

Undoubtedly the meeting was ill-prepared and near chaotic in its final phase. The timing and agenda for the meeting had been driven by U.S. initiative, but the Americans had not presented a clear set of priorities and, more important, had not developed support for their agenda from major trading partners. Solidarity among industrialized countries was lacking while developing countries stood unified in their grievances about the increasingly protectionist policies of the industrialized nations. Specific issues were debated more in polemical than analytical terms. After two days of fruitless talk, the conference chairman, Canadian Deputy Prime Minister Allan MacEachen, hosted a small Friday breakfast meeting for key delegates that lasted eight hours. The Europeans complained about the chairman's heavy-handed pressure against EC farm policy. Developing-country delegates, most of whom were not there, complained about their exclusion. A weekend of round-the-clock haggling ended at 5 A.M. Monday with a press conference that produced a sixteen-page communique of nuanced compromise language which pleased no one.

The diplomatic disarray, moreover, masked the important underlying differences among major trading nations about trade strategy for the early 1980s. Internal economic difficulties preoccupied the European Community. Japan was on the defensive about its nationalistic industrial policy, which it was not prepared to submit to international scrutiny. The developing countries preferred to press the industrialized countries to act on past promises rather than to seek new trade liberalizing initiatives. The United States had the politically sound instinct to organize a broadly based new effort to maintain and enhance access to world markets, but it did not have a well-articulated strategy to do so. There was, in short, no consensus for concerted action, and it would take another four years of patient consultation and technical preparation before such an effort—the Uruguay Round—would be formally launched.

The ministerial communique of November 29, 1982, though blurred by compromise language on key points, nevertheless provided the framework for a comprehensive GATT study-and-action program over the ensuing two years. As one member of the U.S. delegation later commented, "The bottom line is a work program in the GATT," and he was right.[13] The most important components of the 1983–1984 GATT work program were:

1. *Safeguards.* "A comprehensive understanding" was to be drawn up for Council adoption no later than 1983. The understanding would include transparency, criteria for defining serious injury or the threat thereof, the temporary nature and degressivity of restrictions, and compensation or retaliation. These were the same elements that eluded Tokyo Round negotiators, and the 1983 deadline, too, would pass without agreement.

2. *Textiles and clothing.* A study to be completed by 1984 would examine the "modalities of further trade liberalization" in this sector after assessing the consequences "of a phasing out . . . or of the continued maintenance, of the restraints and restrictions applied under the existing textile and clothing regimes, principally the MFA, i.e., multi-fiber arrangement." All options remained open in this sensitive sector.

3. *Agriculture.* A committee was established to examine and make recommendations by 1984, "with a view to achieving greater liberalization in the trade of agricultural products." For export subsidies, the most contentious issue between the United States and the European Community, explicit direction was given to examine "subsidies affecting agriculture, especially export subsidies, with a view to . . . avoiding subsidization seriously prejudicial to the trade interests of contracting parties." This language was, in fact, more explicit on export subsidies than would appear in the 1986 Punta del Este declaration.

4. *Dispute settlement.* Despite three pages of laborious text in the communique, the principal U.S. objective—eliminating the consensus rule that allowed either party in a GATT dispute procedure to veto a decision or judgment—was not achieved. Even the hortatory language, that "obstruction in the process of dispute settlement shall be avoided," was footnoted with a proviso that this did not prejudice the consensual (i.e., veto) provisions of decision making in the GATT. The European Community had objected vigorously to any weakening of the right to veto.

5. *Trade in counterfeit goods.* The GATT Council was instructed to determine "the appropriateness of joint action in the GATT framework on the
trade aspects of commercial counterfeiting . . . having full regard to the
competence of other international organizations." The World Intellectual
Property Organization (WIPO) was specifically referenced. Unauthorized
use of trademarks and copyrighted material had been discussed from
time to time in the GATT, and its inclusion in the 1982 ministerial communique is noteworthy in that the United States, at that point, still limited its interest in the GATT to trade in counterfeit goods. It would be another three years before the much broader issue of protection of
intellectual property rights would become a U.S. priority for the Uruguay
Round.

6. *Services.* Bringing trade in services within the GATT mandate was a central U.S. objective at the 1982 GATT ministerial meeting, and developing
countries forcefully resisted. Indian Minister of Commerce Shivraj Patil
stated flatly, "the proposal for a study of services in GATT . . . is clearly beyond the competence and the present workframe of GATT. . . . We have
no doubt that GATT has no mandate to discuss these issues."[14] The European Community and other industrialized countries gave only lukewarm
support to the U.S. initiative, and the best the United States could manage
was a final brief section in the communique recommending that each
contracting party with an interest in services undertake a national examination of the issues in this sector. It suggested inviting "contracting parties to exchange information on such matters among themselves, inter
alia through international organizations such as GATT." The results of
these examinations would be reviewed at the 1984 GATT session of contracting parties. However tenuous and voluntary, the service-sector cam-
el's nose was under the GATT tent.

TOPICAL ADDENDUM: TRADE IN SERVICES

The transition to predominantly service-based national economies has been
apparent for several decades. The share of the U.S. labor force in the service
sector increased from 51 percent in 1950 to 62 percent in 1970 to 72 percent
in 1990. Other countries followed in the U.S. wake, including most developing
countries. The corresponding figures for the Mexican labor force, for example, are 23, 32, and 51 percent, bringing Mexico in 1990 to the U.S. level
of 1950.

International trade in services and the implications for trade policy, however, received no significant attention until the mid-1970s. In part, this re-

flected the preoccupation of the trade policy establishment with trade in goods and border restrictions on such trade. GATT negotiations through the Kennedy Round agreement of 1967 were overwhelmingly devoted to tariff reductions and elimination of import quotas. Trade in services also suffered from inherent problems of definition and an extreme scarcity of pertinent statistics.

The first public document to address "trade in services" was the 1972 OECD report of a group of eminent persons chaired by former EC President Jean Rey.[15] The chapter on services concluded that "the services sector, like the industrial sector, is experiencing a measure of internationalization. . . . for some countries trade in services is at least as important as, and in some cases more important than, merchandise trade." Moreover, the services sector, "poses problems similar in nature to those met in merchandise trade," and therefore, "action should be taken . . . to ensure liberalization and non-discrimination in the services sector." There was no explicit recommendation that the GATT should incorporate trade in services, but the link between service industries and trade policy had been established.

A parallel pioneering effort was undertaken by Hugh Corbet, director of the Trade Policy Research Centre in London. Observing from an international center of banking, insurance, publishing, and transport, Corbet understood the importance of trade in services, and he commissioned a study by Brian Griffiths of the London School of Economics. The resulting 1975 book, *Invisible Barriers to Invisible Trade*, provided seminal thinking for the subsequent surge in policy analysis and public debate.

The focus of political attention and initiative for bringing trade in services within the international trading system, however, was in the United States. It was an extraordinary experience in public education, based on mutually reinforcing activities by the private sector, independent research institutions, and the government. Corporate leaders included James Robinson, CEO of the American Express Company; Maurice Greenberg, CEO of the American International Group (AIG); and John Reed, CEO of Citicorp. In the early 1980s, the American Enterprise Institute embarked on the most ambitious research initiative, which produced seven volumes on specific sectors—including aviation, banking, construction, and telecommunications—and a comprehensive overview volume by Geza Feketekuty with 181 references, of which 129 were from the 1980s.[16] The central theme was that trade in services was an important and integral part of overall trade, while remaining outside the international trading system.

The U.S. Congress took the public-sector lead while drafting the 1974 Trade

Act, which gave the president authority to negotiate the Tokyo Round. The act includes in the definition of international trade "trade in both goods and services," and the Advisory Committee on Trade Negotiations is stipulated to include representatives of the service sector. Service industries are a clearly implied target for "the extension of GATT articles to conditions of trade not presently covered in order to move toward more fair trade practices."[17]

The 1974 Act came too late, however, to bring trade in services into the Tokyo Round in any major way. The round had already begun in 1973 with a firmly established agenda. Nevertheless, the United States was able to include provisions relating to services in three of the nontariff codes in the final 1979 agreement. The government procurement code was extended to trade-related services such as transportation and insurance, the standards code included foreign testing, and the subsidies code explicitly disallowed subsidies for services used to export goods.

From 1979 to 1981, U.S. initiative to bring services into the trading system shifted to the OECD Trade Committee. Other industrialized countries agreed to study the issue, and the United States quickly assembled a comprehensive inventory of barriers faced by American businesses drawn from surveys by the U.S. Chamber of Commerce. The ensuing OECD discussions educated and gradually convinced other industrialized-country governments that trade in services was indeed an important matter. Parallel discussion and data gathering by private sector groups reinforced this view, and by 1981 the industrialized countries had begun to work together to include trade in services in some way on the GATT agenda.

Developing countries, however, were not convinced of the need even to discuss services in the GATT, and some were firmly opposed. Lack of information on developing-country interests in services trade was an inhibiting factor. It would take several years of discussion and diplomatic debate before consensus would be reached that open trade in services was a mutual interest that should be part of the broader trading system. The GATT ministerial showdown in November 1982 was only the first round in this process.

The substance of the ultimate Uruguay Round negotiations to bring trade in services within the GATT system can be separated into four parts: (1) Definition and statistics; (2) general principles; (3) market access; and (4) implementation procedures.

1. *Definition and statistics.* The education process for Uruguay Round negotiators required a definition of trade in services and a measure of its scope. The distinction between "goods" and "services" contains many gray areas and is ill-defined within national economies. Defining interna-

tional trade in services is even more complicated. Should it be based on the residency of the buyer and the seller or the nationality of the firms involved? In the former case, how is residency defined? When an American tourist buys a prepackaged Big Mac on the Champs Elysees, is he acquiring a good or a service, and is the transaction part of international trade? What if the American lives in Paris?

The only standardized set of statistics on trade in services in the early 1980s came from the International Monetary Fund (IMF) balance-of-payments accounts, based on transactions between residents of one country and nonresidents. Three categories from the IMF "invisibles" account—transportation, travel, and other private services and income—can be used to approximate "commercial services," as was later done by the GATT secretariat.[18] Table 2.2 shows that in 1989 such trade in services totaled $680 billion, or 19 percent of total world trade. During the 1980s, services trade grew at an annual rate of 10 percent in current dollars, slightly faster than the 9.5-percent rate for merchandise trade.[19] By 1993, the GATT estimated services trade at $1 trillion, or 21 percent of world trade in goods and services.

Important distinctions exist among the three sub-categories of services. Transportation—the cost of shipping goods in trade—has been declining as a share of world trade, from 7.5 to 6.5 percent during the 1980s, reflecting more efficient methods of transport and the decline of bulk cargoes in overall world trade. Travel, in contrast, including business and tourist trade, has been increasing at a rapid rate. The "other private services and income" category is the single largest and potentially fastest growing of all. It includes financial services, insurance, communications, engineering, royalties and license fees, and worker remittances.

The interests of developing countries in services trade were central to the Uruguay Round negotiations and, as more was learned, it became increasingly apparent that developing countries had major stakes involved. Smaller and lower-income developing countries received an especially high share of export revenues from service industry, such as tourism and labor-intensive services transmitted by telecommunications. Overall, commercial services had roughly the same importance for both industrialized and developing countries relative to total trade.[20]

Many developing countries received large worker remittances of hard currencies from nationals working abroad in service industries, and thus pressed in the Uruguay Round for more open immigration policies for service workers. This demonstrated how trade in services, as compared with goods, can be more intrusive in other areas of national policy. Industrialized countries

TABLE 2.2: World Exports of Merchandise and Commercial Services

	Value ($ billions) 1989	Share in World Trade (percent) 1980	Share in World Trade (percent) 1989	Average Annual Growth (percent) 1980–89
Merchandise	3,095	83	81	9.5
Commercial services	680	17	19	10
transportation	225	7.5	6.5	6.5
travel	195	4	5.5	13.5
other private services and income	260	6	7	10

Source: International Trade, 89–90 (Geneva: GATT, 1991), vol. 1, tables 1, 8.

were highly reluctant to negotiate in the GATT any aspects of immigration policies for unskilled service workers.

The Uruguay Round experience represented only a beginning in understanding the importance of service industry in world trade. Basic statistics remain woefully inadequate. In general, they are substantially underreported, particularly in the rapidly growing information technology sector, such as telecommunications services and cross-border data flow. IMF statistics are on a value basis only, with no volume indices to adjust for change in prices, and there is no breakdown by country supplier or destination. Developing-country submissions are sketchy at best. A beginning was made in the Uruguay Round to agree on nomenclature for services trade and to develop a program for data collection and dissemination. It will take at least several more years to fully implement such a program.

2. *General principles.* The Punta del Este ministerial declaration called for negotiations aimed at the establishment of a multilateral framework of principles and rules for trade in services. This apparently straightforward objective went to the heart of the question of the possible role of services trade in the GATT trading system. To what extent should the principles and norms of trade in goods apply equally to services? This subject became the principal focus of negotiation during the first two years of the Uruguay Round. The most important principles involved were:

a) *Non-discrimination or most-favored-nation (MFN) treatment.* This concept of extending the benefits of any agreement on services equally to

40

all signatories is the counterpart to GATT Article I for trade in goods. An early concern for the Uruguay Round services negotiation was the possibility that not all GATT members would sign the agreement—thus setting up a dual status within the GATT, a form of "conditional MFN" whereby the benefits would apply only to those GATT members who signed the final agreement. In the end, all Uruguay Round participants had to adopt the services agreement to become members of the World Trade Organization. Conditional MFN still became an issue in the closing phase of the negotiations, however, when the United States linked it to market access in certain sectors.

b) *National treatment.* The GATT principle of national treatment for imported goods, as contained in Article III, is relatively simple. Barriers to imports should be at the border, and domestic policy measures should not be used to disadvantage imports relative to domestically produced goods. For services trade, national treatment has a broader context since the provision of services often requires the ability to establish and operate within the foreign market. It involves such things as access to local distribution networks, customers, and operating licenses. Foreign investment laws and regulatory practices often do not permit unlimited national treatment in all service industry. The national treatment principle is thus far more operative for trade in services than it is for trade in goods. In formal GATT terms, the relationship between commitments under Articles I and III is more balanced and critical.

c) *State monopolies.* The GATT provides that state monopolies follow market principles, and the GATT government procurement code proscribes government monopolies from discriminating against foreign suppliers in their purchasing practices. These objectives are exceedingly difficult to implement in practice, however, and do not deal with the extreme case of a state monopoly as sole supplier of specified goods and services. In such cases, there will be no trade. This was the case for important segments of service industry, especially in the transportation and communications sectors.

d) *Subsidies.* The GATT generally prohibits subsidies that distort trade, although the existing subsidies code only vaguely defines proscribed subsidies. The GATT also provides for the use of countervailing duties by other countries adversely affected by export subsidies. Some service industries are heavily subsidized, including shipping, aviation, and telecommunications, and bringing these activities within GATT

41

norms for subsidies would require major change from existing practices.

e) *Transparency.* The requirement of governments to provide information on trade barriers and other measures affecting trade is fundamental to the GATT system, as it would be for an agreement on trade in
services. Many measures used by governments to control services are
only indirectly related to trade, and transparency provisions would require timely notification of government actions regarding both intended and unintended effects on foreign services.

f) *Progressive liberalization.* The GATT system has been devoted, in large
part, to the principle of progressive reduction of trade barriers on a reciprocal basis among members. In the Uruguay Round, the U.S. services industry, in particular, was at least as interested in a substantial
liberalization of services trade as in the negotiation of a framework
agreement of general principles and procedures. The Punta declaration gave balanced treatment to both objectives, but as the negotiations proceeded, a more sequential approach was adopted, with most
specific commitments on trade liberalization left until after the Uruguay Round. The round's challenge became centered, rather, on the
initial conditions of market access from which further liberalizing
steps could be taken.

3. *Market access.* The complex subject of market access for trade in services includes such issues as the right of establishment for foreign companies supplying the services and the application of national regulatory policies in politically sensitive sectors, including transportation,
telecommunications, and financial services. The services agreement covered all service sectors, but this did not mean that every participant
would provide market access in all sectors. In defining the scope of country commitments, a basic question was whether all sectors should be included except for a "negative list" of country exclusions, or whether a
"positive list" of included sectors should be submitted by each participant. A subsidiary issue involved the degree of market access provided to
foreign firms for sectors included within the agreement. These fundamental questions of market access were put off until the later phases of the
round. Initial priority went to negotiating the framework agreement of
principles and procedures, and negotiators on market access then got
bogged down on debate over the negative versus positive list approach. In
the end, participants all submitted positive lists, but the scope of sector
coverage, particularly by developing countries, varied considerably, and

many specifics of market access were left for post–Uruguay Round deliberations.

The most important challenge to broad sectoral inclusion among the industrialized countries came late in the negotiations in 1990, when the United States insisted on improved market access commitments from others before agreeing to inclusion of basic telecommunications and financial services on its positive list. Specifically, the United States made its MFN commitment conditional on such improved access on the grounds that the U.S. market was more open than others. This belated linkage between MFN and liberalized market access by sector came as a surprise to some others and became one of the most difficult issues at the very end of the Uruguay Round.

4. *Implementation procedures.* Trade in services is inherently ill defined and rapidly evolving. Any Uruguay Round agreement, therefore, would depend greatly on the implementation procedures adopted and the political will of governments to abide by them. The importance of transparency, whereby governments would provide prompt notification of actions affecting trade in services, has already been noted. The linkage between an initial framework agreement and future trade liberalization was another central procedural matter of negotiation.

The most contentious question was whether an agreement on services should be linked to GATT commitments on trade in goods. The final compromise at Punta left the matter open, with the negotiating group on services set apart from the other groups but still reporting to a common senior body. The opposition by Brazil, India, and a few others to bringing trade in services within the GATT, however, gradually lost strength over the course of the round. From the beginning, the GATT secretariat provided staff support for the negotiating group on services and soon acquired the reputation as the leading authority in this new and somewhat arcane field. In the land of the blind, the one-eyed man is king! A new secretariat function, to provide overall trade policy reviews of member countries, began in 1989 and included trade in services as an integral part of the assessment. Most pointedly, negotiation of a draft framework agreement for services, which contained a set of principles very similar to those applying to trade in goods, clearly demonstrated the logic of integration.

Two critical procedural issues for determining the future relationship between the GATT and trade in services were dispute settlement and the degree of participation of developing countries. A strengthened dispute settlement mechanism—vital to strengthening the multilateral trading system—would be prominent in the broader Uruguay Round. The question was whether the same strengthened mechanism should be used for disputes over commitments within the services agreement. Closely related was the issue of "cross-retaliation," that is, the right of an aggrieved party to apply retaliatory restrictions on trade in goods in response to violation of a commitment in the services sector. An integrated dispute mechanism that included the right of cross-retaliation would inextricably integrate trade in goods and services within one trading system.

Developing-country participation in a services agreement became an issue in the preparatory stages and remained through the later negotiating phase of the Uruguay Round. One early question was whether a weaker set of overall commitments would be necessary to obtain agreement by all major developing countries, and if so, was it desirable to do so? Closely related was Special and Differential Treatment (S&D), a controversial GATT concept whereby developing countries were not generally bound by commitments of the industrialized countries. If S&D were fully incorporated in a services agreement, the result would have little meaning for trade with developing countries. Yet a principal objective of the negotiation all along had been to provide such meaning. S&D for trade in services lurked in the shadows throughout the negotiations and infiltrated the final agreement, but in much attenuated form.

)(

This synopsis of services trade in the Uruguay Round concentrates on the early roots and preliminary stages of negotiation. The issue will continue to unfold in ensuing chapters to become a central accomplishment of the round. The emphasis here on U.S. leadership is also most clearly justified for its early initiative to conceptualize the issue and to launch formal negotiations. Interest and leadership would broaden as the importance of trade in services became more clear. A prominent early leadership role was played by Ambassador Felipe Jaramillo, Colombian permanent representative to the GATT, who chaired the services group during the critical preparatory period leading up to the Punta del Este meeting. He was later joined by Australian Ambassador David Hawes in managing the complex mandate of the services-sector negotiating group during the round. Hamid Mamdouh, Gary Sampson, and later David Hartridge added strong secretariat support. A large number of other country representatives from industrialized and developing countries also became deeply involved. Particularly noteworthy were the highly able Brazilian and Indian ambassadors during the later phases of the negotiations, Rubens Ricupero and Balkrishan Zutshi, who came to realize their countries' self-

interest in a services agreement and consequently played a far more constructive role than their predecessors. Considerable strengthening of the services
agreement during the later years was also attributable to the "Quad" group
experts, David Lee of Canada, Jonathan Scheele of the EC, Tadamichi Yama-
moto of Japan, and Richard Self of the United States. Overall, the negotiation
of the services agreement became a truly multilateral achievement for what
was to be the most creative component of the final Uruguay Round
agreement.

THREE

Establishing the Agenda, 1983–1986

The GATT work program established at the November 1982 ministerial meeting would eventually evolve into an agenda for the Uruguay Round, but the immediate effect on the trading system was decidedly negative. Expectations that the GATT would resolve outstanding issues of contention were low to nil, while recession mired the world economy. The economic leadership of the industrialized nations had no coherent response to interacting trade and financial problems and was preoccupied with an emotional transatlantic dispute over the supply of gas pipeline equipment to the Soviet Union. Many developing countries, particularly in Latin America, faced staggering external debt payments, which forced them to reduce imports by every feasible means, often without regard for GATT principles of open trade.

The ensuing four years, in fact, began a process of fundamental reappraisal of national trade strategies that would continue through the decade. The existing GATT multilateral system was clearly inadequate, but views differed as to what to do about it. Newly emerging patterns of regional trade and investment would receive distinctive regional policy responses from governments. Growing political pressures to resolve trade disputes would put increased emphasis on bilateral negotiations outside the GATT. In the process, a universal system of common trade rules for all nations would lose support and credibility.

By the early 1980s, the European Community had lost its economic momentum and faced an identity crisis. Low economic growth, high unemployment and structural rigidities in labor and capital markets were diagnosed as "Euro-sclerosis." External competition from the United States, Japan, and the newly industrialized Asian exporters became a growing concern, especially for high-technology industries. Most fundamental, the EC was increasingly viewed as an ineffective institution that could not achieve economic recovery and perhaps even inhibited that goal. A respected study undertaken for the European Parliament in 1983 faulted member states: "Instead of looking for a driving force that can pull them along together, they are squandering their energies on quarrels that serve only to slow them all down." The study concluded that while it was "economic growth of the member countries that

46

welded the foundations of European unity in the beginning," the new unifying factor that "is gaining ground rapidly . . . is decadence."[1]

Work on EC-92—the European program of market unification, which would instill a new sense of purpose, albeit with a greatly strengthened regional orientation, remained two years away. In the interim, Euro-pessimism prevailed, and the mood hardly encouraged ambitious new trade liberalization within the GATT.

Japan began its definitive rise to economic superpower status in the early 1980s through a direct assault on key U.S. industries. Superior Japanese manufacturing in the automotive sector figured most prominently, with the Japanese share of the U.S. market for automobiles rising from 4 percent in 1970 to 21 percent in 1980. "Voluntary export restraints" then imposed by the United States induced Japanese companies to establish production facilities in the United States, resulting in a further rise in the Japanese share of the U.S. automobile market to over 30 percent by 1989. Growing competition in high-technology industry proved even more consequential. The Japanese share of the world market for the semiconductor industry rose dramatically, from 30 percent in 1980 to 52 percent in 1989, while the U.S. share shrank from 57 to 35 percent, signaling a looming struggle between the United States and Japan in the strategic information technology sector.

Japanese economic success was nevertheless troubled. Economic growth primarily depended on exports to the U.S. market, and by 1985 the burgeoning U.S. trade deficit, particularly vis-à-vis Japan, had become unsustainable. Japan needed a more broadly based trade strategy but faced hostility in Europe and developing countries because of its aggressive export penetration and the fact that the Japanese market remained largely closed to competing manufactured products. A more open multilateral trading system was clearly in Japan's interest, but Japanese trade policy through mid-decade remained generally defensive and overwhelmingly absorbed in nonstop bilateral negotiations with the United States to maintain access to the American market.

The developing countries were also experiencing a profound identity crisis after the oil shocks of the 1970s. Indeed, the dichotomy between developed and developing nations became less and less relevant to trade policy as countries such as South Korea, Singapore, and Brazil became strong competitors in world markets in a broad range of manufacturing industries. A strategy of bloc-to-bloc confrontation—with developing countries seeking market regulation and resource transfer in their favor, which had characterized the 1960s and 1970s—was increasingly viewed as futile. In April 1983, when the Group of 77 developing countries met to coordinate trade strategy, a senior Argentine official aptly commented that not much could be accomplished without the agreement of the industrial world. "There is also an understanding that the more aggressive you are, the harder it is to get things."[2]

But while the old North/South approach lost credibility, an alternative, more cooperative approach had not yet taken form. The key proved to be a revised development strategy based on export-led growth and private sector investment, which some Asian and Latin American countries had already embarked upon. Such market-based "development dialogue" with the World Bank and other aid agencies did not, however, spill over to trade negotiations. Most developing countries rightly saw their principal trade interest as the elimination of quotas limiting their exports of textiles, footwear, electronics, and agricultural products in industrial-country markets, but they were still not willing to offer a major opening of their own markets in return. This was the basis for the hard-line solidarity of developing countries at the November 1982 GATT ministerial meeting, which would not crack for another four years.

The basic reordering of trade interests in Europe, Japan, and the developing countries was thus at a formative stage from 1982 to 1986, which, in each case, would take on more definitive form in the latter part of the decade. In contrast, the trade-strategy debate in the United States started earlier and became a driving force for a fundamental evolution of world trading relationships.

Washington Trade-policy Debate

The GATT ministerial impasse of November 1982 threw U.S. trade policy into disarray and helped trigger the most profound national debate over trade since the 1930s. Brazilian and Indian opposition to a broadened GATT and European resistance to deal with growing protection for agricultural products frustrated Trade Representative Brock. If a multilateral approach could be blocked by a few, perhaps liberal trade should proceed on a more selective basis. In August 1983 President Reagan signed into law the Caribbean Basin one-way free-trade arrangement. Talks leading to a U.S.-Canada free-trade agreement began in February 1984, and similar talks aimed at a U.S.-Mexico framework agreement to liberalize trade began three months later. A U.S.-Israeli bilateral free-trade agreement was reached in 1985. At one point, Brock floated the idea of a limited-participation "GATT for the like-minded." On another occasion he proposed free trade agreements with the members of ASEAN.[3]

Beyond the beginnings of a North American free-trade grouping, however, these initiatives did not add up to a coherent overall trade strategy. The uncertain framework of trade relationships was, in fact, more the cause than the consequence of an ongoing U.S. reorientation of trade policy. The early 1980s saw two fundamental changes in the U.S. global trading position that unleashed a more activist U.S. policy than was feasible within the existing GATT system alone.

The first change was the massive deterioration of the U.S. balance of trade. A trade deficit of $31 billion in 1980 mushroomed to $122 billion in 1984 and to a high of $170 billion in 1987. Experts agreed that 60–90 percent of the trade deficit resulted from macro-economic policy factors. High interest rates to finance growing fiscal deficits caused a rapid rise in the value of the dollar, making imports cheaper and exports noncompetitive. Strong economic growth in the U.S. economy, beginning in 1983, further contributed to the import surge. The Reagan administration, however, split over the policy implications. Treasury Secretary Donald Regan considered the strong dollar a positive development while Chairman Martin Feldstein of the Council of Economic Advisers urged a sharp reduction in the budget deficit to bring down interest rates, the value of the dollar, and the trade deficit. Policy drift resulted while the trade balance worsened.

The political as well as economic consequences of a $100 billion plus annual trade deficits were momentous. Industry after industry faced disruptive adjustment to either import competition or loss of export markets. The dramatic shift of the United States from the largest net creditor country to the largest international debtor caused deep concern. The country could never again rest complacently on its assets as lender of last resort. Washington needed a macro-policy strategy and a more assertive trade policy for the other 10–40 percent of the deficit. Consensus quickly developed that the U.S. market was the most open to imports, and that the asymmetry of market access was no longer tolerable.

The second fundamental change in the U.S. trade position was loss of the comfortable, broadly based technological lead the United States had enjoyed for half a century. Japan, in particular, had closed or narrowed the gap in high-technology sectors such as semiconductors, computers, telecommunications, and robotics. This historic realignment of economic capability in advanced technologies would have pervasive and long-term influence on U.S. export competitiveness. It also raised national security issues since the most advanced technology was critical for superiority in weapons systems.

The prospect of high-tech parity with Japan and perhaps other countries intensified the trade-policy debate within the United States. Wide-ranging government support abroad for technology development—direct subsidies, national preference for public procurement, patent protection, regulatory practices—was often decisive for commercial competitiveness, and none of these policy areas were effectively covered by GATT commitments.

Anticompetitive practices also raised questions about reliance on free trade principles. The semiconductor industry was a prime example wherein huge investment costs for development, large economies of scale, and product life cycles of only two to three years led integrated Japanese computer companies to cut initial prices below cost in order to obtain dominant market share and to stifle competition. A school of American economists developed a "strategic trade policy" approach to deal with such imperfect market conditions through targeted import protection and industry subsidy. Most investigators came to the conclusion that implementation of such a strategic trade policy would be extremely difficult, if not counterproductive, in view of highly politicized trade policy decision-making in the United States. Nevertheless, unqualified adherence to free trade based on comparative advantage was no longer intellectually sustainable.[4]

These two fundamental changes in the U.S. trade position—mounting trade deficits and a sharp decline in the nation's technological lead—produced a groundswell of public calls for urgent remedial action. The administration went on the defensive. Pressures for immediate protection against imports led to tightened restrictions for textiles and steel and to higher tariffs on Japanese motorcycles. A series of bilateral negotiations to open the Japanese market for U.S. exports, orchestrated through the close personal relationship between President Reagan and Prime Minister Yasuhiro Nakasone, produced only modest results that pleased no one. Indeed, the trade deficit and decline of technological leadership problems converged on the U.S.-Japan relationship, which became the focal point of debate. The U.S. trade deficit with Japan reached $59 billion in 1986, with imports more than three time exports.

The momentum for new directions in U.S. trade policy came mainly from the Congress, but the process was anything but orderly. Legislative proposals proliferated. Among the more prominent were the domestic-content provision for automobile imports, a far more restrictive quota regime for textiles and footwear, and a ban on imports of telecommunications products from Japan. Bilateral trade-balance targets became popular. Senator Lloyd Bentsen and Congressman Dan Rostenkowski proposed legislation that would impose a 25 percent import surcharge on countries recording large trade surpluses with the United States, such as Japan, South Korea, Taiwan, and Brazil.

By 1985, some three hundred legislative proposals were before the Congress. A common objective was "fair trade" as distinct from "free trade," with the latter viewed as utopian. For the sports-minded American public, the catchphrase became "a level playing field." Implicit was a rejection of the GATT system of market-oriented trade within multilaterally bound levels of tariff protection.

Finally, in September 1985, President Reagan counterattacked with a comprehensive action program. He called on the Congress to "work with me" to avoid "a mindless stampede toward protectionism."[5] He had recently rejected import quota recommendations for footwear and copper, and he proposed instead a "strike force" to negotiate the elimination of unfair trade practices abroad. Authority for such unilateral initiatives, including the threat of trade retaliation, rose from the obscure and rarely-used Section 301 of the 1974 Trade Act, soon destined for notoriety. The president also proposed a $300 million fund to counter the unfair trade advantage of so-called tied aid export credits used by other countries. The trade proposals coincided with the September 22 announcement by finance ministers of the principal industrialized countries of the "Plaza Accord" to manage a decline in the U.S. dollar.

President Reagan also pledged to accelerate efforts to launch a new GATT round of negotiations, but warned that "if these negotiations are not initiated or if insignificant progress is made, I am instructing our trade negotiators to explore regional and bilateral agreements with other nations."[6]

The more aggressive administration stance clearly checked somewhat congressional momentum toward protectionist legislation. Members of Congress also reacted favorably to Clayton Yeutter, who succeeded William Brock as U.S. trade representative in July 1985, after Brock became Secretary of Labor. Yeutter took a tough line in his initial dealings with other governments, and his previous experience in trade policy was reassuring. More ominous, he was a Nebraska farmer with a Ph.D. in agricultural economics, and his articulate talk was especially blunt when he addressed the iniquitous, trade-distorting impact of the European Common Agricultural Policy.

New-round Agreement

In parallel with these politically charged, national debates over trade strategy, deliberations within the GATT proceeded on an uneven, uninspiring, and generally contentious course. Surprisingly, the committee on trade in agriculture agreed that quotas, subsidies, and technical barriers should be negotiated— even that a ban on most export subsidies should be considered. EC Commission representatives and their French member-state watchdogs had been uncharacteristically complacent, while a determined Dutch committee chairman with a difficult name to pronounce, Aart de Zeeuw, pressed ahead for agricultural reform. This obscure technocrat would later enjoy brief international notoriety. Discussion of trade in services also proved to be a useful educational exercise, aided by a four-hundred-page study submitted by the United States in December 1983, although developing countries continued to oppose a GATT role for this sector.

No progress was made on issues of interest to developing countries, which had been given priority for early action in the GATT work program. As the November 1984 deadline for completing the work program approached, the Uruguayan delegate, on behalf of the developing counties, laid it on the line, urging the industrialized countries to "immediately take adequate measures to redress the present imbalance." He specified, among other measures, the lifting of restrictive measures inconsistent with GATT (i.e., wide-ranging quotas), utmost restraint in countervailing and antidumping procedures, and immediate steps to liberalize imports of textiles and clothing. Such actions "would amount to no more than fulfilling previously accepted commitments." Moreover, until such steps could be taken, "any initiative such as a new round of negotiations in GATT would be lacking in credibility and devoid of relevance particularly for developing countries."[7]

The November 1984 annual meeting of the GATT contracting parties was predictably inconclusive. Delegates agreed to study further whether trade in services could be brought within the scope of the GATT, although only after strong pressure from the United States, including the withholding of approval for the GATT budget for the following year. A proposal by the industrialized countries to deal with the problem of counterfeit goods was opposed by developing countries and a compromise adopted whereby an experts group would be appointed by both the GATT and the UN World Intellectual Property Organization (WIPO). The developing countries made no headway on their priority agenda. Industrialized nations expressed hope that the follow-on work program for 1985 would lead to a new round of negotiations in 1986, but such aspirations remained wishful thinking.

Waning support for the GATT had led Director-General Arthur Dunkel in November 1983 to establish a panel of seven distinguished persons to develop a report on problems affecting the international trading system. The panel represented industrialized and developing countries, and Fritz Leutwiler, chairman of the Swiss National Bank, presided. The report, completed in February 1985, roundly rejected the protectionist trend and made an articulate case for a strengthened and more open multilateral GATT system as the basis for renewed growth and economic development. Fifteen specific recommendations were put forward for "immediate action to meet the present crisis in the trading system." The GATT did not widely publicize the report, however, in part because Dunkel did not want to alienate developing countries, and it thus had minimal impact in rallying support for new GATT negotiations.[8]

The mechanism that finally triggered the Uruguay Round came not from within the GATT but from discussions among industrialized-country leaders, most prominently at annual economic summits and OECD ministerial meetings, and more discreetly through a series of meetings among the Quad (i.e., U.S., EC, Japanese, and Canadian) trade ministers.[9] The protracted process lasted from 1983 to 1985, with the United States as an impatient proponent and France, in particular, raising various roadblocks.

At the Williamsburg, Virginia, economic summit in May 1983, the United States proposed a joint call for a new GATT round, but the leaders could only agree "to continue consultations on proposals for a new negotiating round in the GATT." Moreover, France used the occasion to press for a parallel conference to reform the international monetary system. Despite considerable discussion, the summit and OECD meetings in the spring of 1984 were similarly inconclusive, giving only cautious support to the idea of a new round. In September 1984 President Reagan raised the issue at the annual meeting of the IMF and the World Bank: "Join us. Support with us a new, expanded round of trade liberalization." Dutch finance minister Onno Ruding, however, cautioned that the timing of a new round was uncertain because "we still have to make good on existing commitments from previous trade rounds."[10]

The decisive phase was the spring of 1985. The United States urged a target of early 1986 for the beginning of a new round—a necessary step to counter protectionist pressure. Trade Representative Brock pleaded: "We need multilateral negotiations, and we need them now." Otherwise, "our business community will be able to accuse us with some justification that we fiddled while the trading system was breaking down around us."[11]

At the April OECD ministerial meeting, France resisted a target date, and the compromise language adopted called for a new round to begin "as soon as possible." In addition, it called for "a preparatory meeting of senior officials" that "should take place in GATT before the end of the summer to reach consensus on subject matter and modalities for such a negotiation."

At the Bonn economic summit in May, France hardened its preconditions for a new round. President Mitterand reiterated his linkage to the world monetary system and was assuaged by U.S. willingness to host such a conference in Washington. He also stressed the need to assure developing-country participation in advance. Most important, a new precondition was made to exempt the European Common Agricultural Policy (CAP) from a new round. Belatedly, France realized that the GATT work program in agriculture was well advanced, and President Mitterand accused the Americans of using the GATT round as a pretext to destroy "everything that had been built up for European agriculture within the framework of Common Market policy."[12] Excluding the CAP from the new round was unacceptable to the United States, and a frustrated Secretary of State George Shultz responded, "We intend to move forward in trade, we hope on a multilateral basis. But we'll do so on bilateral terms if we have to . . . excluding the French from the resulting benefits of reductions in trade barriers."[13] The bitter summit stalemate ended with a communiqué endorsing the earlier OECD language for a new round "as soon as possible" and adding plaintively, "Most of us think that this should be in 1986."

The proposed call for a meeting of GATT senior officials bogged down during debate in Geneva in July, with developing countries resisting inclusion of trade in services at such a meeting. The United States then took the unusual step of requesting a postal ballot of GATT members. A majority vote would initiate the meeting in September, and if Brazil and India wanted to stay home, so be it. U.S. ambassadors around the world received instructions to urge their host governments to get their ballots in the mail. The pressure tactic worked, and all GATT members participated in the meeting of September 30–October 2, 1985, which followed by a week the announcement of President Reagan's new tough trade policy. The GATT meeting ended with agreement to begin formal preparations for a new round, and a group of senior officials then struggled for another six weeks to decide how to organize the preparations. Finally, on Thanksgiving day, November 28, weary delegates agreed to establish a preparatory committee to develop a negotiating mandate by July 1986, for adoption at a ministerial meeting to be held in September 1986.

Thus, after more than four years, the United States had achieved its goal of launching a new round of trade negotiations, but it was not an inspiring achievement. Years of deliberations within the GATT had accomplished almost nothing of the immediate-action program agreed to by ministers in 1982. Divisiveness among the industrialized countries, as at the Bonn summit, and strident opposition by developing countries to trade-in-services negotiations and other new issues cast a pall over the prospects for the round. U.S. negotiating behavior was also upsetting. Washington rationalized a new round in large part as a tactical move to avert rampant protectionism at home. Others received an ultimatum. Either they go along or the United States would jettison the multilateral approach and negotiate a series of bilateral and minilateral arrangements. The credibility of the GATT trading system suffered greatly during the protracted process.

The new round did not yet have a name, and there was informal talk of a Reagan Round or a Brussels Round. The latter implied Brussels as the location for the ministerial meeting to launch the round, a setting that would have a disappointing reprise five years later. Of course, the name became the Uruguay Round, reflecting the September 1986 meeting at Punta del Este. It also symbolized the more prominent role of developing countries in world trade. Nineteen eighty-six would, in fact, become a watershed for developing-country participation in the GATT trading system.

Preparing the Agenda

The *Financial Times,* assessing the prospects at the close of 1984, warned that the success and survival of the GATT would "ultimately depend on confidence and consensus." With respect to developing countries in particular, "there is now a distinct and apparently cohesive Third World lobby in the GATT, led by India and Brazil. If the traditionally pragmatic GATT becomes like UNCTAD, a North-South shouting shop more concerned with ideology than with commercial relations, then the prospects for a successful new round of talks on trade liberalization will be bleak indeed."[14]

This assessment accurately reflected the official debate within GATT during the ensuing year, but it masked a rethinking of trade strategy within many Asian and Latin American countries that would lead to a breakdown of developing-country cohesion in the summer of 1986. The issue for developing countries was whether to continue pressing for unilateral actions based on the 1982 work program endorsed by ministers, or to agree to negotiate these objectives in a new round through reciprocal commitments in the new areas of trade in services, protection of intellectual property, and trade-related investment measures. One practical reason for the latter course was that the unilateral approach had gotten nowhere after three years, while new protectionist measures were being applied and threatened in industrialized countries. The tactic of North/South confrontation simply didn't work.

Another cause for the rethinking by developing countries related to changed attitudes about underlying development strategy and the new issues. Trade liberalization in the new areas of policy would give immediate benefits principally to companies in industrialized countries, but it would also help development. A modern, efficient services sector was critical to export competitiveness, and an improved climate for foreign direct investment, including reasonable protection for intellectual property, was becoming a more prominent development objective as the debt crisis closed the door on public sector borrowing from commercial banks. The more advanced developing countries, moreover, had competitive service sectors of their own, in construction, transportation, data processing, and telecommunications. A trade strategy linking market access for exports of goods to a more open system in these new areas made sense. It nevertheless constituted a fundamental shift in developing-country participation in the GATT, from passive *demandeur* to active negotiator of reciprocal commitments.

This evolution of attitudes by developing countries had benefited from a series of meetings in the GATT in 1985. Initial meetings in January, May, and July addressed the desirability of a new round and the possible issues to be negotiated. Although the North/South impasse over services continued, there was detailed discussion for the first time within the GATT of the pros and cons for a new round. The Preparatory Committee (Prepcom), established in November 1985 and chaired by Director-General Dunkel, met nine times during January-July 1986. Members systematically discussed the full range of trade issues that would constitute the Uruguay Round. These deliberations served principally as the technical basis for what came later, but two developments are noteworthy, one concerning what did later occur, the other concerning what did not.

The first was the belated U.S. initiative to broaden greatly the scope of intellectual-property protection as a priority Uruguay Round objective. Through 1985, GATT discussions of the issue had been limited to the problem of counterfeit goods, for which a draft code had been developed but not adopted in the late 1970s. Views differed within the U.S. government over whether the broader questions of adequate standards, enforcement, and dispute settlement, which were of increasing importance to American companies, should be pursued in the GATT or elsewhere. By late 1985, however, the decision was made for a comprehensive approach in the GATT as a high priority, and coordination with other industrialized countries to this end was under way.

The first GATT presentation came at the April 1986 Prepcom meeting. The U.S. representative pressed to discuss in the new round not only counterfeit goods but better protection of patents, trademarks, copyrights, and other intellectual property. In a key statement, the U.S. argued, "GATT had the appropriate legal and institutional framework to deal with the problems, including the machinery for ensuring transparency, notification, consultation, and dispute settlement."[15] At that point, the European Community still felt that the broader questions of intellectual-property protection needed further discussion, but by the subsequent Prepcom discussion in May, the industrialized grouping was united in support of the comprehensive approach. Brazil, India,

Argentina, and Cuba opposed dealing with any aspects of intellectual property in the new round, while the only other developing country to intervene in the Prepcom discussion was Zaire, which did not oppose including the subject in future negotiations. By July, the phrasing of the issue in GATT documents changed from "Trade in Counterfeit Goods and Other Aspects of Intellectual Property" to "Trade Related Aspects of Intellectual Property Rights, including Trade in Counterfeit Goods."

The second noteworthy development at the March Prepcom meeting was the European Community proposal on "balance of benefits," directed at Japan, which the EC considered "the first priority in the new round as far as substance is concerned." The Community representative explained that "a very small number of contracting parties had found a way to obtain benefits from the GATT system which far exceeded their contribution. . . . there was seemingly an impenetrable barrier between the internal market of these contracting parties and the outside world. . . . It was achieved without countervailing the letter of the GATT but nevertheless posed a great danger to the trading system. . . . If this problem was not dealt with in the new round, the system would not survive. . . . If this exercise were not undertaken, there was an increasing risk of recourse to self-defensive actions, or worse, bilateralism." The Japanese representative countered that he "could not accept the alarming picture that the European Communities had painted of the imminent demise of the GATT. It was disconcerting to hear . . . that a complete change in the trading rules was necessary if the system were to survive. . . . Any attempt to dismantle the GATT now would deal a fatal blow to the . . . developing countries."[16]

This unusually accusatory exchange, by GATT standards, reflected growing resentment in Europe about Japanese trading practices and about the elusive government-industry relationship in particular. It paralleled political debate in the United States, including exchanges over draft legislation to set bilateral trade targets for Japan. The U.S. delegate, however, did not engage in the Prepcom discussion, and when the EC-Japan issue flared up again at the Punta del Este meeting, the United States was instrumental in excluding "balance-of-benefits" from the Uruguay Round agenda. By doing so, it implicitly decided to deal with this central aspect of the Japan trade relationship bilaterally rather than together with kindred European spirits. The U.S. decision was based on the well-founded judgment that injecting structural aspects of the Japanese trading system into the new GATT round could indeed have dealt a fatal blow to the GATT.

The lengthy Prepcom process covered a lot of substantive ground, but on the central objective—a consensus mandate for the new round—it was hopelessly polarized. Brazil, India, and a few other hard-line developing countries continued to oppose inclusion of the new issues while the industrialized grouping pressed for a comprehensive mandate. Chairman Dunkel and the GATT secretariat were committed to the tradition of working for consensus, which by June had become futile, and discussion fragmented into smaller groups outside formal GATT auspices.

A catalytic step was then taken that would lead to the ultimate Uruguay Round mandate and would have permanent impact on the GATT as an institution. An informal group of industrialized countries, the "Dirty Dozen," held a series of private meetings and produced the first comprehensive ministerial declaration. For tactical reasons, the three large members—the United States, the EC, and Japan—temporarily withdrew from the group while the smaller industrialized countries joined with about twenty moderate (i.e., non-hard-line) developing countries to further develop and circulate the draft. Other developing countries joined, the big three rejoined, and the now forty-eight participants formally constituted themselves as the G-48. Pierre-Louis Girard, Swiss representative to the GATT, and Colombian representative Felipe Jaramillo chaired the group, which convened in the conference facilities of the EFTA delegations, half a mile from GATT headquarters. Beginning the third week of July, the G-48 met daily for about ten days, working late into the night, and completed the final draft declaration, which Girard and Jaramillo presented to Director-General Dunkel as the basis for ministerial discussion at Punta del Este in September.[17]

The cohesion of the G-48, cutting across North/South lines, put the hardliners on the defensive and forced them to produce their own G-10 draft, reflecting ten cosponsors. Argentina, a hesitant member of the G-10, submitted yet a third draft for ministerial consideration. Thus the stage was set for a showdown between the G-48 and the G-10 at Punta.

A separate yet overlapping country realignment that took place during the summer of 1986 related to the agricultural sector. During the Prepcom discussions, six agricultural exporters—Australia, Chile, Colombia, Thailand, New Zealand, and Uruguay—submitted a joint paper calling for substantial trade liberalization in this sector. The group expanded to fourteen—adding Argentina, Brazil, Canada, Fiji, Hungary, Indonesia, Malaysia, and the Philippines—and formalized in a meeting at the Australian north coast resort town of Cairns in August 1986. The Cairns group threatened to walk out if substantial trade liberalization for agriculture were not achieved in the new round. This created a basically three-cornered inner framework for agricultural negotiations between the European Community, the United States, and the Cairns group. It also pushed agriculture, the most intractable sector in past negotiations, further toward center stage in the Uruguay Round, even though it accounted for a declining share of only about 10 percent of world trade.

The realignment of country groupings and, in particular, the split in developing-country solidarity constituted a fundamental change in the negotiating context of the GATT. The decision by most developing countries to embark on negotiation of reciprocal commitments reflected a revised assessment of their economic self-interest. It also meant that they had bargaining leverage to insist on specific commitments in return on issues of export interest to them—relating to textiles, for example—which was not fully recognized by the industrialized countries at the time.

The regional breakdown in the developing-country splits was especially indicative of shifting trade strategies. In Asia only India stood among the hardliners, while the G-48 grouping included the generally more export-oriented Bangladesh, Hong Kong, Indonesia, South Korea, Malaysia, Pakistan, the Philippines, Singapore, Sri Lanka, and Thailand. The split within Latin America and the Caribbean was even more significant in view of traditional solidarity in support of the anti-GATT, protectionist, import-substitution approach to development. Brazil was joined in the G-10 by Argentina, Cuba, Nicaragua and Peru, while G-48 members included Chile, Colombia, Jamaica, Mexico, Trinidad and Tobago, and Uruguay. Mexico's decision in 1985 to join GATT under terms of a radically liberalized import regime produced a stark contrast between the two largest economic powers in Latin America.

The realignment also influenced the role of Director-General Dunkel and the GATT secretariat in the new round. Until summer 1986, Dunkel, in longsuffering deliberations to reach consensus, maintained a scrupulously neutral stance between the hard-line views of Brazil and India and those of the industrialized grouping. Americans became outspoken critics of Dunkel's attempts to curry favor and thus compromise moves from the hard-liners. With the split among the developing countries and the triumph of the G-48 at Punta, however, the director general, a free trader by deep conviction, shifted to a more assertive role in support of a major trade liberalizing agreement.

Punta Declaration: Synopsis

A detailed account of the Punta del Este meeting was given in the prologue, and the text of the ministerial declaration adopted by the ministers on September 20, 1986, is contained in Appendix B. The following is an annotated synopsis of the declaration geared to an understanding of the ensuing course of negotiations.

The Punta declaration language was most specific on the four principal objectives pressed by the United States—agriculture and the three new areas, which were the focus of negotiations at Punta. The scope of the negotiating mandate was far broader, but other important issues received less attention and, in some instances, were incorporated into the declaration in cursory fashion. As a result, the relative importance of issues, as well as linkages among them that would emerge in the final bargaining phase, are only partially revealed by the text.

The agricultural debate at Punta centered, as it had during the years of preparatory discussion, on the trade-distorting effects of the European Community farm policy. This involved three related elements—internal price supports, access for imports, and export subsidies. Export subsidies threatened world trade the most, and the United States and the Cairns group tried to obtain a specific commitment in this area. The operative declaration language for the agricultural sector called for "improving market access through, *inter alia,* the reduction of import barriers," and with respect to subsidies and price supports "increasing discipline on the use of all direct and indirect subsidies and other measures affecting directly or indirectly agricultural trade, including the phased reduction of their negative effects." The French had resisted explicit reference to "export subsidies," but the reference to "all" subsidies clearly included them. Attempts to insert "possible elimination of export subsidies," which had gotten as far as the 1984 GATT agricultural committee report, met unyielding EC resistance and was dropped, although such a goal was still possible within the broadly drawn ministerial mandate.

The three new areas were all included in the declaration but with differing levels of commitment. The objectives for trade in services were the most explicit in substantive terms, having benefited from several years of detailed discussion: "Negotiations in this area shall aim to establish a multilateral framework of principles and rules for trade in services, including elaboration of possible disciplines for individual sectors, with a view to expansion of such trade under conditions of transparency and progressive liberalization." Clearly an agreement of some sort was to be negotiated. The organizational compromise separated the Group on Negotiations on Services from the other negotiating groups, but the same GATT procedures would apply, including technical support from the GATT secretariat, and the services group, like all others, would report to the more senior Trade Negotiations Committee. There was no commitment that the final agreement on services would be linked to the GATT, but the momentum was all in that direction.

The declaration was more tentative with respect to protection of intellectual property, and uncertainty remained until the final hours of the Punta meeting as to whether agreement could be reached at all. The final text called for negotiations "to develop a framework of principles, rules and disciplines dealing with international trade in counterfeit goods," but for the broader subject of trade-related aspects of intellectual property rights, the negotiations were more vaguely defined, "to clarify GATT provisions and elaborate as appropriate new rules and disciplines." Nevertheless, the United States achieved the broader scope it sought, and the detailed discussion on protection of intellectual property, in contrast to that on services, would only begin in the post-Punta negotiations.

The third new area, trade related investment measures, was limited to one sentence in the declaration, never getting the same emphasis as the other two. Debate focused on whether the issue should be subject to negotiation at all, or merely referred for further study. The final text called for negotiations, but with greatly hedged terms, to "elaborate, as appropriate, further provisions that may be necessary to avoid such adverse effects on trade."

Agreement by the developing countries on the three new areas reflected a strategy to negotiate a package of reciprocal commitments, but the quid pro quo from the developing-country vantage was not clearly delineated in the declaration. Under general principles governing negotiations, the traditional language about nonreciprocity and "differential and more favorable treatment" for developing countries was included. The lengthy section on "Standstill and Rollback" consisted of unilateral commitments by the industrialized countries, "commencing immediately," not to take new restrictive measures and to phase out existing measures inconsistent with the GATT. It included explicit provision that "there should be no GATT concessions requested for the elimination of these measures." This was the last attempt to maintain the 1982 ministerial declaration to dismantle unilaterally bilateral quotas and other informal restrictions. The Punta language on standstill and rollback was agreed to disingenuously by the industrialized countries, who later stretched the meaning of "GATT consistency" to cover virtually all past and future actions.

The principal developing-country objectives to be negotiated in the Uruguay Round, in addition to agriculture, were a comprehensive safeguards agreement and trade liberalization for the textile sector. Most elements of a safeguards agreement were elaborated in some detail in the declaration, although the most difficult issue, nondiscrimination versus selectivity in applying quota restrictions, was not even mentioned. For textiles and clothing, negotiations would be aimed at integrating this sector (i.e., that covered in the Multifiber Arrangement on quotas) into normal GATT rules, and thus to "further liberalization of trade." Two other subjects of particular interest to developing countries, tropical products and natural resource-based products, were to achieve "the fullest liberalization of trade," but the potential trade impact from actions in these areas was more limited.

Some subjects for negotiation were not elaborated, and their significance would only become apparent as the negotiations unfolded. Reductions in tariffs and nontariff barriers, which had been the principal substance of previous GATT trade liberalization, were inscribed briefly as objectives, but with no indication of the anticipated degree of reductions or the formula for achieving them. Improvement in the existing GATT agreements on subsidies and countervailing duties was listed as an explicit negotiating objective, but antidumping practices, which would become a major area of contention before the end of the round, were not mentioned by name and were subsumed under the broad heading, "MTN [i.e., multilateral trade negotiation] Agreements and Arrangements." Another catch-all heading, "GATT Articles," included several issues of significance, most prominently the provisions of Article XVIII that permit developing countries wide latitude to apply quotas and other selective import restrictions for balance-of-payments reasons.

The remaining subjects for negotiation related to strengthening of the GATT as an institution. One negotiating group would develop a more prompt and effective dispute-settlement mechanism, while the Group on the Functioning of the GATT System (FOGS) would deal with GATT surveillance of trading practices, more effective decision-making within the GATT, and a strengthened relationship between the GATT and the international financial institutions in order to achieve the nebulous goal of "greater coherence in global economic policy-making."

This was the negotiating mandate adopted by ministers from ninety-six countries at Punta del Este. Some proposed issues were not included in the declaration, including labor standards, commodity agreements, and restrictive business practices. The U.S. negotiators, reflecting congressional intent, had pressed for inclusion of labor standards against strong resistance by others to linking such standards to possible GATT trade sanctions, and the issue was dropped to be reengaged for the post–Uruguay Round agenda by a more labor-friendly U.S. Democratic administration. The EC proposal for a balance-of-benefits objective was rejected, as explained by conference chairman Enrique Iglesias, on the grounds that it might lead to a trading system incompatible with the GATT, "the guarantor of the open and non-discriminatory trading system."[18] The long U.S. quest for negotiations on high-technology trade also had been left out of the G-48 draft. Three of these issues—restrictive business practices, balance-of-benefits, and high-technology trade—however, would become more closely interrelated and better understood through actions outside the GATT by the time the Uruguay Round was concluded.

The Uruguay Round mandate, nevertheless, exceeded the scope of anything attempted before, and the active participation of major developing countries made it truly multilateral in nature. But inscribing subjects on the agenda was a long way from specific, final agreements. The ministers agreed to complete the negotiations within four years, which some GATT veterans considered unduly optimistic.

TOPICAL ADDENDUM: PROTECTION OF INTELLECTUAL PROPERTY

Agreements on trade in services and protection of intellectual property were the two major Uruguay Round accomplishments for broadening the mandate of the GATT trading system, but their negotiating roots stood in sharp contrast to one another. Trade in services, as described in the previous topical addendum, was subject to a deluge of public discussion and economic analysis for more than a decade before being inscribed on the agenda at Punta del Este. Efforts to bring intellectual property rights into the GATT, in contrast, started much later and focused predominantly on direct trading interests rather than analytic debate.

One common root was the almost exclusive U.S. initiative at the outset. In the early 1980s, U.S. industry became increasingly worried about the growing cost of inadequate protection for patents, trademarks, copyrighted material, and other intellectual property rights, particularly in newly industrialized Asian countries. The computer, pharmaceutical, motion picture, publishing, and apparel industries were the most seriously affected. The U.S. International Trade Commission, based on industry surveys, estimated the annual loss to U.S. industry at $40 billion.[19]

There was no agreement, however, as to how to respond to the problem. The existing policy framework centered on the Paris Convention for patent and trademark protection and the Berne Convention for copyright protection. Both provided for national treatment—that is, treatment of foreign intellectual property according to national laws and standards—and were administered by the World Intellectual Property Organization (WIPO), a UN agency. The WIPO had no authority to make binding decisions or to impose sanctions, and thus policy differences had to be pursued elsewhere. The U.S. trade laws included Section 337, which banned imports that infringed on intellectual property, and Section 301, applying sanctions against countries that engaged in "unreasonable" or "unfair" trading practices, which could include inadequate protection of intellectual property.

The U.S. private sector considered existing standards unreasonably low in most developing countries and felt that the lack of enforcement of even these standards constituted unfair trading practices. The question, rather, was whether to pursue strengthened standards and enforcement in the WIPO and bilateral negotiations or to seek to place the full range of intellectual-property issues within the GATT framework. GATT Article XX contained an exception to general obligations in order to permit protection for intellectual-property rights, but the GATT did not address possible trade distortions from inadequate protection of such rights.[20] A new GATT mandate for protecting intellectual property rights, however, would be strongly resisted by developing countries, who were already opposing discussion of services trade in a new round. Some trade experts thus opposed adding intellectual property to the already troubled GATT agenda. Intellectual property experts within the U.S. government and private sector also tended to resist a change in policy venue from their controlled, WIPO-oriented domain to the trade policy bureaucracy and the GATT. Proponents of the GATT approach built their case on the growing importance of intellectual-property rights in international trade and investment, and the nonoperational character of the WIPO.

Differences of view prevailed through mid-1985, and only in April 1986, shortly before the Punta meeting, did the U.S. government formally announce that it would seek an agreement in the new GATT round against "trade-distorting practices arising from inadequate protection of intellectual property."[21] The decision of Chairman John Opel of IBM to support the GATT approach, despite opposition or indifference from his in-house legal staff, was the most noteworthy conversion that tipped the balance.

The Punta declaration called for the elaboration of new rules and disciplines for intellectual-property rights, and the United States provided prompt follow-up with a detailed proposal for a GATT-based intellectual-property agreement.[22] It focused on three elements:

1. *Dispute settlement.* The United States simply proposed adoption of GATT procedures for consultation and dispute settlement, including possible retaliation by withdrawing "trade benefits elsewhere." In other words, the cross-retaliation issue arose here as it had in the services negotiating group.

2. *Domestic enforcement.* Commitments covering both imported and domestic goods would be undertaken to ensure "prompt, fair, reasonable, and effective" administrative and legal procedures against infringers of intellectual property rights. Remedies could include injunctions, monetary awards, seizure and destruction of infringing goods, and criminal procedures.

3. *Standards.* In this most controversial area, the United States wanted standards of protection raised to levels existing in the industrialized countries, which were much higher than those prevailing in most developing countries. The initial U.S. proposal contained an annex that elaborated "agreed norms" for patents, trademarks, copyright, trade secrets, and semiconductor design. Patents, for example, would be protected for twenty years from the date the patent was sought or seventeen years from the date it was granted. Severe restrictions would be placed on compulsory licensing.

The U.S. proposal polarized the initial phase of Uruguay Round negotiations on intellectual property rights. The other industrialized countries, which had earlier been hesitant about a frontal assault in the round, quickly closed ranks with the Americans. As in the United States, the private sectors in Europe and Japan led their governments in assessing the growing commercial stakes involved. Close collaboration developed between the U.S. Intellectual Property Committee, the Union of Industrial and Employers' Confederation of Europe, and the Japanese Keidanren. Their definitive joint statement of June 1988, *Basic Framework of* GATT *Provisions on Intellectual Property: Statement of Views of the European, Japanese and United States Business Communities,* took as the reference point for dispute settlement the standards of protection that currently existed in the industrialized countries. It stated that any negotiated GATT provisions "must not permit a reduction in protection from levels already afforded."[23]

Developing countries were not as unified in their response, but neither were they openly split, as was the case in the services sector. Again, Brazil and India led the opposition, while many others held back, raising questions and remaining uncommitted. The developing-country response was based on the Uruguay Round mandate to consider "trade-related aspects of intellectual property rights" in the context of trade expansion, and the existing levels of protection were judged to be trade-restricting, particularly for developing countries. A Brazilian presentation concluded that "the rigid monopoly situation created by excessive protection of IPRs [intellectual-property rights] constitutes . . . a serious restriction to trade, for in such cases, countries granting protection . . . can neither freely acquire and adapt foreign technology, nor freely import new processes and products from alternative foreign sources."[24] India, in a comprehensive twenty-page, single-spaced presentation, concluded: "India is of the view that it is only the restrictive and anti-competitive practices of the owners of intellectual property rights that can be considered to be trade-related because they alone distort or impede international trade." As for a GATT role in this area, "the protection of intellectual property rights has no direct or significant relationship to international trade. . . . It would therefore not be appropriate to establish within the framework of the General Agreement on Tariffs and Trade any new rules and disciplines pertaining to standards and principles concerning the availability, scope and use of intellectual property rights."[25]

In any event, initial debate within the negotiating group was largely a dialogue of the deaf. The industrialized participants, under growing pressure from companies with specific complaints, pressed for strengthened standards, effectively enforced. Developing countries argued a more theoretical case, with few specifics. The $40 billion losses claimed by U.S. industry were never examined in detail or compared with the alleged losses to developing economies. The crux of the matter, in analytic terms, was that a limited monopoly is granted to holders of patents and other intellectual-property rights in order to stimulate new invention for commercial application. But measuring the costs and benefits of such monopoly rights is extremely difficult, if not impossible, and existing standards are thus highly subjective if not arbitrary. Why seventeen- and twenty-year protection for patents, and why the same length of time for all industries?[26] The Indian presentation noted that "many economists have questioned the very hypothesis that a patent system is essential to encourage inventions and investments in research and development,"[27] but no economists were called to debate this fundamental issue during the Uruguay Round. It is also doubtful that they would have had much to contribute to the question of optimum levels of protection for intellectual property.[28]

The ideological impasse lasted two years, and at the mid-term ministerial review at the end of 1988, the status of intellectual-property rights in the overall negotiation remained tenuous. Then, during the second half of the Uruguay Round, two largely unanticipated developments changed greatly the context of the intellectual-property negotiations. First, developing-country opposition to a broad GATT mandate in this area collapsed. Second, several major issues of contention emerged among the industrialized countries, which broadened the negotiations from a strictly North/South to a multilateral context.

A reevaluation by developing countries came, in part, from the growing emphasis placed on foreign direct investment in national development strategies, and the realization that intellectual-property protection was important for attracting such investment. Export-competitive industries required state-of-the-art technology, which multinational corporations would only transfer abroad if the embodied intellectual property was adequately protected. The more dramatic changes by the end of the Uruguay Round included a sweeping new Mexican law to protect intellectual property and a basic reversal of the Brazilian "informatics" policy, which had either prohibited or failed to protect foreign-owned information technologies and related software.

Equally important, the United States aggressively pursued strengthened protection for intellectual property through the enhanced Special 301 provision of the 1988 Omnibus Trade Act. Priority countries were targeted for bilateral negotiation, and trade retaliation loomed if changes were not forthcoming. Some East Asian exporters, enjoying large yet politically vulnerable trade surpluses with the United States, yielded to U.S. pressure and strengthened intellectual-property standards and enforcement procedures. Retaliatory import restrictions were levied against Brazil and threatened against India and China, among others. This unilateral U.S. approach made it easier for some developing countries to sign on to a GATT agreement, since their national standards had now become more acceptable. Others came to realize that a multilateral agreement in the GATT could be the lesser evil to unilateral U.S. demands outside the GATT.

The emergence of major contentious issues among the industrialized countries demonstrated the scope and complexity of intellectual property rights. While these countries already applied the same general standards of protection, important issues of application still prevailed, and the European Community, to the surprise of the United States, used the latter phase of the Uruguay Round to try to resolve some of them.[29] One issue was patent entitlement on the "first-to-file" principle, as practiced in most of the world, versus the "first-to-invent" principle of the United States. Another was appellations of origin—that is the use of geographic names for products, such as "burgundy" for a California wine. Yet another was "neighboring rights" for copyright of sound recordings, which would extend copyright to "neighboring" performers' and broadcasters' rights.

The final agreement that emerged in the Uruguay Round provides a basic set of standards and procedures but is only the beginning of what will be a steadily evolving area of international rights and obligations. Intellectual-property rights for such things as semiconductor design, computer software, and biotechnology will be developed at various levels, within national judicial systems, through bilateral agreements, and more broadly within the European Community, the OECD, and the WIPO. More elaborate standards can then be incorporated within the World Trade Organization, and disputes addressed through its consultative and dispute-settlement procedures.

FOUR

Specifying the Objectives, 1987–1988

The ministers at Punta agreed to a quick start for the negotiations. The senior body for managing the negotiations was the Trade Negotiations Committee, chaired by the Uruguayan foreign minister when meeting at ministerial level and by Director-General Dunkel at official level. The first meeting at official level was held in October 1986 to organize the work schedule. By January fifteen negotiating groups were established, covering: (1) tariffs, (2) non-tariff measures, (3) natural resource base products, (4) textiles and clothing, (5) agriculture, (6) tropical products, (7) subsidies, (8) safeguards, (9) GATT articles, (10) dispute settlement, (11) multilateral trade negotiation (MTN) agreements and arrangements, (12) functioning of the GATT system, (13) trade-related aspects of intellectual property, (14) trade-related investment measures; and (15) services.[1] Chairmen for the groups were among the most able Geneva representatives to the GATT and, in a few cases, officials from capitals. All groups had met at least once by April, and the intent was to have detailed proposals for negotiation from all participants by the end of the year.

The early months of 1987, however, were greatly troubled in the trade-policy field, which spilled over to the fledgling Geneva talks. The U.S. record trade deficit of $150 billion in 1986 increased domestic pressures for immediate action. Protectionist trade legislation that had been sidetracked in the previous Congress could no longer be avoided because the president needed new legislative authority to negotiate the Uruguay Round. Japan remained the principal target for acrimonious statements by members of the Congress and for intensive bilateral negotiations involving semiconductors, supercomputers, auto parts, and construction contracts for the new Osaka airport. On April 29, the eve of Prime Minister Nakasone's visit to Washington, the House of Representatives approved a proposal by Congressman Richard Gephardt calling for retaliation if Japan did not stop unfair trade practices and reduce its trade surplus with the United States to specified levels.

The United States and the European Community were also embroiled in a dispute over $430 million of U.S. corn and sorghum exports that would be terminated when the Common Agriculture Policy was applied to its new member, Spain. The United States threatened to retaliate with 200 percent duties on European wines, brandy, and cheese if market access were not retained. After much public posturing on both sides, the European Community agreed to permit Spanish feed-grain imports for four more years, until 1991, thus effectively linking expiration of this accord with the final Uruguay Round bargaining in the agricultural sector.

In this conflicted context, the fifteen negotiating groups launched their work, which over the ensuing two years would accumulate a prodigious amount of technical and policy-oriented material on the wide range of issues being negotiated. Country proposals were supplemented by analytic work requested from the GATT secretariat and from other international bodies. The most interesting debate involved the groups on services, chaired by Ambassador Jaramillo, and on intellectual property, chaired by the Swedish representative to the GATT, Lars Anell. These groups were breaking new, uncertain ground, and the documentation of their efforts in the GATT archives provides rich insight as to how complex and ill-defined issues were molded into specific negotiating objectives. During 1987–1988, there were more than 150 official meetings of the negotiating groups, plus countless smaller, unofficial gatherings.[2]

The group approach, however, tended to compartmentalize discussion and thus ignore the inevitable linkages among issues that would emerge as negotiations reached a more definitive stage. There were, in any event, too many groups, the large number stemming from the fifteen headings in the Punta Declaration. No mechanism linked the groups, and the fifteen chairmen never met together. In addition, the four-year time frame for negotiations was vague, threatening a desultory pace until the final months, when all issues would have to come together for the final bargaining phase. The Americans, especially anxious to show early results, proposed a midterm ministerial meeting in 1988, at which time a selected package of agreements would be adopted, leaving the remaining issues for 1990. The idea of a midterm ministerial was appealing, and a December 1988 meeting in Montreal was set. The proposal for a selected package of early agreements was received more warily, however, since much depended on what was in the package. The United States, unsurprisingly, wanted to include a framework agreement for services and immediate action to liberalize agricultural trade. To emphasize the agricultural connection, the package approach was labeled, "early harvest."

The two U.S. priorities for early decision provoked the initial skirmishing over linkages among issues that would determine the outcome of the Uruguay Round. Agriculture was clearly the most difficult issue for the Europeans, and the EC was not prepared to do anything in this sector unless movement took place on all other fronts. In fact, the United States had tried to incorporate a "fast track" priority into the mandate for the agriculture negotiating group and ran into a French stone wall.[3] With respect to an early harvest at Montreal, the EC countered with a "global" approach in which all issues would move ahead in parallel.

The singling out of a services agreement for early decision triggered an even more complicated reaction. The majority of developing countries were prepared to negotiate a service-sector agreement but only in return for commitments by the industrialized countries to liberalize imports of textiles, curtail bilateral quotas elsewhere, and reduce tariffs and other impediments to rapidly growing developing-country exports of manufactured products. This alone precluded an early harvest that left textiles and other such priority issues for later.

More fundamental, a deal consisting of a services agreement in exchange for industrialized-country actions in the manufacturing sector left out the highly protected industrial sectors that generally prevailed in developing countries. Some degree of reciprocal North/South trade liberalization in the dominant manufacturing sector was in order. At stake was fuller participation in GATT commitments by the increasingly competitive newly industrialized countries of Asia and Latin America. The principle involved was Special and Differential Treatment (S&D) for developing countries.

Developing-country Participation

GATT rules did not bind developing countries to an open and nondiscriminatory trading system even though they constituted the large majority of the membership. In 1966 the GATT had been amended by adding Part IV, entitled "Trade and Development." It elaborated principles and commitments affording special treatment for developing countries. For trade negotiations, the industrialized countries would "not expect reciprocity for commitments" to the trade of developing countries. At the conclusion of the Tokyo Round in 1979, the so-called Enabling Clause was adopted, which restated the nonreciprocity principle and added the concepts of "differential and more favorable treatment" for developing countries with respect to nontariff measures, and of "special treatment" for the least developed among the developing countries.

The Enabling Clause also provided that "with the progressive development of their economies and improvement in their trade situation," developing countries would be expected "to participate more fully in the framework of rights and obligations under the General Agreement." This language could be interpreted as leading to "graduation" from developing to industrialized status. The GATT does not define a developing country, however, and the question of criteria for developing-country treatment has never been discussed within the GATT.[4] Developing-country status has been a matter of self-selection, and no developing country had ever chosen to graduate.

By the early 1980s, the industrialized countries became more focused on the need to integrate the advanced and more competitive developing countries into the GATT system. Trade Representative Brock's proposal for a North/South trade round at the 1982 OECD ministerial was one such manifestation, and lengthy discussion of the graduation issue took place within the OECD Trade Committee. The preoccupation at Punta del Este to get the new issues on the agenda, however, including maintenance of the coalition of industrialized and moderate developing countries against the hard-liners—shunted aside the underlying issue of special and differential treatment. The Punta declaration reaffirmed by reference the provisions of Part IV and the Enabling Clause, and with respect to reciprocity generalized the principle that developing countries should not be required to make concessions that are inconsistent with their development, financial, and trade needs. This could be read to mean that while developing countries would negotiate, for example, agreements on services and intellectual property, they would not themselves have to abide by its provisions. The fifteen negotiating groups began their work on this ambiguous basis.

The industrialized countries agreed that something needed to be done during the Uruguay Round to integrate developing countries into the GATT system, but their objectives and tactical approaches differed. The Europeans worried most about surging imports from Asia's newly industrialized nations following in the Japanese wake. Outside the GATT, they applied a growing array of "grey area" quotas and other informal restrictions against the Asians. The issue was a broader version of the "balance of benefits" dilemma. The Europeans were not prepared to open their markets fully to Asia unless there was fundamental change in the trading practices of the newly industrialized, an unlikely prospect within the Uruguay Round.

Japan, as a matter of principle, was reluctant to confront the issue of special and differential treatment within the GATT context. Japan was rapidly deepening its trade and investment relationships in East and Southeast Asia, supported by large amounts of economic aid, and viewed the relationship in terms of positive economic complementarity rather than conflict. The Asian newly industrialized nations, over time, would progressively liberalize their trading systems, as had Japan. In any event, the policy process should center on pragmatic bilateral consultations and not on a multilateral debate in the GATT.

The U.S. market was the most open, absorbing about two-thirds of the manufactured exports of developing countries, and congressional criticism that the Asians were getting a free ride in the GATT had increasing validity. The United States was thus the most determined to get results in the Uruguay Round, but did not have a clear strategy for doing so. One approach would be to seek revised general provisions in the GATT that would tighten criteria for special treatment and accelerate graduation. Another was to deal with the S&D issue on a case-by-case basis in each of the negotiating groups. Yet another approach was to press for early graduation of at least a few developing countries as a precedent for others at a later point. The complete withdrawal of U.S. tariff preferences from Hong Kong, Singapore, South Korea, and Taiwan in January 1988 was a signal in that direction.

In December 1987, more than a year after Punta, the United States finally established an interagency group to form a strategy for developing countries in the Uruguay Round, and most of its recommendations were adopted in the spring of 1988.[5] The underlying conceptual question was whether to continue to treat all developing countries in the same way within the GATT. Analysis of a wide range of economic and social criteria indicated that the four Asian economies no longer granted tariff preferences had broken away from the pack, had become developed or industrialized by any reasonable definition of those terms, and had reached a level of development comparable with the lower tier of OECD countries. About forty countries, less rigorously defined, were widely viewed as the "least developed." In between lay another forty or so middle-level developing countries, many with important stakes in the trading system. The Uruguay Round involved a basic policy decision. Should three distinct negotiating strategies be adopted for the three sub-groups, or should each country be dealt with individually within a more general concept tying progressively greater GATT obligations to higher levels of development? After considerable debate, the latter course was adopted to avoid confrontation in an already heavily burdened negotiation.

By avoiding a showdown on the graduation issue, however, greater attention had to be given to specific S&D provisions in each of the negotiating groups, and in this respect the U.S. strategy became more precise. For some groups, such as those considering dispute settlement and reform of the GATT, no special treatment was warranted. Where developing countries were highly competitive, such as in the textile sector, increased market access should be reciprocal. In general, special treatment should involve longer time periods for phasing in new GATT obligations rather than exemption, although in some areas, such as agriculture, development-related exceptions to free-market principles were acceptable.

The most important issue, in terms of trade impact, involved GATT Article XVIII, which permits developing countries to apply selective quotas on imports to protect infant industries or to respond to "temporary" balance-of-payments problems. The balance-of-payments provision, in particular, had been greatly abused, and 85 percent of quotas notified to the GATT by developing countries over the years were so justified. South Korea, an export powerhouse with a strong balance-of-payments position in 1988, still used the Article XVIII balance-of-payments provision to justify import quotas in violation of GATT commitments. The United States sought revision or a severely restrictive interpretation of Article XVIII, and in this instance the priority was fully shared by other industrialized countries. Article XVIII was basically the developing-country counterpart to the Article XIX safeguards clause, which should restrain industrialized country use of "temporary" quotas, and the possibility of an "18/19" package as the basis for a broad market access agreement had long been recognized. Revising Article XVIII, however, was a matter for the negotiating group on GATT Articles, and developing countries, aware of its importance, refused even to discuss possible changes.

The U.S. interagency group recommended that the United States clearly state its overall position on developing countries in the GATT system, emphasizing the complementarity between good development strategy and the GATT open-trading system, and suggested a statement by the secretary of treasury in view of his broad responsibilities in the international economic policy field. On September 14, 1988, the acting secretary, Peter McPherson, who had previously served six years as administrator of the U.S. Agency for International Development, gave a strongly worded speech in which he condemned the traditional import substitution, protectionist approach to development as "built on false assumptions" that have engendered "a powerful constituency for continued protection, regardless of the economics."[6] The resulting S&D provisions of the GATT "not only encouraged bad development policies, they are used as cover for protectionism that has nothing to do with development." He highlighted the Article XVIII balance-of-payments provision, which "is used to provide lasting cover for import substitution policies," and advocated its use only for "true crisis situations" in conjunction with financial adjustment policies. He also criticized the concept of nonreciprocity, which reduces the incentive of industrialized countries to open their markets to developing-country exports. "The cumulation of special exceptions and arrangements for developing countries," he concluded, had effectively removed these countries from GATT obligations, and for many, "membership is without substance." Thus, the United States issued a clarion call for a change in the dual GATT status of industrialized versus developing countries. Some developing-country delegations in Geneva reacted negatively to the U.S. frontal assault, but for most it came as no great surprise. The world economy was changing and developing countries were becoming more integrated into the open trading system. The Uruguay Round nevertheless was deeply enmeshed in a complex negotiation on many specific issues. Agriculture, services, and intellectual property would dominate the first three years of deliberations. S&D would never come to a head in conceptual terms, and the negotiating groups dealt with it on the periphery. S&D remained elusive and mostly below the surface, awaiting the final phase of negotiations on an issue-by-issue basis.

GATT Institutional Issues

One area of negotiations that did move toward an early harvest was strengthening the GATT as an institution. This involved the negotiating groups on Functioning of the GATT System (FOGS) and dispute settlement. Both had highly able and respected chairmen. Chairman Julius Katz of the FOGS group was a veteran U.S. State Department trade negotiator who had moved on to the private sector and was recalled to government service part time for this task. In 1989 he would return to full-time service as the principal deputy U.S. trade representative. The chairman of the Dispute Settlement Group was the Uruguayan representative to the GATT, Julio Lacarte-Muro, who had long experience in GATT affairs and trade policy. He was unique among the Uruguay Round negotiators in having participated in the 1947 Havana conference that created the GATT.

The FOGS group dealt with four issues, for which it produced results on two, was split on the third, and had no coherent response on the fourth. The easiest task was to respond to the Punta del Este mandate to increase the involvement of ministers in GATT decision-making. It was an anomaly that an international organization of such stature, dealing with an important area of policy, did not convene regularly at ministerial level. Discussion by the FOGS group revolved around whether meetings should be on a fixed or somewhat flexible schedule, at intervals of one, two, or three years. The consensus agreement was that ministerial meetings should be held "at least once every two years."

The second issue with mid-term results involved creation of a trade-policy review mechanism. The objective was to have regular reviews of GATT member trade policies to evaluate their impact on the multilateral trading system. Policies would thus become more transparent in their application and effect on trade. The country-review approach was based on longstanding practice in the IMF and the OECD, which included peer assessment. Some resistance developed in the FOGS group, especially from India, to submitting developing-country policies to such scrutiny, but forceful pressure by Chairman Katz drew broad support within the group and produced a formula by which the four largest trading entities—the EC, the United States, Japan, and Canada—would be reviewed every two years, the next sixteen largest members every four years, and the remaining GATT members every six years.

The FOGS group split on whether to establish a restricted ministerial grouping of about twenty members, with smaller countries represented on a rotational basis through a group representative. This objective had been modeled on experience elsewhere, particularly the IMF Interim Committee and the World Bank Development Committee, which meet twice annually at ministerial level for more focused, less formal discussion than is possible in plenary sessions. The deputies groups for these committees also play an important role in developing issues for ministerial review. As GATT membership approached one hundred, a more flexible, smaller body was needed if serious trade-policy debate was to take place within the GATT. During the 1980s, at U.S. initiative, ministers and senior officials of major countries tended to meet outside the GATT, among the Quad, as noted earlier, or in a larger group of about twenty ministers from major trading nations, developing as well as industrialized. The GATT had established a Group of Eighteen at official level, which met twenty-nine times between 1975 and 1987. These meetings grew in size, however, as alternate representatives were permitted to participate, and discussion tended toward formal statements of existing positions.[7] In the FOGS group, however, many developing countries resisted any limited-membership GATT bodies, and this important issue, in terms of GATT operational effectiveness, ended at impasse.

The fourth FOGS issue was, "to increase the contribution of the GATT to achieving greater coherence in global economic policy-making through strengthening its relationship with other international organizations responsible for monetary and financial matters." More precisely, the idea was to integrate overlapping jurisdictions of the GATT, the IMF, and the World Bank, a very tall order for a relatively obscure GATT negotiating group, and it was not surprising that the FOGS group came up empty handed. IMF financial stabilization and World Bank structural-adjustment programs place heavy emphasis on trade-policy measures while the GATT deals with balance-of-payments–related trade restrictions for developing countries under Article XVIII and more generally under Article XII. Studies of trade/finance institutional linkages have provided specific recommendations for better coordination,[8] and there is broad agreement on the substantive issues involved, namely that progressive trade liberalization facilitates financial adjustment and that selective import restrictions are counterproductive in dealing with balance-of-payments problems.

Two specific and important trade/finance linkage issues did arise during the Uruguay Round, but one was never addressed seriously and the other was handled outside the FOGS group. The first involved credit in the Uruguay Round to developing countries for trade liberalization undertaken within a World Bank structural-adjustment program. President Barber Conable of the bank suggested this at Punta, and other delegations voiced support. A meaningful GATT linkage, however, would require binding lower tariff levels in the GATT against future increase, since such bindings constitute the basis for reciprocal GATT commitments. The developing countries resisted GATT bindings in the context of World Bank adjustment programs, as nonreciprocated unilateral obligations on their part. An integrated approach would have consisted of enhanced trade concessions by industrialized countries in the Uruguay Round and of more World Bank financing in support of trade liberalization as the quid pro quo for developing countries to undertake GATT bindings within World Bank–sponsored adjustment programs. Such a far-reaching arrangement, however, went well beyond the purview of the FOGS group, and no delegation chose to pursue it in a broader context.

The second objective was to limit trade restrictions permitted by the GATT for balance-of-payments reasons to situations where an IMF financial stabilization program was being implemented, and even in these cases to permit only comprehensive and not selective restrictions. This approach constituted a frontal assault on Article XVIII, which was initially resisted strongly by developing countries in the GATT Articles negotiating group, and the FOGS group had no jurisdiction to consider this issue.

On both of these issues—as well as other aspects of strengthened relations between the international organizations considered by the FOGS group—strong underlying forces resisted closer linkages. Institutional resistance by the GATT, IMF, and the World Bank to turf-sharing was one factor. Finance ministers similarly opposed constraints on their financial domains by a trade organization. Developing countries generally feared reinforced leverage against them by linking GATT trade commitments to access to multilateral financial facilities. After two years of relatively abstract and inconclusive discussion, the FOGS group meekly invited Director-General Dunkel "to approach the heads of the IMF and the World Bank, as a first step, to explore ways to achieve greater coherence in global economic policy making." As chairman Katz later explained: "We punted."

The Dispute Settlement Group proceeded with low profile deliberations that steadily grew in importance during the course of the Uruguay Round. A more effective dispute-settlement mechanism had been on the GATT workprogram agenda since 1982, but little progress followed the U.S.-EC impasse in the Tokyo Round. The existing process had become discredited over the years for two related reasons. First, the GATT consensus rule allowed any member, including an accused party, to block or indefinitely delay dispute settlement at a number of points, and such obstruction often happened. Second, until the mid-1980s, relatively few trade problems were referred for GATT dispute settlement. Disputes were settled outside the GATT, often ignoring third-party interests and thus undermining the credibility of the GATT as a multilateral system of rules and obligations.

Interest in the Uruguay Round dispute settlement negotiations increased because, from about 1985, members began using the process more frequently for significant trade problems. The United States brought a complaint against Japan on certain agricultural restrictions, and Japan accepted the panel finding and took remedial action. An EC complaint against Japan concerning alcoholic beverages brought similar results. The European Community, in turn, challenged provisions of the U.S.-Japan semiconductor agreement, which established floor prices in third-country markets, and won its case. Japan complained about EC antidumping duties on components to be assembled in Europe, and the GATT panel supported Japan. The surge in GATT dispute settlement was, in part, a reaction to the parallel growth in bilateral actions outside the GATT. It also reflected recognition by some countries, such as Japan, that unpopular political decisions against vested domestic interests can be more palatable as part of an international adjudication process than as a result of bilateral political pressure.

In this context, Lacarte-Muro's negotiating group became more prominent.[9] Debate centered on the consensus rule. The United States proposed important changes whereby the complainant would have an automatic right to a panel and no one party engaged in the dispute could veto adoption of a panel report, the "consensus minus one" principle. Support for the consensus rule still ran deep, however, and opposition to the U.S. proposals, including from the EC, resulted in a more modest package of recommendations for the early harvest. The ability to delay decisions was curtailed to sixty days for initial bilateral consultations and to about two months during the decision to establish a panel. A panel's terms of reference were to be standard unless otherwise agreed, and in the event of an impasse on panel membership, the GATT director-general could be requested to decide. These steps would prevent the accused party from indefinitely delaying the process, but the right to block the establishment of a panel remained ambiguous, and the consensus rule for adoption of a panel report was unequivocally reaffirmed.

Immediately after the midterm ministerial meeting, this package of revised dispute-settlement procedures was to be applied on a trial basis until the conclusion of the round. Meanwhile, the Dispute Settlement Group would continue its work "for the full achievement of the negotiating objective." In other words, another assault on the consensus rule would come during the second half of the Uruguay Round. The second-half scenario, in fact, would be stimulated by another important development, emanating from the U.S. Congress, that catapulted GATT dispute settlement into the center of debate about the future of the trading system and caused the EC to reconsider its support for the consensus rule.

Congressional adoption of an expanded version of Section 301 of the existing trade act would pose an alternative to multilateral adjudication of trade problems. It mandated a unilateral U.S. approach to deal with alleged "unfair trading practices" of others. It reached beyond existing GATT obligations to deal with the vaguely defined and rarely addressed GATT doctrine of "nonviolation nullification and impairment." In plain English, this phrase means that reasonable market access for trade can be denied even when all GATT obligations are maintained. Moreover, unilateral Section 301 actions would center on the new areas of policy being negotiated in the Uruguay Round, linking them indirectly to GATT dispute settlement. The issue would boil down to whether a greatly strengthened and broadened GATT dispute settlement procedure would be sufficient to induce the United States to back off or at least greatly restrain its unilateral approach for dealing with unfair trade practices. The stakes were being raised on both sides, and the negotiating group on dispute settlement became the critical linchpin.

Bilateral and Regional Initiatives

The showdown between President Reagan and Congress over trade legislation came in the summer of 1988. On August 23, after prolonged negotiation between the White House and the congressional leadership, the president signed the Omnibus Trade and Competitiveness Act of 1988. It gave him authority to negotiate reductions in tariff and nontariff trade barriers in the Uruguay Round under the "fast track" procedure, as utilized in the Tokyo Round, whereby the Congress would cast a yes or no vote on the final agreement, with no amendments, within sixty legislative days. The fast track authority ran until May 31, 1991, with provision for a two-year extension if requested by the president and if neither house of Congress opposed it.

The quid pro quo for Uruguay Round negotiating authority was a broad congressional mandate for a more aggressive U.S. trade policy in other areas.[10] The antidumping law was tightened to deal with repeat dumping offenders and "circumvention" of dumping penalties whereby components of dumped products were imported for assembly in the United States. Protection of intellectual property was strengthened by making violations in the U.S. market easier to demonstrate and relief procedures more responsive. In the telecommunications sector, deadlines were set for obtaining negotiated agreement to improve U.S. access to foreign markets—under the threat of retaliation.

The most sweeping and controversial provision of the 1988 Act was the greatly expanded Section 301, which authorized the president to take actions to improve access for U.S. companies in foreign markets. Section 301 was first incorporated in the trade act of 1974 but was not actively utilized until 1985. The 1988 act strengthened this authority through shorter time limits for action, an expanded definition of unfair trade practices abroad, priority investigation of foreign violations of U.S. intellectual property rights, and new "super" and "special" 301 provisions. "Super 301" directed the president to identify and negotiate changes in generic or systemic unfair trade practices of targeted countries, while "special 301" actions focussed more narrowly on countries that did not provide adequate protection for intellectual property. Unfair trade practices included denial of opportunities for the establishment of an enterprise, denial of intellectual property protection, export targeting, denial of workers rights, and foreign government tolerance of anticompetitive activities.

Through super 301, in particular, Congress called for unilateralism in dealing with the "uneven playing field" of market access for U.S. exporters. The principal, although by no means only, target was Japan. Super 301 was also an implicit repudiation of the adequacy of the GATT multilateral system for opening international markets, at least in the short run. Over the longer run, rivalry between the unilateral and multilateral approaches would depend, to a large extent, on the outcome of the Uruguay Round. A broader GATT mandate to include major areas of unfair trading practices elaborated in Section 301 and more effective GATT procedures for dealing with them could preclude the need for the unilateral approach. But the unilateral genie, once out of the bottle, would be difficult to put back in. Initial Section 301 actions under the 1988 act would prove to be expeditious, effective, and increasingly popular in the U.S. Congress.

The 1988 trade act also gave the president authority to negotiate bilateral trade agreements, utilizing a similar fast track procedure for congressional approval. That established another dimension in U.S. trade policy—regional free trade agreements. Ronald Reagan, in his final State of the Union address in January 1988, hailed the "historic free trade agreement" just concluded between the United States and Canada: "I can also tell you that we're determined to expand this concept, south as well as north. . . . Our goal must be a day when the free flow of trade, from the tip of Tierra del Fuego to the Arctic Circle, unites the people of the Western Hemisphere in a bond of mutually beneficial exchange." The quest for regional free trade had a Pacific as well as a hemispheric dimension. In early 1988, Prime Minister Nakasone of Japan and Senate majority leader Robert Byrd discussed a possible U.S.-Japan free-trade agreement, and Chairman Lloyd Bentsen of the Senate Finance Committee requested the International Trade Commission to assess the pros and cons of such a bilateral negotiation. The venerable American ambassador to Japan, Mike Mansfield, was an outspoken advocate for U.S.-Japan free trade, although his view was not shared elsewhere in the executive branch. In July 1988, a trans-Pacific study group, including senior officials and academics, was formed to produce ASEAN-U.S. Initiative, recommending an ASEAN-U.S. free trade agreement as a long-term objective.[11]

The big question was whether the United States viewed regional free-trade agreements as building blocks toward eventual global free trade or as an alternative to multilateralism. One did not preclude the other, but the "either-or" approach appeared to be more authoritative. The strategy of a U.S.-centered trading bloc to counter the European Community had been raised in the early 1970s by the tough-talking Texan, Treasury Secretary John Connally, and senior U.S. officials had repeatedly alluded to it as a veiled threat during the prolonged preparatory phase of the Uruguay Round. In February 1988, Secretary of the Treasury James Baker, another product of Texas, gave a widely quoted speech lauding the trade-creating potential of the U.S.-Canadian agreement. He then warned bluntly: "The rewards of this agreement offer an incentive to other agreements. If possible, we hope this follow-up liberalization will occur in the Uruguay Round. If not, we might be willing to explore a 'market liberalization club' approach, through minilateral arrangements or a series of bilateral agreements." He noted that Japan, South Korea, and Taiwan had shown interest in participating in such negotiations.[12]

The United States, in brief, had lost its longstanding faith in the multilateral GATT approach as the all-dominant structure for trade relations and had embarked on a three-track approach: gradual trade liberalization at the multilateral level through the GATT, more ambitious free trade at the regional level, and unilateral actions for enhanced foreign market access on specific issues in targeted countries. This three-track strategy was not clearly articulated, however, nor was it clear whether the three tracks would be mutually supportive or working at cross purposes.[13]

Other countries uniformly opposed U.S. unilateralism, as expressed in Section 301, but were of different minds about regional free trade. By the summer of 1988, the European Community had shaken off Euro-pessimism and found renewed self-confidence through its EC-92 program of internal market unification. EC President Jacques Delors and Lord Cockfield, commissioner for the internal market, had collaborated on a June 1985 commission white paper, "Completing the Internal Market," including an annex with three hundred specific areas for action. This led to adoption of the Single European Act for implementing the action program, which entered into force in July 1987, wherein EC members expressed their "firm political will" to complete market unification by the end of 1992.

Initial public reactions to EC-92 were skeptical, given past Community performance, but by mid-1988 it became clear that major changes would take place in such areas as integration of financial markets, border controls, and Community-wide standards, and that progress was being made on ever tougher issues such as public procurement and tax harmonization. A commission assessment of market unification projected the creation of 2 to 5 million jobs and additional economic growth of 4.5 to 7 percent.[14] The private sector turned bullish, corporate mergers within the EC doubled between 1984 and 1987, and a catchphrase objective called for European companies of global stature—in other words, firms capable of competing with American and Japanese rivals.

The renewed vigor of European economic integration produced strong reactions abroad. The European Free Trade Association (EFTA) countries, predominantly dependent on the EC market, saw deeper ties with the European Community as imperative for their own economic well-being, and they began to reconsider membership. Japan and other Asian exporters feared that a burgeoning European bloc would turn inward, become a "Fortress Europe," and restrict imports from Asia. The United States belatedly realized the potentially important consequences of EC-92 and expressed alarm. On August 4, 1988, Deputy Secretary of the Treasury McPherson warned that some Europeans wanted to erect a "protective curtain" around their European market and that the United States would view as "unacceptable" an EC-92 program that curbed American access to the Community.[15] The EC Commission calmed the fears of its trading partners somewhat with a statement in October reaffirming its "fundamental stake in the existence of free and open international trade." It referred to concerns about an inward directed Europe as "senseless and groundless."[16]

EC-92 also had an impact on the Uruguay Round. The EC wanted a successful outcome for the round, if for no other reason than to assuage its trading partners about Fortress Europe, but at the same time it didn't want to limit flexibility, through new GATT commitments, for building a strengthened Europe. European officials were outspoken about not permitting European industries to be overwhelmed by the Japanese, as had happened in the United States. They were also increasingly reluctant to undertake fundamental reform of the European farm subsidy program, which the United States was pressing for in the Uruguay Round. The EC decision-making apparatus—painstakingly complex—was now more than fully engaged with internal decisions related to EC-92. The preoccupation among Europeans in late 1988 with deeper and broader regional economic integration, however, was only a prelude to the historic, mind-boggling European events that would unfold in the year ahead.

Japan and other East Asian economies were uniformly concerned about the growing momentum toward regional economic blocs in Europe and North America since their own economic success during the 1980s was highly dependent on those export markets. This gave them particularly high stakes in a strengthened multilateral framework for open trade. The performance of East Asians in the Uruguay Round, however, did not match their evident self-interest in the outcome. Japan maintained low-profile support for the round but rarely took the initiative to move issues forward. South Korea, now a formidable industrialized exporter, chose refuge behind developing-country status to resist major commitments on its part and thus lost the opportunity to significantly influence the negotiations. The ASEAN countries generally supported framework agreements for services and intellectual property but remained wary of easing access to their highly protected internal markets.

East Asian reaction to regional economic integration was also not entirely negative. On a practical level, trade and investment dependencies within East Asia were growing rapidly. The revaluation of the yen beginning in 1985, and later of the Korean won and the Taiwanese dollar, produced lucrative economic complementarity between these high-wage, technologically advanced economies and the populous ASEAN nations and China. Large amounts of official finance as aid, export credits, and support for private investment enhanced deepening economic ties. The huge East Asian trade surplus with the United States was unsustainable, and policy orientation, in general, redirected exports toward neighbors within the East Asian region.

There were no concrete proposals for an East Asian trading bloc, and to the extent that free trade agreements were discussed during 1988, they involved linkages between the United States and East Asia. Contingency planning for a future comprised of a Fortress Europe and a protectionist United States, however, inevitably pointed to a countervailing East Asia response. In terms of straightforward commercial interests, the Japanese Ministry of International Trade and Industry (MITI) was developing its New Asian Industries Development Plan, or New AID, which was an industry-by-industry blueprint aimed at offshore production in Southeast Asia.[17]

Ministers arriving at Montreal in December 1988 for the mid-term Uruguay Round meeting were thus faced with a trading environment greatly changed from the days of Punta del Este just two years earlier. Protectionist pressures in the United States had been translated into a comprehensive legislative program of unilateral actions centered on Section 301. More fundamental, the interaction of a multilateral set of GATT rules and regional free-trade agreements had become a major issue of debate. The GATT permitted free-trade agreements under Article XXIV, but through the 1970s this provision was viewed principally as a vehicle for West European integration, with the positive political/security implications at least as important as the economic effects. Nondiscrimination or most-favored-nation treatment, as enshrined in GATT Article I, had stood as the overriding norm for trade relations. Now, regional free-trade agreements were taking on a broader role within the trading system and were becoming more widely viewed in a positive though carefully qualified light.

The regional issue was catapulted to attention at Montreal by the political debate within Canada over the free-trade agreement with the United States. Prime Minister Brian Mulroney was forced to call a parliamentary election over the issue, which took place on November 21, only two weeks before Canada was to host the GATT ministerial meeting. The early election campaign indicated a majority against the agreement, but public support steadily grew and Mulroney achieved a resounding victory. He and his trade minister, John Crosbie, arrived triumphantly in Montreal and proclaimed the U.S.-Canada pact a major step toward more open trade. Other ministers echoed the view that U.S.-Canada free trade was a catalyst, or building block, for trade liberalization at the multilateral level. GATT Director-General Arthur Dunkel, during the initial press conference at Montreal, was asked about the relationship between free-trade agreements and the multilateral GATT system. He replied that if such agreements conformed to the provisions of GATT Article XXIV, they should not be considered as exceptions to the rule and, indeed, should be viewed as *"une évolution souhaitable,"* a desirable evolution.

Montreal Ministerial Meeting

The run-up to the Montreal meeting within the GATT negotiating groups did not match the ardor of the triumphant U.S.-Canada free-trade agreement. Recommendations from the FOGS group on periodic ministerial meetings and country reviews were ripe for ministerial adoption. The group on tropical products, of particular interest to developing countries, had produced a package of tariff cuts and other liberalizing measures covering $20 billion[18] of trade in such products as bananas, tea, coffee, and liichi nuts. An outline for a framework agreement on trade in services had broad support. But other difficult issues—including intellectual-property protection, textiles, and safeguards—were far less advanced.

Agriculture, however, had clearly emerged as the major stumbling block for the Montreal meeting. The United States had proposed a complete phasing out of trade-distorting government farm supports over ten years—in effect, free trade—while the European Community was only willing to discuss limited, short-term measures. The Cairns group proposed a compromise combining a specific short-term commitment to freeze existing levels of protection and reduce government farm supports by 20 percent over two years, with a longer term plan for free trade, but it was frustrated by the intransigence of the two dominant participants. As the conference date approached, positions hardened. U.S. Trade Representative Yeutter stated flatly that no agreement would be preferable to a bad agreement, and that if the talks collapsed, the United States would retaliate against countries deemed to be violating trading norms. EC Commissioner for External Relations Willy de Clercq characterized the U.S. ultimatum as a dangerous nonstarter and elaborated on American "Rambo" thinking: "They very often adopt a menacing attitude, affirming the intent to turn towards bilateralism if they don't find satisfaction at the multilateral level. In other words, it is the law of the jungle, the right of the strongest to prevail. . . . This tendency bothers us (*Ce penchant nous préoccupe*)."[19]

Nevertheless, the purpose of the midterm ministerial was to raise the most difficult issues to the political level. The idea of a major early harvest had proved to be unrealistic, but the Montreal meeting could serve the purpose of narrowing differences and specifying more precise negotiating objectives for the final two years of the round. So despite bitter arctic winds outside, the mood at the conference opening on Monday, December 5 was warm and hopeful. The spacious conference center and neighboring modern office buildings symbolized Canada as a vibrant, industrialized trading nation and no longer the "hewer of wood and hauler of water" of yore. The mayor of Montreal hosted a reception for the hundreds of accredited journalists in the observation tower built for the 1976 Olympics. Surrounded by a breathtaking view of the city, he extolled the high-tech entrepreneurial spirit and international orientation of the new Quebec, committed to free trade.

Prime Minister Brian Mulroney set the initial tone of the conference with a rousing call to action: "We, the members of the GATT, are now engaged in an historic effort, not only to liberalize international trade, but also to free up the spirit of innovation and enterprise that exists in all countries. . . . Our negotiators must leave Montreal more determined than ever to bring the negotiations to a timely and successful conclusion." He predicted that the U.S.-Canada free-trade agreement would "stand in the history of international trade negotiations as a significant and beneficial contribution," but quickly added that "our faith in the GATT, as the prime instrument of international trade policy, is as strong today as it was 40 years ago." On a more ominous and parochial note, Mulroney warned of the need for progress on agriculture: "Think of our farmers. They must confront not only the challenges of nature, but also the devastating impact of shortsighted and trade distorting agricultural subsidy policies. . . . Farmers are looking for results at Montreal. They can no longer survive on a diet of promises."[20]

Other speeches included similar combinations of high sounding political goals and reinforcement of key negotiating positions. In the latter category, Indian Minister of Commerce Dinesh Singh warned that for intellectual property, approaches should be avoided that would "generate new tensions in the trading system through linkages . . . between these issues and rules for trade." The head of the Brazilian delegation, Ambassador Paulo Tarso Flecha de Lima, affirmed that "due account must be taken to apply the principle of special and differential treatment." Referring to recent U.S. trade restrictions against Brazil under Section 301, he claimed, "Unjustifiable actions to curb imports are taken and pressures to force parties to change their legislation on intellectual property rights have become new and worrisome features." President Barber Conable of the World Bank painted a somber picture of recent developments in trade policy affecting the developing countries, with particular concern about the growing trend to bilateralism: "Trade preferences are being increasingly granted only to neighbors—in the Antipodes, in Europe and America. . . . The result is a growing and massive discrimination against other countries' products."

Clayton Yeutter focused on "the three most difficult areas," agriculture, services and intellectual property. For agriculture, he vaunted the U.S. "bold proposal calling for the removal of all *trade-distorting* subsidies and market access barriers by the year 2000" and warned, "We would rather leave unable to resolve an issue than paper over differences." Willy de Clercq responded: "We have within our reach an agreement on a freeze, a short term concrete reduction of farm support and a commitment to negotiate towards a further lowering of the level of support in the longer term. . . . Those who refuse to seize this opportunity for the sake of unrealistic expectations for some hazy faraway future, will bear a heavy responsibility indeed."

Serious negotiations, paralleling ministerial speeches, made some progress. The tropical-products package was quickly approved for immediate implementation, although the United States conditioned its approval on progress on the broader agricultural issue. Tariff reductions, which had not received much attention, were agreed to be "at least as ambitious" as those achieved in the Tokyo Round. In other words, they would amount to at least 33 percent. Support for the elements of a framework agreement on services approached consensus. The intellectual-property issue was more difficult, but India was becoming isolated in opposing any negotiation in the Uruguay Round. Brazil, however, as an active member of the Cairns group, linked its willingness to negotiate intellectual property to progress on agriculture.

The growing abuse of antidumping duties for protectionist purposes became prominent for the first time at Montreal. World Bank President Conable laid out the problem with biting clarity: "While anti-dumping began as a favorite United States way to enforce its view of fair trade, this tactic is now being exported quite successfully. . . . It is flexible; little Trinidad and Tobago's urea exports—0.3 percent of the EEC market—were found to be causing 'material injury' to one of the largest markets in the world. This decision was taken, of course, when the European Communities were dumping $2 billion worth of sugar and beef on the world market."[21] Japan, Korea, and other advanced developing countries were the principal targets of antidumping actions, and they formed a coalition to do something about it.

By the second day, however, the U.S.-EC impasse on agriculture had moved to center stage, and it stayed there. Packed-house daily press briefings elaborated the intransigence on both sides. The United States maintained the high ground with its "Zero 2000" proposal for a total elimination of protection and refused to discuss short-term measures until the long-term goals were established. French Agriculture Minister Henri Nallet expressed widely shared cynicism about the Americans: "Faced with a Congress supposedly hostile to any reform program that would impose sacrifices on farmers, *la position maximaliste* which they espouse is very comfortable for them, because they would be incapable of adopting short term measures."[22] The EC proposal, in turn, proved to be equally evasive. The offer to freeze the level of price supports was based on 1986, substantially above the actual levels in 1988, and no specific offers were forthcoming for short-term reductions in import barriers and export subsidies.

The likelihood of a major breakthrough on agriculture was reduced by the fact that the key negotiators were lame ducks. George Bush had been elected president a month earlier, and Trade Representative Yeutter and Secretary of Agriculture Richard Lyng were in their final weeks of office. During the conference, President-elect Bush announced in Washington that his new trade representative would be Carla Hills. The press reported that her law firm had prominent Japanese clients, but little else about her was known to the trade-policy establishment gathered in Montreal. Similarly, the EC Commission term expired at the end of the year, and Willy de Clercq was scheduled to depart. The taciturn Dutch commissioner for agriculture, Frans Andriessen, known for his rigid views on the farm issue, had been chosen to succeed the more pro-active Belgian, which was not encouraging to the Americans. Clayton Yeutter would later be selected as U.S. secretary of agriculture, providing parallel continuity for the hard-line U.S. stand on farm-trade liberalization.

The tone of the agricultural debate hardened and tempers rose. Andriessen became so angered by Lyng's attack on the EC farm policy that he stalked out of a meeting on Tuesday and said he wanted no more contact with the U.S. delegation. The United States called for a thesaurus to find a synonym for *eliminate* in the U.S. export subsidy proposal, but the Europeans didn't appreciate the joke. Other negotiating groups lost their momentum and the bulk of the three thousand delegates became, more and more, spectators to the bilateral agricultural debate. Developing countries were especially bitter because they had negotiated in good faith on services and intellectual property only to see the negotiation bog down in a squabble between the two largest industrialized participants. Strong pressures on the United States from Cairns group members to offer a compromise from the Zero 2000 maximum position received some sympathy from Yeutter, who believed almost to the end that he could work out a compromise with de Clercq. But Lyng and senior agricultural adviser Daniel Amstutz insisted on holding firm. The Cairns group frustration was summed up by the outspoken Australian trade minister, Michael Duffy: "The United States and the European Community really do deserve one another. They're a pair of rippers. I think we're staring down the barrel of an all-out farm trade war."[23]

By Thursday afternoon agricultural negotiations had clearly failed. The United States then proposed that ministers adopt the agreements reached on eleven of the subjects negotiated, including services, while leaving the four remaining issues—agriculture, intellectual property, textiles, and safeguards—for further discussion. Others refused to split the package, and the Latin American agricultural exporters were particularly adamant. Argentine delegation head Bernardo Grinspun put it simply: "We don't like to pay and have nothing to receive."[24]

Later in the evening, Director-General Dunkel met with Yeutter, de Clercq, and Andriessen, and proposed that the midterm review be "suspended" until the first week in April, allowing time for President Bush's economic team to join the negotiations. Meanwhile the results achieved at Montreal would be put "on hold." Yeutter agreed and further suggested that Dunkel be given the job of consulting in capitals during the interim to seek solutions on the outstanding issues. The Europeans assented, and the unassuming yet tough-minded Swiss diplomat was thrust into the middle of the negotiating process for the first time. It would not be the last.

Ministers quickly adopted the suspension proposal on Friday morning and were on their way. A total collapse of the negotiations had been avoided, but there was little to cheer about. Prime Minister Mulroney's opening appeal that ministers leave Montreal "more determined than ever to bring the negotiations . . . to a successful conclusion" went unfulfilled. Trade Minister Crosbie, at the close, could go no further than to say, "It is time for a cool re-examination." His laconic appraisal: "Nobody blinked. The EC and the U.S. just closed their eyes."[25]

Mid-term Package

The outcome at Montreal provoked wide-ranging press commentary: "The collapse of the Montreal trade talks . . . has derailed the most ambitious attempt in 40 years to rewrite the rules of the world trading system"; "The trade talks were a flop. . . . it was unwise to plan a critical review session . . . when the Reagan administration's trade bargainers would be lame ducks"; "The fiasco at Montreal only stoked the bilateral conflicts between the EC and the United States"; "not unusual midway into a major trade liberalization effort"; "Temporary crises and impasses . . . serve as a warning and are, in this sense, useful for the negotiations"; "No one was expecting a miracle. . . . what was most noteworthy . . . was the wide range of issues on which the 96 GATT members have found consensus"; "Once again, GATT meetings have brought together 'as many egoisms as registered members' (*autant d'égoïsmes que de membres inscrits*)."[26]

The ambiguity and diversity of views about the ministerial outcome reflected growing doubts about the ability of the GATT system to cope with the accelerating pace of events in world trade relations. Carla Hills, at her Senate confirmation hearing, carefully hedged her bets on the adequacy of the GATT: "Our strategic goal is to open markets. . . . we must prefer to use multilateral negotiations to achieve this end, but we will engage in bilateral and plurilateral efforts and take selective unilateral action where such can be effective in opening foreign markets and establishing equitable and enforceable rules."[27] Steve Dryden, in *Business Week*, was more direct: "The problem is, the tiny steps the GATT is making are less and less significant as the world moves increasingly into trading blocs."[28]

A new nadir in GATT credibility came at the annual meeting of the international economic elite at Davos, Switzerland, in January 1989. Lester Thurow, dean of the Sloan School of Management at MIT, came close to impinging on Nieztschean intellectual property in pronouncing, "GATT is dead!" He labeled the Montreal meeting a "total failure," adding, "what is now being negotiated cannot be negotiated." In Thurow's view, the EC-92 program would be "the event that visibly destroys the post–World War II GATT era." The world economy was moving toward a tripolar bloc relationship, and "given this reality it is far better to channel what is . . . an irresistible movement toward trading blocs in a benign direction." Government officials and businessmen decried Thurow's pessimism and emphasized the need for progress on the stalled Uruguay Round, but defenders of the GATT were on the defensive.[29]

Despite the supposed demise of the GATT, Director-General Arthur Dunkel remained undaunted in his efforts to bring the negotiating parties back together on the four outstanding issues. Bilateral consultations and group meetings through mid-March narrowed the gaps or papered over the differences. High-level officials gathered in Geneva on April 5 and worked intensively for ten days, with little public fanfare, to finally achieve the midterm package of agreements. Public reactions were muted but relieved. Lester Thurow's obituary was, at least, premature.

The salient results of the midterm package and their significance for the ensuing two years of negotiation were as follows:[30]

Tropical Products. The trade-liberalization package was adopted, covering a large volume of trade, but since trade barriers were already quite low for these products, the resulting trade impact was limited. It was thus beneficial to developing-country exports but not central to their interests in the round.

Dispute Settlement and FOGS. The negotiating-group proposals for streamlined dispute settlement, a trade-policy review mechanism, and biannual ministerial meetings were adopted. The dispute-settlement procedures were implemented on an interim basis until the end of the round, when further revisions were anticipated. The review mechanism began in 1989, and the first national trade policies to be scrutinized were those of the United States, Australia, and Morocco. The quest to achieve "greater coherence in global economic policy making" was left with Dunkel and his IMF and World Bank counterparts.

Tariffs. The ministerial agreement on reductions of at least one-third did not specify how the cuts would be made. Most countries wanted a general formula, such as a given percentage cut across the board. The United States, however, resisted the formula approach, in part to avoid any significant reductions in sensitive areas such as textiles. It preferred a process of "request and offer lists" of individual tariff items as a basis for negotiations. The absence of a formula approach would make the achievement of major tariff cuts more elusive until a zero-for-zero sector approach took hold later in the negotiations.

Services. Considerable progress took place on a multilateral framework agreement for trade in services, "and its entry into force by the end of the Uruguay Round." Principles and rules would include transparency, progressive liberalization, national treatment, most-favored-nation nondiscrimination, market access, increasing participation of developing countries, safeguards and exceptions, and regulatory practices. A significant aspect of the midterm agreement, however, was a substantial decoupling of the framework agreement commitments from actual liberalization of trade in services, for which provisions were to be established "for further negotiations after the Uruguay Round." Although little noticed at the time, this decoupling would later become a major problem for U.S. negotiators in view of strong interest in the American private sector.[31]

Intellectual Property. India and other hard-line resisters to any negotiation on this subject finally accepted "the importance of the successful conclusion of the multilateral negotiations" for trade-related aspects of intellectual property rights. The negotiations would encompass the applicability of the basic principles of the GATT, adequate standards and principles, effective national enforcement of intellectual property rights, and expeditious procedures for multilateral dispute settlement. A framework agreement for trade in counterfeit goods was also specified. A reservation stated that "the outcome of the negotiations is not prejudged" as to the GATT institutional relationship, but the industrialized countries succeeded in making this issue an integral part of the final agreement.

Textiles and Clothing. Given the strong resistance in industrialized countries, this highest-priority issue for many developing countries was the last to be resolved. The midterm agreement contained a substantial commitment beyond the Punta declaration, even though press reports gave it little attention and the industrialized governments tended to play down its significance. The midterm agreement recognized this sector as "one of the key elements of the Uruguay Round" and stated that "substantive negotiations will . . . reach agreement . . . on modalities for the integration of this sector into GATT. . . . Such modalities . . . should *inter alia* cover the phasing out of restrictions under the Multifiber Arrangement and other restrictions on textiles and clothing not consistent with GATT rules and disciplines."

Safeguards et al. No progress was made on "a comprehensive agreement on safeguards," even while noting that "such an agreement is vital to the strengthening of the GATT system." Other issues that produced nil or only modest results were nontariff barriers, natural-resource-based products, GATT articles (including the contentions balance-of-payments provisions of Article XVIII), multilateral trade negotiation (MTN) agreements and arrangements—despite rising concern over abuse of antidumping procedures, subsidies and countervailing measures, and trade-related investment measures. For subsidies, a framework for negotiations was adopted, significantly including a distinction in categories between "nonactionable" (i.e., not subject to countervailing duties) and prohibited subsidies. For investment measures, "further work" was directed to the negotiating group, but with little indication as to what the final result might be.

Agriculture. This had become the central roadblock, and the final compromise text required five pages. It elaborated short- and long-term elements of "a framework approach" as well as arrangements on sanitary and phytosanitary regulations. A short-term freeze provided that support prices to producers would not be raised and that import access would not be reduced during 1989 and 1990. No immediate reduction in farm support and import barriers was adopted, as had been pressed by the Cairns group. The long-term objectives remained vague: "to provide for substantial progressive reduction in agricultural support and protection." "Substantial" could range from 100 percent, as proposed by the United States, to a much lower level acceptable to the EC. The most important and difficult issue, export subsidies, was explicitly cited: "the commitments to be negotiated should encompass all measures affecting directly or indirectly import access and export competition, in particular: . . . direct budgetary assistance to exports, other payments on products exported and other forms of export assistance." The EC thus did undertake to make substantial progressive reductions in its export subsidy program, but translating this general commitment into a specific proposal was another matter. Finally, the esoteric dimension of a multilateral framework for sanitary and phytosanitary regulations was elaborated in an attempt to harmonize national regulations and to ensure that such regulations would be based on sound scientific evidence and not used as an indirect means of import protection. Environmentalist groups had not yet noticed that such harmonized international standards might conflict with maximum environmental goals. Their arrival on the trade scene was still two years away.

Overall, the midterm agreements mixed substantial progress with fuzzy compromise and stalemate. Agreements on tropical products, dispute settlement, and FOGS provided at least a mini early harvest. A major step forward involved services and intellectual property. At a minimum, framework agreements for incorporating them into the international trading system would be part of any final Uruguay Round accord. In return, developing countries obtained an explicit commitment to phase out the Multifiber Arrangement for textile quotas. The services-intellectual property-textile linkage had been firmly established.

The U.S.-EC standoff on agriculture clearly emerged as the critical challenge to a successful final, overall outcome. This was ironic in that the Uruguay Round was conceived as an initiative to deal with the new issues facing world trade, while the transatlantic dispute over the Common Agricultural Policy had been an unyielding stalemate for twenty-five years. However, it was sensible to face up to this political reality at the midterm so as to give the negotiators another two years to develop a reasonable solution. Unfortunately, even the tenuous language adopted by ministers would fall by the wayside as positions polarized in the year ahead.

If there was one point of unambiguous consensus, it was recognition that the real political-level decisions were yet to come. A wide-ranging negotiation like the Uruguay Round only comes together at the final stage, during the final weeks or days. At that point a short list of key issues is brokered out among ministers or even heads of state. The midterm agreements had vetted the issue list somewhat, but a lot more preparatory work remained to be done before that conclusive stage would be reached.

TOPICAL ADDENDUM: AGRICULTURE

A U.S.-EC political showdown over the European Common Agricultural Policy (CAP) became the critical issue that delayed and almost destroyed the entire Uruguay Round agreement. An agricultural Armageddon, however, was not anticipated during the preparatory phase of the round in the early 1980s or even at the official launching at Punta del Este in September 1986, and there were plausible reasons for such relative complacency.

The CAP was universally acknowledged to be highly protectionist and costly. Farmers received unlimited internal support prices, well above world prices. In 1986 the EC support price for wheat was more than double the world market price. Imports were treated as residual supplies through a variable levy that kept the import price above the support price. When EC production exceeded internal demand, the surplus was dumped on world markets through subsidy payments that undercut nonsubsidized exporters.

This foolproof protectionist system had been tolerated within the GATT for twenty-five years, in large part because the agricultural sector was in general treated on a different basis. To accommodate the U.S. Agricultural Adjustment Act of 1933, the United States had insisted on special rules for agriculture when the GATT was created in the late 1940s. GATT Article XVI prohibits export subsidies for manufactured products while only restraining agricultural products within ill-defined criteria. Similarly, Article XI permits quotas for agricultural exports and imports under broadly drawn circumstances. In 1955 the United States forced through the GATT Council the notorious "temporary" waiver that fully exempted U.S. import restrictions on sugar, peanuts, and dairy products, and which continued in effect through the Uruguay Round.[32]

Attempts had nevertheless been made to liberalize the CAP in earlier GATT rounds. In the Kennedy Round, the EC offered to bind its internal level of price supports for three years, while reserving a share of its domestic grains market for imports. After prolonged negotiations, the EC offered a 10 percent market share for imports while the United States held out for 13 percent. In the end they reached no agreement on basic agricultural commodities.[33] As recounted earlier, the Tokyo Round was triggered by a U.S.-EC dispute over export subsidies for dairy products, although the final agreement on a subsidies code largely exempted agriculture.

In view of this unsuccessful and unpromising background, a central question is why the United States chose to make fundamental change in the EC agricultural policy a make-or-break issue in the Uruguay Round. The impetus for this round, during the preparatory stage, had been new issues to broaden the GATT mandate, particularly trade in services and protection of intellectual property, and fuller application of GATT commitments to burgeoning trade in manufactures between industrialized and developing countries. Trade in agriculture had declined to only about 10 percent of world trade, while trade growth was concentrated in the manufactures and services sectors.

Two underlying developments helped precipitate the U.S. decision to force a showdown over the CAP in the Uruguay Round. The first was greater awareness of the cost of agricultural protection and the perceived political will, even among Europeans, to do something about it. The OECD nations began a study program in the mid-1980s to measure the total costs of farm protection, including price supports, income payments, and export subsidies, on a common basis. The resulting "producer subsidy equivalent" (PSE) calculations for 1987 revealed a staggering total cost for farm support by industrialized countries of $177 billion. The EC paid the highest price, $73 billion, but the negative impact on other economies was large as well, costing the United States $45 billion, Japan $35 billion, and Canada $7 billion.

The political will to reduce these costs was less graphic, but there was plausible reason for hope. During the GATT work-program deliberations of 1982–84, the Committee on Agriculture reached surprising consensus on the need for substantial change. French President Mitterand tried to exclude agriculture from the Uruguay Round at the 1985 economic summit, but his EC colleagues overrode him, and signals from U.K. and other member-state representatives indicated that something could be accomplished this time around. Likewise, some commission officials viewed the Uruguay Round as the means to force change in the budget-busting EC farm policy. Farmers remained a potent political force in Europe, but their share of the labor force had declined from 21 percent in 1960 to 7 percent in 1989.

The second and more compelling reason that the United States took on the CAP frontally in the Uruguay Round was the emergence of large export subsidies by the EC for wheat and other grains. Community export subsidies during the Kennedy and Tokyo Rounds had been most prominent in dairy products, which did not pose a direct challenge to U.S. exporters.[34] Then, as shown in Table 4.1, the EC shifted from a major importer to a growing exporter of grains beginning in 1980. Total Community farm export subsidies averaged $2.3 billion per year during the Tokyo Round, 1975–78, and then rose sharply during the 1980s to reach more than $12 billion in 1991. Export subsidies for grains rose from $394 million in 1977 to $4.6 billion in 1991.

TABLE 4.1: EC Net Imports of Grains and Agricultural Export Subsidies

	(1) EC net Imports of Grains (millions of metric tons)	(2) EC Export Subsidies (million U.S. $)		(3) U.S. Export Subsidies (million U.S. $)	
		Total	Grains	Total	Grains
1974[a]	12.3	740	96		
1975	11.7	1,279	454		
1976	21.8	1,858	480		
1977	11.5	2,765	394		
1978	6.5	3,696	1,305		
1979	2.7	6,483	1,623		
1980	−3.8	7,579	1,633		
1981	−5.5	5,531	1,351		
1982	−10.0	4,669	1,044		
1983	−11.1	4,699	1,373		
1984	−19.6	4,901	725		
1985	−17.1	5,008	818	22	23
1986	−18.6	7,094	1,678	256	214
1987	−18.8	10,520	3,630	928	754
1988	−25.0	11,548	3,638	1,014	916
1989	−25.1	10,679	2,927	339	322
1990	−22.6	9,790	3,175	312	289
1991	−25.5	12,477	4,628	917	880
1992	−26.5	12,272	4,245	968	893
1993	−23.7	11,137	3,692	967	901

Sources: Column 1: 1974–85, Dale E. Hathaway, *Agriculture and the GATT: Rewriting the Rules* (Washington, D.C.: Institute for International Economics, 1987), p. 10; 1986–91: U.S. Department of Agriculture, Economic Research Service, *Western Europe Agriculture and Trade Report, 1992* (Washington, D.C.). 1992–93: COMEXT Trade Database, EUROSTAT. Column 2: *The Agricultural Situation in the Community, EC annual reports, 1975–94* (Brussels). Column 3: 1985–89, *Background for 1990 Farm Legislation* (Washington, D.C.: U.S. Department of Agriculture, 1990); 1990–93, internal USDA figures.
[a]For crop year ending in listed year.

The introduction of large Community grain export subsidies in the late 1970s and early 1980s triggered several reactions that tended to force a confrontation in the Uruguay Round. The U.S. Congress took the initiative to establish a countervailing U.S. subsidy program, the Export Enhancement Program, which began operations in 1985. Congressional agricultural committees, as a result, had to contend with growing export subsidy payments within tight overall budgets and took a strong bipartisan stand that unless the Uruguay Round substantially resolved this problem, members would vote against the final agreement.[35]

Third-country grain exporters, most prominently Argentina, Australia, and Canada, were caught in the crossfire of the expanding U.S.-EC export subsidy war and lost market shares. The Cairns group of agricultural exporting countries, established just before the Punta meeting, agreed to walk out of the negotiations if results in agriculture were not forthcoming.

Nevertheless, the U.S. decision to provoke a showdown over the CAP in the Uruguay Round was still not inevitable. The Punta declaration had clearly called for reduction in trade-distorting farm support, implicitly including export subsidies, but it was flexible as to the form and degree of specific commitments. For example, a more limited set of objectives to freeze subsidies at existing levels and to undertake longer-term supply adjustments could have constituted a reasonable response.[36]

Instead, during the period from the Punta meeting in September 1986 to July 1987, the United States developed its proposal for a total phaseout of trade-distorting agricultural supports—including internal price supports, border restrictions on imports, and export subsidies—over ten years, the Zero 2000 proposal. The ten-year transition was negotiable, but the long-term commitment to free trade was essential. In other words, the EC had to agree to phase out the CAP.

This critical decision for the course of the Uruguay Round was essentially the work and inspiration of three committed people within the U.S. government. The leading player was Trade Representative Clayton Yeutter, a farmer, agricultural economist, former assistant secretary of agriculture, and long-standing opponent of the CAP. He had enjoyed ultimate decision-making authority at the Punta conference, unchallenged by cabinet colleagues, and the successful outcome strengthened his bureaucratic hand for post-Punta policy formulation. Yeutter's senior agricultural adviser and negotiator was Daniel Amstutz, the former undersecretary of agriculture. Amstutz entered government from the agri-business sector and was ideologically the most committed to free trade and destruction of the protectionist CAP system. The third player was Secretary of Agriculture Richard Lyng, a trusted friend of President Reagan since serving as California's secretary of agriculture. Lyng had earned his international negotiating spurs through his tough yet deft dealing with European counterparts at Punta del Este.

This strong and committed USTR–Department of Agriculture axis controlled the policy process that produced the free-trade proposal for agriculture. There was relatively little cabinet-level discussion. Secretary of State

George Shultz, who had the greatest potential cause for concern about the political consequences of a U.S.-EC confrontation, was himself a free trader frustrated by French intransigence at earlier economic summit meetings, and his senior economic adviser, Allen Wallis, was an even more committed economist from the Chicago school. Both strongly supported the free-trade approach. President Reagan responded enthusiastically to Zero 2000. He especially liked the target date, which was analogous to the U.S. proposal to the Soviet Union for elimination of medium-range nuclear warheads.

On July 6, 1987, the United States threw down the gauntlet for free trade in agriculture at Geneva, and the unfolding diplomatic drama shifted to Brussels. The initial EC reaction was predictably negative, including the political argument that the U.S. proposal would undermine the cohesive fabric of the Community. The U.S. proposal, from the outset, provided for non-trade-distorting income payments to farmers, which could help small farmers in particular, but Community criticism ignored this alternate means of support and predicted dire consequences for all farmers.[37] A continual EC debating point was that the U.S. free trade approach was so extreme that it inhibited the Community from formulating a reasonable response. In fact, the outspoken public denunciations by EC spokesmen became a self-fulfilling prophesy when thousands of European farmers converged on Brussels during the ill-fated ministerial meeting in December 1990.

Tactics and histrionics aside, a real question remained: what would the Community propose as an alternative to the U.S. maximum demand? Other Uruguay Round participants, including the Cairns group, considered the extreme approach to be unrealistic. They were disposed to negotiate concrete trade liberalization of lesser magnitude. The EC adopted a package of agricultural reform measures in February 1988, including production cuts in specified circumstances, but the United States and others viewed these measures skeptically, considering them likely to be ineffective. In any event the reforms did not address directly the issues of access for imports and export subsidies. The agricultural negotiating group in Geneva waited for a complete EC response. The wait lasted more than four years.

The EC's difficulty in developing a credible proposal reflected the integrative nature of the ultimate protectionist mechanism that was the CAP. A limit on export subsidies below existing levels, always the most important specific objective, could back up surplus production and lead to unbearable storage costs. The conversion of various forms of import restrictions, including the variable levy, into a consolidated fixed tariff, which became the general Uruguay Round approach for dealing with access for imports, could tend to undermine internal price supports. And a major reduction of internal price supports without offsetting income payments to small farmers was a political nonstarter. In other words, any substantial move by the EC would entail a fundamental restructuring of the existing CAP.

Many EC leaders and officials understood this basic point and indeed wanted a change in agricultural policy, but they faced institutional and political hurdles that proved overwhelming. The agonizing complexity of EC decision-making was at its worst when dealing with agriculture. Differences of approach between the EC directorates-general for external affairs and agriculture laboriously worked their way up to compromise between their respective commissioners, only to have the result rejected by the committee of member-state agricultural ministers. Positions finally adopted could be ambiguous, with poor communication and differing interpretation between commission officials and member state representatives. One determined member state, usually France, could block or even roll back an earlier decision at semiannual summit-level meetings.

The political hurdles to European farm reform were internal and external. Domestic agricultural lobbies were organized and vocal, while at least one member government usually faced elections in any given year. The competing external interests involved the extraordinary events, beginning in 1989, that ended the cold war and transformed the map of Europe. The EC became predominantly absorbed with unprecedented regional issues, including how to accommodate resurgent agricultural production in newly democratized Central European states. The former German Democratic Republic suddenly became part of the EC and a beneficiary of the CAP.

The U.S.-EC Uruguay Round confrontation over agriculture dragged on and marginalized the important agricultural stakes of other participants. Multilateral trade liberalization for agriculture could have great impact on developing countries, shifting some of them from net importers to substantial net exporters of farm products.[38] Japan and South Korea were large importers of food and also highly protectionist concerning key commodities, particularly rice. Yet they remained on the sidelines while all attention focused on the U.S.-EC standoff. The Cairns group kept political pressure on the two largest participants, but except at a few specific junctures, such as the Brussels ministerial meeting in December 1990, they became more of a Greek chorus of lament than a fully engaged negotiating party.

The broadest cost of the agricultural impasse fell upon the GATT trading system. Five years of delays and overall paralysis, beginning at the Montreal ministerial meeting in December 1988, further undermined confidence in the

multilateral system, and trade-policy momentum shifted to deepening regional blocs and bilateral arrangements. The agricultural specter of a protectionist European *deus ex machina,* a widening export-subsidy war between the
two dominant world trading partners, and prolonged political inability to do
anything about it produced public cynicism about a General Agreement based
on free-trade principles. Agriculture was different in some respects from trade
in manufactures and accounted for a relatively small share of world trade. In
the Uruguay Round, however, it became the litmus test for a credible GATT
system because the United States chose to make it so.

FIVE

The Road to Brussels, 1989–1990

The second-half period of negotiating group meetings, from April 1989 through the summer 1990, was definitive in shaping the package of final Uruguay Round agreements. The midterm decisions of April 8, 1989, left some issues more advanced than others. All key areas of negotiation would now be engaged. The period of initial diplomatic maneuvering was over, and most of the necessary technical analysis had been accomplished. The U.S.-EC impasse over agriculture continued to lurk in the shadows, but on all other issues, the time for specific proposals and counterproposals was at hand.

Director-General Dunkel, at the Trade Negotiations Committee meeting following the midterm decisions, outlined a three-phase work program. During the first phase, through the end of 1989, governments would present specific proposals in each of the negotiating groups. Phase two, through July 1990, would aim to narrow differences and to reach broad agreement. The final phase, through the end-year ministerial conclusion of the round, would be devoted to refining the agreements and preparing the necessary legal instruments for final adoption. Viewed in retrospect, phases one and two tended to overlap, and phase three never fully achieved it goals. Nevertheless, the basic objective—developing a limited number of well-defined key issues for ministerial review and decision—was accomplished in most areas. The Trade Negotiations Committee agreed on the first week in December 1990 for the ministerial meeting. It also accepted the invitation of the European Community and the government of Belgium to host the meeting in Brussels with the portentous comment, "the Community stressed the important political and symbolic nature of the decision."[1]

Several working groups got off to a quick start on issues pertaining to bilateral quotas and related selective import restrictions affecting, in particular, trade between industrialized and developing countries. The long-suffering safeguards issue was addressed through a draft comprehensive agreement prepared by negotiating group chairman George Maciel, the former Brazilian ambassador to the GATT. Temporary import restrictions to avoid market disruption would be subject to time limits and accompanied by adjustment measures for the protected industry. The right of retaliation would not apply as long as parties adhered to the provisions of the agreement. The use of tariffs would be preferable to quota restrictions. Concerning restrictions selectively employed against a few countries, which developing countries had long opposed, Maciel opened the door slightly to compromise by proposing that the negotiating group "examine the possibility of selective measures in special situations and subject to tighter discipline and surveillance."[2] The EC, which had insisted on selectivity since the Tokyo Round, responded with a proposal for limited selectivity, leaving blank the maximum time limit for such restrictions. The United States, an opponent of selectivity in the Tokyo Round, did not take a clear stand. The stage was thus being set for an agreement with some selectivity, but within specified conditions monitored by a GATT Safeguards Committee.

The GATT secretariat had compiled a tally of 250 "voluntary restraint" agreements outside the GATT, which would have to be brought within a new safeguards agreement, but almost a third of them applied to the textiles and apparel sector.[3] The negotiating group on textiles was thus closely linked to the safeguards issue, and it focused its work on the phaseout of the Multifiber Arrangement (MFA) bilateral quotas. A series of proposals was put forward during 1989 and early 1990. The International Textile and Clothing Bureau, representing twenty-three developing-country exporters, proposed a quick, six-year phaseout of existing quota restrictions. The ASEAN countries were willing to stretch out the transition until the year 2000. The EC and Japan proposed differing approaches to a ten-year phaseout of the MFA, but they were vague on the pace of quota liberalization.

The United States, later joined by Canada, took a very different approach, suggesting that bilateral textile quotas be converted immediately to global quotas (i.e., a single quota for imports of a product from all sources), which would then be progressively liberalized.[4] Everyone but Canada opposed the U.S. approach, in part because it entailed extending new quota restrictions to all trade in the sector. It was also suspect as the system long advocated by the highly protectionist U.S. industry, and indeed, the textile lobby by the spring of 1990 was campaigning in support of a textile bill along these lines that would reduce rather than liberalize access to the U.S. market. By mid-1990, other Uruguay Round participants agreed to phase out the MFA over a maximum period of ten years. The United States became increasingly isolated in its global quota approach, and negotiations turned more toward the specific phaseout rates for MFA quotas.

Negotiations to phase out MFA textile quotas inevitably led to the issue of other restrictions on textile and apparel imports, particularly by developing countries. The United States, the EC, Canada, and Japan together insisted that developing countries, who were highly competitive exporters of textiles, should also phase out wide-ranging quota restrictions on their part, bind remaining tariff protection within the GATT, and subject any temporary restrictions to the provisions of a new safeguards agreement. Such commitments, and particularly developing-country compliance with safeguards provisions, were related, in turn, to the contentious issue of balance-of-payments based import restrictions under Article XVIII. The industrialized countries coordinated closely in the GATT Articles negotiating group to seek stringent limits on balance-of-payments–justified restrictions through revision of the 1979 Tokyo Round Declaration on Trade Measures for Balance-of-Payments Purposes.[5] Developing countries continued to resist any commitment related to Article XVIII, as well as reciprocal trade liberalization within the textile sector, but these negotiating linkages were becoming firmly established, and they would stick.

Revision of the GATT antidumping code was yet another interrelated dimension of selective import restrictions and came to dominate the work of the MTN negotiating group. Antidumping actions had increased sharply during the 1980s and were becoming the instrument of choice for industries seeking protection. The United States and the EC accounted for almost half of such actions, but some developing countries were adopting antidumping laws on the U.S. model, at times with encouragement from the World Bank.[6] Antidumping actions were subject to abuse, for example, through questionable procedures for determining prices at which imports were allegedly dumped and the criteria for assessing injury. The threat of dumping duties—which could involve lengthy and costly litigation—was also used as leverage to negotiate "voluntary" export restraints. In the MTN negotiating group, Hong Kong and South Korea proposed amendments to the existing code to strengthen disciplines on use of antidumping measures, and Singapore suggested a revised set of principles and objectives to ensure that antidumping would not be used for protectionist purposes. The United States and the EC, in response, raised problems from the importing-country point of view, principally that of "circumvention," whereby dumping duties were evaded by exporting components for assembly in the importing or third countries. In March 1990, in view of the growing complexity of the issue, negotiations shifted to a more informal group chaired by GATT Deputy Director Charles Carlisle, who prepared a draft comprehensive agreement as a basis for final negotiations. Country positions remained far apart, however, and a broadly supported draft antidumping agreement was not achieved by the time of the Brussels meeting.

The negotiating groups dealing most directly with market access—those on tariffs and nontariff measures—moved ahead more slowly. The nontariff-measures group concentrated on two issues, preshipment inspection and, more important, rules of origin. By the spring of 1990, draft agreements on both were taking shape. The rules-of-origin agreement would focus on greater harmonization of national rules and the basic principles for a more ambitious post–Uruguay Round negotiation linked to a technical work agenda carried out by the Customs Cooperation Council. The tariffs negotiating group bogged down over U.S. insistence on an item-by-item, request-offer approach, while the EC, Japan, and Canada each proposed a formula approach of across-the-board cuts with some degree of harmonization through deeper percentage cuts for the highest rates.[7] In January 1990, the group agreed to the submission of initial proposals on either basis. By June thirty-six participants had done so, but the content of the proposals fell far short of the minimum one-third average reduction agreed by ministers.

Other negotiating groups became more targeted on key issues. The dispute-settlement group, building on the interim agreement adopted at the midterm review, tackled the central question of decision-making by consensus. The United States, under pressure to refrain from unilateral dispute settlement under Section 301, made clear that this issue was related to a more prompt and reliable multilateral GATT mechanism and proposed the establishment of an appellate body that could review panel reports, after which the reports could be adopted with something less than a full consensus. Others, however, remained reluctant or opposed. The FOGS group continued to come up empty handed with respect to "greater cohesion in global economic policy-making" vis-à-vis the World Bank and the IMF, but did consider Swiss proposals to strengthen the GATT management framework by giving the secretariat independent policy analysis capability and by establishing a small ministerial level steering group.[8] The subsidies and countervailing measures group struggled to distinguish more precisely three categories of subsidies, those prohibited by the GATT; those "actionable" (i.e., subject to countervailing duties), depending on trade impact; and those that would under specified circumstances be permissible, such as subsidies for R&D, regional policies, structural adjustment, and environmental upgrades. The categories were referred to as red, amber, and green light, respectively. The subsidy debate, however, to the extent it became more specific also became more polarized. The United States wanted to circumscribe greatly any green-light subsidies, and almost everyone else, for varying reasons, supported some permissive subsidies.[9]

The most complex and prolonged deliberations continued to be in the negotiating groups on intellectual property rights and trade in services. The intellectual-property negotiating group debated the basic elements of an agreement—such as national treatment, transparency, and GATT-oriented dispute settlement—as well as the critical issue of minimum standards of protection. India, with limited support from other developing countries, was most adamant in seeking to limit negotiations to "restrictive or anti-competitive practices of the owners of intellectual property rights," while allowing developing countries to be "left free to adapt their domestic legislation to their development and other public and technological requirements and interests."[10] Mexico, in contrast, submitted a proposal covering elements of an agreement that highlighted the importance of an appropriate intellectual-property system to attract foreign investment, and stressed the importance of a rapid and efficient dispute-settlement procedure. By the spring of 1990, six separate draft texts of an agreement had been put forward by the United States, the EC, Switzerland, Japan, a group of fourteen developing countries, and a group comprised of Australia, New Zealand, Hong Kong, and the Nordic countries. The EC text raised new issues of contention with the United States, involving most notably appellations of origin and the more esoteric matters of neighboring rights and industrial design. The highly able chairman of the negotiating group, Lars Anell, with strong secretariat support centering around David Hartridge, laboriously molded the various drafts into a consolidated text.

The services negotiating group further developed the general principles and objectives of a framework agreement as well as the more specific aspects of trade in six sectors: telecommunications, construction, transportation, tourism, financial services, and professional services (i.e., legal, health care, and engineering services). Lengthy debate continued over special and differential treatment for developing countries, especially with respect to market access and progressive trade liberalization. The United States singled out dispute settlement as the most important institutional issue, envisaging a common mechanism for the GATT and the services agreement, but the matter remained unresolved. The central issue of sectoral coverage for national treatment and other market access commitments was not seriously addressed until late 1989, and it then quickly bogged down over the procedural question of whether countries should submit a "top down" negative list of industries excluded, as proposed by the United States, or a "bottom up" positive list of included service industries, as proposed by the EC and supported by most others. The United States finally agreed in the summer of 1990 to a Swiss "hybrid" proposal in which industry sectors would be submitted on a positive-list basis but commitments within sectors would be top down (i.e., all inclusive unless specified).[11] This left little time before Brussels to develop the actual offer lists, and the United States would soon dismay others with what was not included.

Various unresolved issues in the negotiating groups, not to mention the agricultural impasse, would have to be engaged at a higher political level. However, negotiating groups had achieved a major accomplishment in specifying most of the decision issues in "profiles" of prospective final agreements. The dimensions of a "big package" final accord compared with less consequential outcomes had been clearly delineated.

Arthur Dunkel, at a Trade Negotiations Committee (TNC) meeting in April 1990, summed up the progress to date in terms of four major themes: "First, there had been a very strong collective plea in favor of multilateralism. . . . Second, participants had clearly expressed their wish to keep to the ambitious objectives defined in the Punta del Este Declaration. Third, there had been a general perception that since the launching of the Uruguay Round, the political and economic map of the world had changed dramatically and in a direction that made a strong multilateral trading system even more indispensable than had been envisaged three years earlier. Fourth, the relevance of the Uruguay Round for the present and future cooperation in the economic and trade field had increased dramatically because of this evolution."

Director-General Dunkel's first two themes erred somewhat on the side of optimism. The third and fourth themes—the dramatically changed role of the multilateral trading system and the relevance of the Uruguay Round—were far more complicated to assess, but they were surely not overstated.

Dramatic Developments Elsewhere

While 1989–90 was a critical period for shaping the final Uruguay Round agreement, the painstaking trade deliberations were only peripheral to the dramatic parallel transformation that took place in the broader world political and economic order. Between the Uruguay Round mid-term agreement of April 1989 and the Brussels ministerial meeting in December 1990, the communist government in East Germany, together with the Berlin wall, were swept away; a unified D-mark economy was created and all-German elections were held; communist regimes elsewhere in East Europe collapsed and were replaced by democratically elected governments committed to capitalist economic reforms; in the Soviet Union, public confidence in communism and a centrally planned economy plummeted while reform movements proliferated; the momentum of change in China erupted in the massacre of Tiananmen Square in June 1989; economic success and modernization elsewhere in East Asia fostered democratization in South Korea and Taiwan; in the Americas, elected civilian governments dedicated to market-oriented economic reforms came to rule everywhere except Cuba. The Russian catchwords were *glasnost* and *perestroika*. A fuller rendering in English was the triumph of economic liberalism and liberal democracy as the basis for a new world order.

This transformation, as noted by Arthur Dunkel, had important consequences for the GATT trading system. The principles of free trade and market-oriented prices embedded in the General Agreement became mainstream thinking for economic reform almost everywhere, replacing the competing ideologies of East versus West and North versus South. The change was evident in the rush of new GATT members: Mexico and Hong Kong in 1986; Botswana and Antigua & Barbuda in 1987; Lesotho in 1988; Tunisia, Venezuela, Bolivia, and Costa Rica (the hundredth member) in 1990; eight other applicants in process at decade's end. Moreover, the conditions for new membership became more stringent in terms of broader commitments to open trade, reduced import barriers, and lower tariffs bound in the GATT. Mexico set a prominent example, followed by Venezuela, Bolivia, and Costa Rica.

By 1990 the only major traders not in the GATT were China, Taiwan, whose application request was linked to that of China, and the Soviet Union. Negotiations for Chinese membership were well advanced when the Tiananmen massacre and a reversal of the economic reform program caused an indefinite suspension. The Soviet Union first requested GATT observer status in 1986 and was turned down on the grounds that GATT-compatible economic reforms were not yet under way.[12] In December 1989, however, at the U.S.-Soviet summit meeting in Malta, President Bush, in response to Soviet withdrawal from East Europe and progress on internal reforms, decided to support Soviet observer status, and the GATT Council approved it in May 1990. GATT membership had thus not only gained respectability but had become a bargaining chip in support of reforms within the two largest communist powers.

The precise role of the GATT multilateral trading system within an only vaguely defined new world order and the degree to which it would be, in Dunkel's terms, more or less indispensable, however, was less clear. The bipolar cold war order was in rapid decline, but whether it would be replaced by a universal system of equal sovereign states or by a reconfiguration of large-power and regional relationships remained an open question. In political-security terms, permanent members of the UN Security Council were far more equal than others, and interest was on the rise for regional security arrangements from the Conference on Security and Cooperation in Europe (CSCE) to new initiatives in the Middle East and Asia. The corresponding debate over the international economic system and the trade policy relationship in particular followed a similar pattern, focusing on the respective roles of the GATT multilateral system and the tendency toward regional trade groupings.[13] The trade-strategy model was no longer limited to the "bicycle theory" with its two settings, forward movement toward trade liberalization or fallback to protectionism. It now also included various forward speeds, for example slow progress within the GATT Uruguay Round and fast forward toward regional free trade. Indeed, the distinct circumstances in Western Europe, North America, and East Asia fostering regional trade and investment, which had been building throughout the decade, coalesced and accelerated during 1989–90.

The dramatic end of the cold war in Europe added a new dimension to regional economic integration. A deepening of Community integration through the EC-92 market unification program and phased monetary union became linked to a geographic broadening of membership as well. East Germany was fully integrated into the EC by the end of 1990. Czechoslovakia, Hungary, and Poland quickly expressed interest in membership over time. Austria cast aside its long-cherished neutrality and formally applied for EC membership in July 1989, joining the queue with Turkey, Malta, and Cyprus. The Nordic countries and Switzerland wanted closer ties if not ultimate full membership. More speculative discussion involved the future Community relationships with unstable Balkan states, potentially independent Baltic republics, and a truly restructured Soviet economy. The vision of a greater "European economic space" captivated the imagination and dominated policy discussion.

The rapid course of events within Europe engulfed the Community decision-making apparatus in frantic activity. The more difficult EC-92 directives were reaching the decisive stage and the path toward monetary union became cluttered with the financial problems of a united Germany. More comprehensive trade agreements were negotiated with EFTA countries, and a new form of associate membership developed for the newly democratic East Europeans. Enhanced political cooperation within the Community became a post–cold war objective, and the Commission needed to coordinate support for economic reconstruction in the East. In this fervid context, the more intractable Uruguay Round issues received little political-level attention. Basic reform of the EC agricultural policy, moreover, faced a new, ill-defined complication. Former East Germany was the historic German breadbasket and had been a small net exporter of grains even under the grossly inefficient communist state-farm system. Now, conversion to private farms and guaranteed Community prices at two to three times world levels held out the prospect of a major economic stimulus for depressed East German states and of greatly increased financial demands on the EC budget.

While world attention centered on the deepening and broadening of European integration, trade policy developments in the Americas were of comparable consequence. The U.S.-Canadian free-trade agreement took force in January 1989 in parallel with intensified U.S.-Mexican discussions for more open trade, although Mexican President Carlos Salinas de Gortari initially sought enhanced access to the U.S. market on a nondiscriminatory basis. In February 1990, however, Salinas returned from a European trip disillusioned with the prospect of expanding trade with regionally preoccupied European countries. Shortly thereafter, to widespread surprise, he announced his intent to seek a free trade agreement with the United States. President Bush responded enthusiastically and, by autumn, Canada had joined in a trilateral initiative for free trade that would include 360 million people and $6 trillion of GNP, slightly more on both counts than the European Community.

On June 27, 1990, President Bush took another major step toward building a regional dimension into U.S. trade policy—his Enterprise for the Americas Initiative. Anticipating a trip to South America, he announced, "Now is the time to make a comprehensive free trade zone for the Americas our long term goal," and stated the readiness of the United States to enter into free-trade agreements, beginning with Mexico.[14] The free-trade objective had a rhetorical ring and did not initially receive prominent press attention in the United States. Circumstances were changing rapidly in South America, however, where almost all countries had embarked on trade-oriented structural reform programs. They were as concerned as Mexico about export prospects in Europe and elsewhere and responded promptly and positively to the Bush initiative. Chile requested early negotiations for a free-trade area, and bilateral economic framework agreements, the precursor step to free trade with Mexico, were quickly established throughout the region. By the end of 1990, Ronald Reagan's vision of free trade from "Tierra del Fuego to the Arctic Circle" was being discussed not so much in terms of whether, but of how and when.

Deepening economic integration within East Asia was the least clearly defined and, to draw an analogy from astrophysics, could be viewed as the black hole of the world economy: enormous economic energy was being generated within the region, but its impact on the global system was not clearly visible to the eye. On the surface, East Asians—from Japan to the newly industrialized economies to lower income ASEAN countries—strongly supported the GATT multilateral system, but the slow pace of the Uruguay Round and the trend toward regional blocs in Europe and the Americas increasingly troubled them. A shared longer view of manifest economic destiny saw East Asia as the center and driving force for the world economy in the next century. A logical conclusion was that East Asia needed a regional trading bloc of its own, and in December 1990 Prime Minister Datuk Mahathir Mohamad of Malaysia proposed an East Asian Economic Grouping. The substance of the proposal was vague but the rationale was to allow members "to counter the emergence of protectionism and regionalism in world trade."[15] Official reaction in the region was not immediately supportive, but neither was it openly negative.

Another possible future course for East Asia was deeper integration within a broader Asia-Pacific region, including at least the United States and Canada on the Pacific rim of the Americas, which would serve to keep the important North American market open to East Asian exporters. In November 1989 a ministerial meeting in Canberra, Australia, established an intergovernmental mechanism called Asia-Pacific Economic Cooperation (APEC).[16] Ministers agreed to meet annually, but the substance of regional cooperation initiatives was initially limited to noncontroversial issues such as trade promotion and environmental problems.

Meanwhile, trade/investment relationships within East Asia continued to deepen. Trade shares were shifting steadily away from the United States, and by decade's end Japan, South Korea, and Taiwan exported as much to East Asia as to the United States, while ASEAN countries imported two to three times as much from regional trading partners as from North America.

Nineteen eighty-nine through 1990 can thus be identified as the period in which the world trading system moved definitively away from a predominantly multilateral, most-favored-nation trading system to a two-tiered structure of regional groups interacting with a more loosely knit multilateral framework. Trade flows became increasingly tripolar, with half the world's trade by decade's end taking place within the three advanced industrialized regions of Western Europe, North America, and East Asia, and another quarter among these three regions. Trade policy commitments were deepening at both the multilateral and regional levels, but with decidedly stronger momentum at the regional level. In this context, Arthur Dunkel's comment that a strong multilateral trading system had become even more indispensable could be interpreted not only in terms of positive benefits from multilateral trade liberalization but also as a countervailing force to the growing regional polarization of the world economy and to the potential negative consequences of trading blocs turned inward and antagonistic.

Faltering Trade Leadership

The more complex geographic configuration of the trading system raised a corresponding question about leadership. The United States had always been acknowledged as the moving force within the GATT. The long struggle to launch and then negotiate the Uruguay Round reconfirmed this role in most respects but raised doubts about it in others. U.S. leadership faced an especially severe test in the spring and summer of 1990, which generated broader concerns about the locus of leadership within the GATT system.

The leadership role of the United States in world trade had evolved steadily during the 1980s. Sustained U.S. initiative had led a reluctant GATT membership into the Uruguay Round and had established the round's broad, forward-looking agenda. Countercurrents in U.S. trade strategy, however, were also at play. The pursuit of free-trade agreements in the Western Hemisphere by Presidents Reagan and Bush constituted a fundamental shift from the previously unyielding commitment of the United States to nondiscrimination as the preferred basis for trade. The surge in unilateral Section 301 initiatives to deal outside the GATT with alleged unfair trading practices and insufficiently open markets was another basic change in trade strategy. Impatience and frustration over the lack of progress during the lengthy preparatory and negotiating stages of the Uruguay Round and continuing threats to turn toward bilateralism and regional blocs provided a far less confidence-inspiring form of U.S. leadership within the GATT.

But while the United States appeared to weaken as leader within the multilateral trading system, alternatives to U.S. leadership were not apparent. The Uruguay Round performance of the European Community and Japan, through 1989, only highlighted inherent weaknesses. The EC was active in all negotiating groups, but its inability to make specific offers in the agricultural sector not only put it on the defensive in this key area but tended to slow down the overall pace of the round. Moreover, the growing preoccupation with deepening and broadening the Community structure within Europe and growing resistance to imports from Japan and other Asian countries raised serious doubts about EC interest in a strengthened GATT system. Another big question of an institutional character was whether the cumbersome member-state–Commission decision-making process would be capable of making politically difficult decisions during the final phase of the negotiations.

Japan had moved dramatically to economic superpower status during the 1980s but was unable to translate its enhanced trade position into a GATT leadership role. The reason was in part cultural, a familiar reticence or inability to formulate and implement initiatives within international organizations. Meanwhile, interministerial decision-making in Tokyo complicated and discouraged bold initiative. Japanese trading practices were also under constant assault, in and out of GATT, putting Japanese negotiators on the defensive. In the Uruguay Round, the most pressing request on Japan was for some relaxation of its total ban on rice imports as part of an overall agricultural package. Japanese negotiators hinted at ultimate flexibility but held back any formal offer until the final days of the round, thus limiting their ability to influence the final agreement elsewhere. More fundamental, the Japanese approach to trade and investment relations was to deal with issues on a pragmatic, informal basis, making discrete demands or concessions as specific situations developed. This approach contrasted with the legalistic GATT framework of general principles and formal procedures. Japan was more concerned with specific trade interests than with the rules of the GATT multilateral system, which tended to preclude an active leadership role.

A logical transition of GATT leadership would be toward some form of trilateral U.S.-EC-Japanese condominium, reflecting the tripolar trend in the structure of the world economy. There were, in fact, meetings of the Quad (which also included Canada) at both ministerial and official levels, but they had been more prominent during the preparatory period leading up to Punta and would become most intense and productive only later, after the Brussels meeting. Nineteen eighty-nine and 1990 were a relatively quiescent phase for Quad activity, inspiring little in the way of joint leadership.

As summer 1990 approached, the political will of the United States to maintain leadership in the Uruguay Round came into more serious question. The United States had prevailed in moving its priority objectives in the round forward—services, intellectual-property protection, and agriculture—but now, faced with corresponding concessions on its own part, it faltered. For textiles, the United States and Canada alone opposed a phaseout of the Multifiber Arrangement. For tariff cuts, the United States had rejected a general-formula approach that appeared most likely to achieve substantial results. For a more disciplined antidumping code, the United States and the EC were resisting any significant curbs on their right of unilateral action. Even in agriculture, the U.S. hard-line stand for total or near elimination of farm supports was suspect as a convenient way to avoid offering specific though more limited reductions in its support programs in such sensitive areas as sugar and dairy products.

The most dismaying development, however, involved the service-sector negotiations, which had been the top U.S. priority at Punta del Este. Under domestic pressure, the United States wanted to exclude air and marine transportation from the agreement. The U.S. Treasury was also advocating strongly the exclusion of financial services on the grounds that GATT jurisdiction would be unsettling to world financial markets. More surprising, in the spring of 1990, AT&T and other U.S. telecommunications companies belatedly requested U.S. negotiators to withhold an MFN commitment on basic telecommunications services from the GATT services agreement. The 1988 Trade Act mandated bilateral negotiations to open state-controlled telecommunications markets in the EC, Japan, and elsewhere, and U.S. bargaining leverage would, in the industry's view, be compromised by an MFN commitment in the GATT to permanently maintain the more open U.S. market. Bilateral negotiations were preferred to multilateral rules, and by July U.S. negotiators in Geneva indicated they could not unconditionally support MFN for trade in basic telecommunications services.

In Washington, a broader question of U.S. negotiating strategy concerned the potential net negative impact on U.S. manufacturing industry. The United States was seeking trade liberalization for farm products and general framework agreements for service-industry and intellectual-property protection, but in return it faced requests to reduce protection for manufacturing industry, including textiles, and to limit recourse to antidumping and other remedies against unfair trading practices. U.S. manufacturing industry, which encompassed the large majority of trade, would be more exposed to imports and get little in return in terms of market access for exports. One senior U.S. negotiator questioned privately whether there had not been a fundamental flaw in U.S. negotiating strategy at Punta. Publicly, a congressional call for projections of the impact on U.S. trade from a Uruguay Round agreement revealed that the administration had no detailed estimates of its own, putting it on the defensive. A private group favoring some form of "managed trade" over GATT market-oriented principles, promptly produced a projected $14 billion deterioration in the U.S. trade balance from the anticipated Uruguay Round outcome.[17]

The apparent faltering of U.S. leadership and the absence of any alternative mode of leadership raised further questions about the adequacy of the multilateral trading system. Part of the problem was institutional in nature, a rigid and constrained GATT structure overwhelmed by a heavily burdened Uruguay Round agenda. In this context, strong leadership was at a premium just when the traditional U.S. lead role needed reinforcement that others were unable to provide. The heart of the problem, however, was political. Could the commitment to a multilateral system—particularly by the United States, the

European Community, and Japan—prevail over competing regional and bilateral objectives. The greatest challenge ever for the GATT would be a successful conclusion of the Uruguay Round, scheduled for December 1990 in Brussels, and the GATT leadership question was one of several storm clouds gathering over the European capital renown for its lack of sunshine.

Negotiating Group Profiles

A key juncture in Director-General Dunkel's negotiating plan came at the Trade Negotiations Committee meeting that began July 23, 1990. All groups were to submit their clearly defined issue "profiles" as a basis for decision-making by senior officials. Only the most difficult decisions were to be left for ministers at Brussels in December. During the spring, however, pessimism grew about the proposed scenario. The agricultural group remained at an impasse. U.S. political will on key issues was in doubt. Developing countries complained about "lack of balance" and the need for greater emphasis on issues of interest to them. An Indonesian negotiator summed it up: "There are moments in discussions when really serious political decisions must be made."[18]

Serious decision-making got sidetracked further by a proposal in April 1990 by Trade Minister John Crosbie of Canada to create a World Trade Organization (WTO) to supersede the existing GATT system.[19] The GATT had existed for more than forty years as a "provisional" protocol, and periodic proposals had been made to give it more permanent status, comparable to that of other international economic institutions. There were also important organizational issues to be confronted at some point in the Uruguay Round, most prominently how the agreements on services and intellectual property would relate to the GATT. An integrated dispute-settlement mechanism, for example, had various implications.

The Canadian proposal went further, however, by proposing a new legal framework to be approved by ministers at Brussels: "The post–Uruguay Round trade policy agenda will be complex and cannot be adequately managed within the confines of the existing GATT system." The official Canadian proposal contained few specifics, except for dispute settlement, which was in any event under discussion in the dispute-settlement negotiating group. The broader substance of the initiative was derived from work done by the American GATT legal scholar, John Jackson, who had published a book about a new WTO in January 1990 and who was later a consultant to the Canadian government.[20] Jackson proposed a permanent organization with universal membership represented on a governing council, within which specific and more limited substantive obligations, such as the GATT, would be sheltered. Dispute settlement—and perhaps provisions for trade-related aspects of such over-arching matters as national security and the environment—would rest with the senior WTO structure.

The Canadian proposal was received coolly, especially by the United States, for two reasons. First, universal membership for a senior governing body could dilute the commitment to a liberal trading system, which was fundamental to GATT membership and had been strengthened by commitments of new members in the late 1980s. The WTO would also enshrine permanently majority one-nation-one-vote decision-making and could become politicized through control by a majority of developing and communist countries, as was often the case in UN bodies. This concern was reinforced when fifteen developing-country foreign ministers at New York, mostly hard-line Uruguay Round participants, complained that the Canadian initiative did not go far enough. They proposed a comprehensive International Trade Organization within the UN system, to be taken up by the UN General Assembly rather than within the Uruguay Round.[21]

The second reason for a cool reception was the fear that negotiation of GATT reorganization would detract from the substantive objectives of the round and could even result in a "successful" final agreement based principally on the creation of a new trade organization. The Canadians were explicit that a new organization would only be justified if there were agreement on the substantive issues in the Uruguay Round, but the Americans were suspicious of EC intentions. The Community, in fact, supported the Canadian initiative in proposing that ministers agree "in principle" at Brussels to a new organization, and a senior European official indiscreetly commented that a new trade organization could be a major accomplishment of the round.[22] Carla Hills, reflecting her legal background, provided the definitive response: "You need to have the rules before you build the courthouse."[23] The World Trade Organization was consigned to languish in the FOGS group while negotiators worked further on the rules.

The rules for agriculture remained at a total impasse. The April 1989 midterm agreement called for detailed proposals by the end of the year on all elements of short- and long-term agricultural reform, but by May 1990 the European Community in particular had yet to put forward specific proposals. The most difficult issue remained export subsidies. The EC opposed any direct commitment to reduce export subsidies and limited its approach to yet-unspecified reductions in domestic levels of support that would, in its view, lead indirectly to diminished export subsidies as well. The United States, in contrast, proposed elimination of all export subsidies over five years and rejected the EC contention that cuts in internal support measures would necessarily lead to reduced surplus production for subsidized exports. The Uruguay Round agricultural stalemate was raised by the United States at the OECD ministerial meeting at the end of May, where a heated five-hour luncheon debate ended in disarray and explicit disagreement in the final communiqué.

As a means to break the impasse, the chairman of the Uruguay Round negotiating group on agriculture was then asked to draw up, by the end of June, a compromise draft agreement as a basis for the final negotiation. This catapulted the reserved, soft-spoken Dutch civil servant Aart de Zeeuw into a flurry of publicity, complete with frequent phonetic help from the press—de-ZAY-ou—and President Bush referred to him by name at the Houston economic summit in early July. The de Zeeuw chairman's report called for "substantial and progressive reductions" in three areas—internal farm support, import barriers, and export subsidies. Moreover, export subsidies were to "result in such assistance being reduced effectively more than other forms of support and protection."[24] De Zeeuw explained the relatively greater reductions in export subsidies in simple terms: "It was logical. Everybody apart from the EC and Austria wanted it that way."[25]

The EC was understandably unhappy with the de Zeeuw report, but its leaders at the Houston summit, after lengthy discussion, agreed to a July 11 communiqué that "commends" the report "as a means to intensify the negotiations." The stage was thus set for the hoped-for breakthrough at the July 23 TNC meeting in Geneva, but nothing happened. The EC representatives were still unable to elaborate specific proposals, and the TNC result was simply to reiterate the summit communiqué language. Even this was marred by a clumsy French attempt to water down the French translation to read "one of several means."[26] October 15 was agreed as the date for all participants to put forward specific offers as provided in the de Zeeuw text.

Not much happened elsewhere at the TNC meeting either, and it ended after four days in a mood of anticlimax and disappointment. Developing countries were particularly upset since many had sent high-level delegations to the meeting in anticipation of serious negotiation of issues of interest to them, such as agriculture and textiles. Brazil's ambassador to the GATT, Rubens Ricupero, in a terse statement on behalf of all developing country participants, expressed "frustration and disappointment at the lack of substantive results. . . . if the current situation is not changed soon, the Uruguay Round will be in serious jeopardy as a result of the lack of political will of the major participants."[27] Delegates agreed to a revised and intensified schedule of meetings for the four remaining months until the Brussels ministerial meeting.

The TNC result, however, was not all negative. The negotiating group profiles represented a major accomplishment in synthesizing large amounts of technical material and wide-ranging country proposals. For intellectual-property protection, the most complicated area of substance, the negotiating group profile of more than one hundred pages, cluttered with brackets, nevertheless did represent a structured basis for final negotiation compared to the plethora of diverse, independent proposals that existed several months earlier. A statement by Director-General Dunkel focused attention by listing the key unresolved issues in need of political attention. The isolated U.S. textile proposal for a new system of global quotas received indirect reference: "I have noted the very wide support in the TNC for a modality based on the (existing) MFA." For the GATT Articles negotiating group, Dunkel singled out the use of trade-restricting measures for balance-of-payments purposes: "There is no sign of a meeting of the minds." And, of course, for agriculture there was a specific list of issues to be addressed on an agreed time schedule.[28]

A busy but not insurmountable agenda was thus laid out for the final months. The question, as raised by Ricupero, was one of political will, and at the end of July the outlook on this score was mixed at best. Press comment tended to be skeptical. Arthur Dunkel concluded his statement with the dubious contention: "It is clear from our discussions this week that all of you feel the need for the Uruguay Round to succeed because history gives us no other choice." The EC spokesman, when asked by the press whether he was optimistic or pessimistic about the outcome, waxed Delphic: "J'ai le pessimisme de L'intelligence et l'optimisme de La Volonté."[29] On August 2, exactly one week after the TNC meeting, Iraq invaded Kuwait and the ensuing Gulf War captivated public attention, relegating all else, including the Uruguay Round, to the shadowy sidelines.

The Brussels Ministerial

Brussels, the capital of the European Community, proudly hosted the GATT ministerial meeting that began on Monday, December 3, 1990, and was to conclude the Uruguay Round. The sprawling Heysel exhibition center, built for the 1958 World's Fair, accommodated comfortably the two thousand delegates, one thousand journalists, and countless private-sector representatives and all-purpose lobbyists. Thirty thousand European farmers converged to protest any reduction in EC agricultural support, but an ample contingent of police kept them from advancing to within sight of the conference hall.[30] Hotels and restaurants bustled with Uruguay Round guests, and complimentary access to the excellent metro system provided prompt transportation to meetings and social functions for those without a chauffeured limousine. The moderately cold and drizzly weather was relatively benign compared with Punta del Este and Montreal. The ubiquitous official poster blazoned the conference motto throughout the city: "World Trade: The Courage to Go Further."

The whirlwind of events elsewhere had upstaged the Brussels meeting and raised questions about the adequacy of political attention given to the GATT negotiations. The UN Security Council, the week before, had finally adopted a resolution permitting the "use of all necessary means," meaning armed invasion, if Iraq did not pull out of Kuwait by January 15. On the previous Thursday, John Major replaced Margaret Thatcher as British prime minister, giving his new trade and agricultural ministers only a couple of days to prepare themselves for Brussels. On Sunday, December 2, the first all-German elections in more than half a century were held.[31] Helmut Kohl won a resounding victory, but his free-trade minister of economy, Helmut Haussmann, resigned on Monday, focusing German ministerial-level representation in Brussels on Agricultural Minister Ignaz Kiechle. President Bush rescheduled his trip to South America, postponed by the Gulf crisis, for the same week as the Brussels meeting, and he appeared each evening on television toasting regional free trade with his South American counterparts .

Many if not most delegates arrived in Brussels deeply pessimistic about the outcome. Nevertheless, there were realistic hopes that the meeting could achieve the definitive breakthrough for a successful conclusion of the Uruguay Round. If the ministers in Brussels agreed on a balanced package of key commitments, subsidiary issues could be worked out in January and February before President Bush's legislative authority expired on March 1, 1991. The four-month calendar of intensive negotiations adopted the previous July had not accomplished much in terms of specific agreements, despite Arthur Dunkel's frequent plaintive warnings that time was running out. But the principal protagonists who held the key to a successful outcome—the United States and the European Community—had positioned themselves for conclusive final bargaining.

Positive positioning by the United States was far more pronounced, and the tottering political will of the previous summer had been replaced by a determination to take the necessary steps to conclude a deal. Preoccupation with bilateral Japanese negotiations had been resolved, at least temporarily, through agreements in April on three super 301 complaints—supercomputers, satellites, and wood products—and in June on a broader program of improved market access through the Structural Impediments Initiative. From July on, the U.S. trade-policy establishment had focused primarily on the Uruguay Round agenda. President Bush barely sustained a veto on a highly protectionist textile bill in October, and then acceded to the broadly supported Uruguay Round approach of a phased elimination of the MFA, including at least some reduction in tariffs. The U.S. delegation was prepared to accept qualified most-favored-nation treatment for basic telecommunications services and to make key concessions elsewhere. For agriculture, the earlier position of a total phaseout of trade-distorting farm support was modified to a 75 percent reduction of internal supports and a 90 percent reduction in export subsidies over ten years. These figures, moreover, were known to be negotiable.

The European Community had a more difficult and checkered experience in developing a proposal for agriculture, and it had been only partially successful. The October 15 deadline passed while member-state agricultural ministers resisted Commission proposals. The EC summit meeting in Rome in late October concentrated on steps toward European Monetary Union and ignored the Uruguay Round agricultural impasse. Finally, on November 6, the Community formally proposed a 30 percent reduction in internal support, but based the offer on higher 1986 levels, which meant only a 15 percent reduction from 1990 levels, and no commitment was offered to limit export subsidies. Strong negative reactions from the United States and the Cairns group led EC representatives to explain that the initial offer was subject to negotiation. Commissioner Frans Andriessen commented, "There is no point that is not negotiable." Italian Trade Minister Renato Ruggiero, who chaired the EC council of trade ministers, elaborated: "In agriculture, we have made a negotiating offer. But we never said this is the Community's position, take it or leave it. . . . If you want to know what my negotiating margin is, ask the U.S. what their margin is."[32] The question was how much further the Community could go in agriculture and, in particular, would it be willing to convert its projection that export subsidies would decline by more than 30 percent as a result of reduced internal supports, into a binding commitment to that end.

The ministerial meeting opened in the cavernous plenary hall with a warm welcome from King Baudouin of Belgium, followed by brief speeches by the Belgian foreign minister, Wilfried Martins, President Jacques Delors of the EC, Conference Chairman Hector Gros Espiell, the foreign minister of Uruguay, and Director-General Dunkel of the GATT. Martins raised a few eyebrows with his assertion that a permanent international trade organization, the missing pillar in the international economic system, could emerge from the meeting, but the conference quickly got down to business, to sort out and resolve outstanding issues in the heavily bracketed 391-page draft comprehensive agreement prepared by the GATT secretariat. As a practical matter, the fifteen negotiating groups were reduced to seven, each chaired by a minister: market access, agriculture, textiles, services, intellectual property/investment, rules of GATT, and "other."

By the second day, reports indicated progress in most groups. One clear sign was growing nervousness among industry lobbyists trying to maintain existing government positions. The largest contingent, from the United States, came together with other nonofficial Americans for daily briefings organized by the private-sector Multilateral Trade Negotiation Coalition. At the Tuesday evening session, the textile people were greatly troubled by U.S. consideration of faster liberalization during the early years of MFA transition and of deeper tariff cuts. The telecommunications representatives worried that an MFN commitment would be accepted without corresponding assurances for balanced market access. Similar concerns were expressed about intellectual property and antidumping agreements.

Agriculture, however, did not move forward. EC Agricultural Commissioner Ray MacSharry insisted that others did not understand the EC proposal. He called for additional technical clarification. Others respected MacSharry's competence but were wary of his political motivation. He was an Irish politician with likely prime-ministerial ambitions, and Ireland had the largest share of population in agriculture among EC members. The chairman of the agricultural negotiating group, Swedish Agricultural Minister Mats Hellström, tried to smoke out the EC by making a compromise proposal: a 30-percent reduction in internal supports, as in the Community proposal, but based on 1990 rather than 1986 support levels; and 30-percent cuts as well for import duties and export subsidies. The Community resisted negotiation on the basis of the chairman's proposal and continued to stress the need for further technical examination of the existing EC offer. EC spokesmen, in lengthy press briefings, tried to convince hundreds of skeptical journalists that 30-percent cuts in internal supports, based on 1986 levels, would likely lead to even greater reductions in export subsidies, but veteran reporters picked apart the EC arguments with growing derision.

More important, and in contrast to Montreal, the United States, the Cairns group, and almost all others united in pressing the EC. Only Japan and South Korea held back, opposed to reducing their own agricultural protection, although Japan, a nonexporter of farm products, supported the general call for cuts in EC export subsidies. Other negotiating groups began to stall, waiting to see what would happen in agriculture. Latin American farm exporters began to talk of suspending the talks. At noon Wednesday, Chairman Gros Espiell gave the EC a twenty-four-hour ultimatum. Either the Community indicate a willingness to negotiate specific commitments for agriculture by noon Thursday or the meeting would be terminated.

A late session on agriculture Wednesday evening among key ministers broke up in bitter recrimination, but an EC Council of Ministers meeting was scheduled for Thursday morning in an attempt to resolve the crisis. There had also been a meeting Wednesday afternoon in Paris between President Mitterand and Chancellor Kohl, with the Uruguay Round an obvious topic. The EC responded early Thursday afternoon with a clear message that it would be more flexible and specific in agriculture if other areas of the negotiation moved forward as well. A feeling of guarded relief and expectation permeated the conference center. Even jaundiced American negotiators were hopeful that a breakthrough had occurred. A 10 P.M. session was scheduled to get down to business.

Negotiations Suspended

On Friday, December 7, the headline "Concessions break trade talks deadlock" led a *Financial Times* story that opened: "The deadlock was broken in the Uruguay Round of talks to reform the world trade system last night after the European Community offered concessions on farm support and the United States shifted its position on services such as banking, telecommunications and insurance." The *Financial Times* prided itself on its full coverage of GATT issues, and all week free copies had been distributed at breakfast in hotels housing Uruguay Round guests. Unhappy hubris. The *Financial Times* story, signed by three senior reporters, got it wrong.[33]

The 10 P.M. meeting Thursday had been a shambles. Despite earlier EC assurances about new flexibility for agriculture, MacSharry simply restated the existing EC position and expressed willingness to study proposals by others. Japan and South Korea, in what can only be described as a tactical blunder, rejected the Swedish chairman's compromise approach for import liberalization and thus became even more uncompromising than the EC.[34] The U.S. delegation was exasperated. The Argentine and Brazilian delegates refused to negotiate further, and Argentina withdrew its delegates from other negotiating groups, which brought the entire conference to a halt. Chairman Gros Espiell concluded that no further progress was possible and called for a plenary meeting in the morning to consider "suspending" the conference.

On Friday morning, the central conference hall, where delegates mingled with press and private-sector representatives, was filled with gloom and confusion. U.K. ministers for trade Peter Lilley and for agriculture John Gummer, surrounded by reporters, tried to explain why it was premature to end the meeting, that the EC was prepared to be more flexible, and that the U.S. demands were "unrealistic" and "unacceptable." A New Zealand delegate was excoriating the EC in highly colorful and emotional terms. U.S. delegates shrugged about the brief period of hope the previous afternoon. Senior EC Commission officials were nowhere in sight, convening in private to prepare a twice-postponed press conference.

At 11 A.M., Chairman Gros Espiell made it official: "Our Brussels meeting has made a substantial contribution to advancing the negotiating process. I have nevertheless reached the conclusion that participants need more time to reconsider and reconcile their positions in some key areas of the negotiations. . . . I therefore propose that Mr. Dunkel, in his capacity as Chairman of the TNC at official level, be requested to pursue intensive consultations in the period from now until the beginning of next year with the specific objective of achieving agreements in all the areas of the negotiating programme in which differences remain outstanding."[35]

The collapse of the Brussels meeting elicited voluminous press analysis and commentary. Few questioned that EC unwillingness to be more forthcoming on agriculture, particularly with respect to export subsidies, had caused the breakdown. Almost all other areas of negotiation had been moving forward, and basic agreements could have been reached with an additional day or two. It would not have been as complete and far-reaching as the agreement finally concluded three years later, but a substantial outcome including all or almost all of the principal areas of negotiation could have been achieved.[36] The real questions was why the Community was unwilling or unable to go further in agriculture, and why others made substantial liberalization for agriculture a sine qua non for the overall agreement.

One major problem at Brussels was the inadequacy of EC decision-making. The Commission negotiated on behalf of the Community, without member state presence, while depending on member state approval for its negotiating mandate. Member states wanted Italian Trade Minister Ruggiero to attend negotiating sessions as an observer, but the Commission refused, leading to significant miscommunication. Early in the conference the Commission erroneously informed member-state ministers that the United States had issued an ultimatum on agriculture, which incensed the Europeans and further polarized discussions. Hopes rose Thursday afternoon when the Commission informed others of its readiness to put forward specific offers, including for export subsidies, only to be later rebuked and reversed at the insistence of French Agricultural Minister Louis Mermaz. Tension also existed within the Commission, between Trade Commissioner Andriessen and Agricultural Commissioner MacSharry, while Commission President Delors did not become engaged after his opening day speech. Overall, the credibility of the EC as an institution suffered, as expressed by a widely quoted senior American delegate: "The Community is an economic behemoth that has no capability of making political decisions."[37]

More fundamental was whether the Europeans were simply unwilling to engage the internal political debate necessary to restructure and liberalize the EC agricultural support system. Chancellor Kohl had not, in fact, pressed President Mitterand to be more forthcoming on agriculture in order to salvage the Brussels meeting. He later complained, "When there are problems it is always the Germans' fault."[38] The U.K. ministers were the most outspokenly critical of the U.S. negotiating stance, and were later criticized at home. The *Times* of London, for example, wrote: "John Gummer, Britain's farm minister, spent this week proving his Eurocredentials by defending the CAP. His outburst yesterday against the Americans for 'intransigence' was outrageous."[39] Germany and the United Kingdom, unwilling to stand up to French agricultural protectionism at Brussels, were described in one account as the "Community dogs that failed to bark."[40] In the eyes of the world, an inwardly preoccupied Europe took on more convincing form.

As for the question of whether substantial liberalization of trade in agriculture was essential for a successful agreement, the answer was yes. It had not come up in earlier rounds because, in large part, the issue had then been limited to import protection, while now it was the more neighbor-beggaring export subsidies. A growing export subsidy war had become a direct cost to the American taxpayer and was cutting nonsubsidized exporters out of markets. Rampant export subsidies undermined the basis of the GATT system and united all others against the EC. Moreover, the United States was no longer the champion of last resort to save the GATT system. When the agricultural impasse set in at Brussels, Secretary of Commerce Robert Mosbacher summarized the new U.S. thinking about multilateralism versus regionalism: "We could be okay either way. The U.S. always could make regional or other agreements. In all truth, we're doing this now."[41]

The "courage to go further" in world trade did not materialize at Brussels. The challenge was put in broader terms by American observers: "In effect, this is the first test of post–Cold War economic cooperation;" if the big industrial nations "fail in trade, it will be difficult for them to cooperate in the Persian Gulf and on other political and strategic issues."[42] These thoughts circulated through capitals as Director-General Dunkel again undertook to repair what ministers had rent asunder.

TOPICAL ADDENDUM: GATT INSTITUTIONAL REFORM

The 1948 draft treaty for an International Trade Organization (ITO) would have provided a permanent organization for international trade and investment with universal membership and a broad yet vaguely defined mandate. Opposition in the U.S. Congress killed the ITO, however, and all that survived was a set of general obligations concerning trade agreed to the previous year on a provisional basis. This temporary undertaking became the GATT trading system, which was described early on as "a slender reed on which to base progress toward a multilateral regime . . . permeated by an atmosphere of impermanence."[43] The GATT remained impermanent through the Uruguay Round, operating on the basis of the 1947 Protocol of Provisional Application.

Attempts had been made over the years to convert the GATT into a permanent institution and to elaborate upon its mandate, but actual changes had been modest.[44] There were also attempts to shift the focus of multilateral trade negotiations away from the GATT. United Nations bodies with universal membership, such as the United Nations Trade and Development Conference (UNCTAD) established in 1964, sought a preferential position over the limited membership GATT. In the other direction, proposals for an even more restrictive grouping of countries willing to take on a more comprehensive and binding set of trade policy commitments, a "GATT-Plus,"[45] challenged GATT primacy. None succeeded, and after three decades the dictum attributed to Napoleon—the temporary oft becomes the permanent—appeared fitting.

GATT reform and a restructuring of trade institutions received far more serious attention during the 1980s, although the Canadian proposal to create a new World Trade Organization (WTO) did not come until the spring of 1990, only months before the scheduled conclusion of the Uruguay Round in Brussels. More limited steps up to that point within the Uruguay Round to strengthen the multilateral trading system moved ahead in parallel with and, at times, were overshadowed by debate outside the GATT over alternatives to the multilateral approach.

The initial Uruguay Round objectives emanating from the Punta del Este Declaration dealt with five specific areas of GATT reform already elaborated: a broadened mandate to include trade in services and protection of intellectual property rights; more expeditious dispute settlement; ministerial level meetings at regular intervals; a strengthened secretariat function through the trade-policy review mechanism;[46] and "greater coherence" between international trade and financial policymaking. By 1989 substantial progress had been made in each of these areas except the "global coherence" objective, which was to elude the Uruguay Round negotiators to the end, except for the limited yet significant issue of trade restrictions applied for balance-of-payment reasons.

Outside the Uruguay Round, the idea of a more limited membership GATT-Plus gathered support in the wake of the stalemate at the 1982 GATT ministerial meeting and the subsequent years of inconclusive deliberations about a strengthened GATT mandate. If hard-line developing countries, led by Brazil and India, were unwilling to assume broader commitments, an inner grouping of industrialized and perhaps newly industrialized countries would move ahead without them. A 1989 study by Professor Gary Hufbauer, in collaboration with a task force of twelve distinguished U.S. trade experts, recommended the creation of an OECD Free Trade and Investment Area, negotiated outside the GATT, since this more limited form "could eventually succeed in realizing the goals of free and open trade that have so long inspired and frustrated the GATT."[47] In the later stages of the Uruguay Round, as the United States and the European Community became deeply divided over agriculture, trade in services, and other issues, a GATT-Plus initiative became less realistic. Nevertheless, as late as April 1991, former U.S. Trade Representative William Brock proposed consideration of a restricted GATT-Plus grouping before the Senate Finance Committee.[48]

Other alternatives to the multilateral approach involved a system of regional trade blocs and various proposals for bilateral trade balancing, the most antithetical to the GATT system.[49] The anti-GATT sentiment and, in particular, the appeal of bilateralism was strongest in the United States, but disenchantment with the existing GATT system was widespread. If the Uruguay Round had, in the end, failed, and many believed throughout 1990–93 that it would, a broadly shared view was that the world trading system would evolve into broadening geographic blocs and bilateral relationships among the blocs and the largest trading nations.

The initiative to create a new WTO as part of the Uruguay Round agreement began in October 1989 in informal Quad discussion among EC, U.S., Japanese, and Canadian officials. Both Canada and the EC supported the idea from the outset, but the United States was decidedly cool if not negative toward major institutional reform at that point. After further inconclusive informal discussion, Canada formally proposed the creation of a WTO in April 1990, but through the Brussels meeting in December little headway was made in defining the specific elements of such a new organization.

With the collapse of the Brussels meeting and the ensuing long period of U.S.-EC stalemate over agriculture, more serious and detailed attention was given to the institutional reform proposal, again principally within the Quad framework during 1991 and 1992, and then, in parallel, through an expanded Geneva-based group in 1992 and 1993. One early change in the Canadian proposal was adoption of the EC's preferred name—Multilateral Trade Organization (MTO) rather than WTO—which had less threatening political overtones. The WTO appellation, however, would have an ironic, last-minute reprieve.

Three central substantive issues developed during this long period of quiet diplomacy. The first was qualified majority voting, particularly with regard to waivers from Uruguay Round commitments. The second was the concept of a "single undertaking" with respect to membership in the WTO—that is, membership would not be universal but conditioned on a commitment to all or almost all of the Uruguay Round agreement. And the third was an integrated dispute-settlement mechanism which, in particular, linked together GATT commitments in trade in goods with commitments in the areas of services and intellectual-property rights. The final result for these three issues, in technical terms, appears in chapter 8, but the underlying political tradeoff was between the developing and industrialized countries. The developing countries wanted a stronger multilateral framework, including more effective dispute-settlement procedures, while the industrialized countries insisted on lasting commitments to the full range of Uruguay Round agreements from developing countries, as defined by these three central issues. The final result embodied this political tradeoff.

The outcome for the WTO proposal, however, remained in limbo until the very end of the negotiations. The Dunkel draft for a comprehensive agreement put forward in December 1991 did not adequately address the three issues, which led to further intensive negotiation among Quad members outside the GATT framework during 1992. The United States continued to resist the creation of a new trade organization, and in fact became more negative, but with mixed motives. The American negotiators were adamant in achieving satisfaction on the voting, dispute-settlement, and single-undertaking commitments. They knew that congressional concerns over "loss of sovereignty," which had contributed to the demise of the ITO forty years earlier, would reemerge during congressional debate over the Uruguay Round agreement. However, they were also using the WTO as a bargaining chip both within the institutional negotiating group and more broadly in the round. Finally, differences emerged within the senior ranks of the U.S. negotiating team. Carla Hills was more negative than her senior deputy, Julius Katz, who had let slip during a public discussion in April 1992: "The Administration still has a number of questions and concerns about the text in its present form. I have no doubt, though, that in the end the MTO will be accepted; the idea will not be jettisoned."[50]

Nevertheless, the prolonged U.S. arguments against the WTO nearly defeated it. Some members of the Congress believed and supported them. Mickey Kantor, who succeeded Carla Hills as U.S. trade representative in January 1993, initially believed them and had to be convinced that at the end of the

125

day the WTO, suitably drafted, should be accepted after obtaining maximum concessions in return. As late as November 1993, the U.S. proposed an alternative legal framework for linking services and intellectual-property rights to the GATT without creating a new trade organization. The WTO was not, in fact, accepted by the United States until the morning of December 15, 1993, the final day of Uruguay Round negotiations.

Farm Subsidy Showdown, 1991–1992

The multilateral acrimony that accompanied the failure at Brussels soon dissi-pated as governments sought ways to salvage the Uruguay Round and orga-nize a new diplomatic endgame. Obviously some compromise was needed on agriculture, and the confusion within EC ranks at Brussels left hope that a more forthcoming proposal was possible. The Brussels meeting had also high-lighted the considerable number of other unresolved issues, but there was general confidence that if a breakthrough could be achieved for agriculture an overall package could be negotiated in reasonably short order. Hope for an early compromise on agriculture, however, was ill-founded. The U.S.-EC impasse had deeply embedded political as well as economic roots.

The immediate issue was the expiration of U.S. negotiating authority on March 1, 1991, less than three months away. The Omnibus Trade Act of 1988 provided the president "fast track" authority—that is, a single up or down vote by the Congress on the final agreement within sixty legislative days. The dead-line for signing the agreement was May 31, 1991, but the trade act also re-quired a prior consultation period of ninety days, thus setting the effective date for an agreement within the GATT at March 1. Without an agreement, the president could request a two-year extension of his negotiating authority, but such a request would also have to be made by March 1.

In this context, the preferred scenario was to move quickly on agriculture so as to reassemble all of the negotiators in January or early February for a final session. Director-General Dunkel traveled to Washington and Brussels to arrange such an outcome and scheduled a January 15 meeting of heads of delegation in Geneva. Expectations rose briefly when EC Agriculture Commis-sioner Ray MacSharry announced on January 4 "revolutionary" proposals to restructure the Community agricultural policy away from price supports and toward direct income payments. Such a restructuring was compatible with the U.S. approach to trade liberalization and could form the basis for an enhanced Uruguay Round proposal. It soon became clear, however, that the Commission proposals faced strong resistance from some member states and would re-quire at least several months of debate. Moreover, EC President Jacques De-lors stated curtly that the proposed reforms were an internal Community matter not directly related to the Uruguay Round, and Arthur Dunkel's January 15 meeting meekly concluded that more time was needed.

By early February, it was clear that no agreement was possible by March 1 and that President Bush would have to ask Congress for a two-year extension of negotiating authority. He was not prepared to do so, however, without tangible progress on agriculture. With nothing to show in this sector after four and a half years, the president would have great difficulty obtaining support from a skeptical Congress, while anticipated opposition from some members of the agricultural committees, the textile lobby, and organized labor would likely prevail. Thus quiet yet intense negotiations continued, principally between the United States and the European Community, with Arthur Dunkel as broker. Finally, on February 20, the EC Commission, at a special session in Strasbourg, France, agreed to a significant change in its agricultural position, which was obscured somewhat by a procedural maneuver within the GATT. Arthur Dunkel convened GATT representatives in Geneva later the same day and announced agreement on a new negotiating "platform," which, for agriculture, would include, "negotiations to achieve specific binding commitments on each of the following areas: domestic support, market access, and export competition." The EC delegate remained silent and thus acknowledged agreement without having to state any formal change in the EC position.[1]

Significantly, the new platform specified explicitly for the first time a binding commitment on export subsidies (i.e., export competition), the critical element entirely absent from the EC offer at Brussels. There was no indication yet as to what that commitment would involve, but the formulation was sufficient for Trade Representative Carla Hills to state that the "major impasse" had been removed and that President Bush would seek a two-year extension of U.S. negotiating authority.

Fast-track Extension

The administration request for a two-year extension of fast-track authority triggered another heated debate over U.S. trade policy. There were, in fact, two major trade initiatives under consideration. The first involved the Uruguay Round, which faced continued uncertainty over EC agricultural policy and general concern that U.S. exports of manufactured products would not achieve significant gains in market access. The second was the proposed negotiation of a North American Free Trade Agreement (NAFTA) among the United States, Canada, and Mexico. A separate provision of the 1988 Trade Act provided authority for such free-trade agreements, which also required the fast-track extension. The ensuing debate over extension of fast-track was technically about the delegation of authority from the Congress to the president since the U.S. Constitution stipulates that the Congress shall regulate commerce. Much of the opposition, in fact, was presented in terms of the need for greater congressional participation in the trade negotiation process, which the single up-or-down vote on final agreements greatly circumscribed. Proponents of fast track recalled that this procedure was indeed created in the 1970s because other nations were unwilling to negotiate, at least in a large multilateral GATT context, if the resulting agreement was subject to uncontrolled congressional amendment.

Underlying the issue of constitutional process, however, was widespread concern and outright opposition to free trade with Mexico. Loss of jobs to low-wage Mexican laborers and allegations of inadequate labor and environmental standards south of the border formed the backbone of the anti-NAFTA strategy. Investment opportunities in Mexico and job-creating export growth for the United States coalesced the supporters. Many specific industry and agricultural interests were at play in the thriving U.S.-Mexico economic relationship, already spurred by the radical market-oriented Mexican reform program. As a result, the fast-track political struggle came to focus on free trade with Mexico, while the Uruguay Round, more abstract and less likely to have a major immediate impact on trade, slipped largely into the background.

On March 1 President Bush made a formal request to the Congress, highlighting the multilateral dimension of trade policy: "At a time when world events have reconfirmed the importance of U.S. leadership in multilateral efforts, maintaining fast track is essential to our leadership in the global trading system." The debate broadened quickly, however, through a March 4 statement of opposition by forty-four environmental, consumer, and other organizations concerned that trade agreements could undermine domestic environmental, consumer, and safety laws. The AFL-CIO had already taken a strong stand against a NAFTA: "The proposed U.S.-Mexico free trade agreement would be a disaster for workers in both countries. It would destroy jobs in the United States, while perpetuating exploitation of workers and inflicting widespread damage on the environment in Mexico. The beneficiaries would be multinational corporations and large banks."[2]

The initial congressional response was a March 7 letter to the president from Senate Finance Committee Chairman Lloyd Bentsen and House Ways and Means Committee Chairman Dan Rostenkowski, citing concerns of members about fast-track extension, "particularly as it applies to the proposed free trade agreement with Mexico." They requested the president to provide, by May 1, his assessment of the disparity between the two countries with respect to environmental standards, health and safety standards, and worker rights, and asked whether the agreement would have "a net positive effect on jobs and wages in the United States." House Majority Leader Richard Gephardt followed up with a strongly worded ten-page letter elaborating these issues and concluding that he would only support an agreement that "fights for American jobs and exports, preserves the world's environment, and defends the rights of Mexican workers."[3]

The lines were thus drawn for ensuing weeks of unbridled lobbying from all sides. The AFL-CIO made defeat of fast track a top priority and thus a critical test of its political clout. Environmentalist groups made their first serious entry into trade-policy debate. The government of Mexico reportedly spent large amounts of money on lobbyists in support of fast track. The Multilateral Trade Negotiations Coalition of fourteen thousand private companies championed the pro–fast track campaign and produced a compendium of more than seven hundred newspaper editorials supporting the president.

The president's May 1 response to the Congress provided a detailed assessment of a NAFTA. Separate sections dealt with economic impact, worker retraining and adjustment, labor and health standards, and environmental matters. It was most forthcoming on environmental concerns, outlining a series of commitments and initiatives with Mexico which, although outside the trade agreement proper, were linked into the same time frame. Administration strategy aimed to split the environmentalist groups and mute their opposition, and it succeeded. A few groups shifted to support the president on the grounds that a comprehensive negotiation with the Salinas government would more likely bear fruit than a rebuff of the free-trade initiative. AFL-CIO opposition, in contrast, was viewed as uncompromisingly protectionist and was left to the showdown vote in Congress.

The final outcome remained in doubt, especially in the House of Representatives, until late May. The Democrats were badly split. The Democratic National Committee, principally representing local party leaders, had formally opposed fast-track authority at the outset. Most of the congressional leadership on trade, however, ended up in support. Chairmen Bentsen and Rostenkowski strongly supported extension. Bentsen explained: "It seems inconceivable that the U.S. would deny itself the ability to negotiate the elimination of barriers to foreign trade."[4] Gephardt took a more qualified stand in support on May 9. Senate Majority Leader George Mitchell and House Speaker Thomas Foley finally voted in favor but played no role in the debate. The large majority of Democratic members, however, especially those from districts with a significant organized-labor constituency, remained opposed. The final votes were comfortably positive in the trade committees, 15–3 in Senate Finance and 27–9 in House Ways and Means, but the margins narrowed in plenary. On May 23, the House voted 231–192 to defeat a proposal not to extend the authority, and on May 24 the Senate did likewise by 59–36.[5]

The president thus won the bruising encounter for fast track extension, with a number of significant consequences for U.S. trade politics. AFL-CIO unyielding opposition suffered a humiliating defeat. Environmentalist groups, in contrast, successfully influenced trade-policy deliberations, and their involvement in the U.S.-Mexico debate would soon extend to the GATT. The Democratic party emerged with serious unanswered questions about its trade-policy objectives.

Finally, the Uruguay Round received a new lease on life, although largely as a lonely addendum to a major national debate over free trade with Mexico. As for the evolving multilateral/regional balance in U.S. trade policy, Department of State Counselor Robert Zoellick, speaking before the Senate Foreign Relations Committee, summed up strategy with respect to a North American Free Trade Agreement: "This agreement would be a key component of a network of global, regional, and bilateral arrangements that promote American interests. It can strengthen the capabilities of North America, enhancing our ability to compete globally." The veiled reference to competing regional blocs did not go unnoticed abroad, especially in Asia.[6]

Quiet Progress

With new fast-track authority in hand, North American trade negotiators got off to a quick start with a flurry of trilateral U.S.-Canada-Mexico meetings. A revival of the Uruguay Round was less evident, however, since the extended U.S. negotiating authority essentially put the agricultural ball back in the European court. The February impasse-breaking agreement to make specific binding commitments in three areas needed elaboration as a formal EC offer. The OECD ministers met on June 4, but the concluding communiqué simply reiterated the language of the earlier GATT commitment. Press commentary that angry clashes over agriculture had been avoided, compared to previous ministerials, only confirmed the lack of serious effort.

Attention shifted to the economic summit meeting of the seven major industrialized countries beginning July 15 in London. President Bush called the Uruguay Round the most important economic issue of the summit and pressed for progress in bilateral and group sessions, but the Europeans weren't prepared to respond. The summit was upstaged, in any event, by the arrival of Soviet President Mikhail Gorbachev for a post-summit meeting, and the issue of Western aid for Soviet reforms dominated discussion. The "Economic Declaration" of the summit leaders called for completion of the Uruguay Round by the end of 1991, with a pledge to remain "personally involved in this process." For agriculture, the identical language on commitments in three areas was repeated yet again. Reactions from the press and Geneva negotiators were skeptical at best, as expressed by Swedish Ambassador Lars Anell: "We had the same experience with the seven leaders of the G-7 in Houston last year where they made personal pledges, but failed to follow through with any personal diplomacy."[7]

The continuing agricultural impasse at the highest political levels appropriately received public attention, and its prolongation for yet another two years would evoke much more criticism of the lack of follow-through by the summit leaders. Nevertheless, the remainder of 1991 and 1992 were productive in advancing Uruguay Round issues other than agriculture. The credit belonged to the professional trade negotiators, who met in less formal settings and built consensus on a wide range of issues unresolved or inadequately developed at the time of the Brussels meeting. Such negotiations went forward in Geneva, both in large and small groups, and in a more intensive negotiating process among the Quad members at various locations.

At Geneva, Arthur Dunkel and the GATT secretariat assumed a more assertive role that would continue to build through the concluding phase of the round. Dunkel's longstanding favorite modality for conducting informal negotiations was the renown "green room" sessions, named after the small conference room of that color adjoining the director-general's office. Its size limited participation to twenty to thirty people, essentially one delegate from each major country, with the EC represented by the Commission alone. The limited participation ran counter to GATT practice of open bodies, and smaller, excluded countries grumbled, but participants provided feedback to others, and the practicality of the intense green-room process, led by the dedicated director-general, prevailed. During the later stages of the negotiations, a series of even more restricted dinner sessions was utilized to good effect, hosted by Arthur Dunkel, usually at an auberge in his home town of Russin.

Director-General Dunkel also proceeded with seven active negotiating groups, as delineated at the Brussels meeting, and the respective chairmen played important roles in producing what would be known as the Dunkel Draft in December 1991. Dunkel himself chaired the agriculture and textile groups, although he delegated the effective chairmanship for textiles to Arif Hussain of the GATT secretariat. Colombian Felipe Jaramillo and Australian David Hawes led the services group, Swede Lars Anell the intellectual-property rights group, Uruguayan Julio Lacarte-Muro the dispute settlement/ WTO group, Brazilian George Maciel the safeguards/antidumping/subsidies group, and Canadian Germain Denis the market-access group.

The more active Quad deliberations centered on the veteran senior negotiators Warren Lavorel of the United States, Hugo Paeman of the EC, Minoru Endo of Japan, and Germain Denis of Canada, who served double duty. Lower-level technical groups functioned in such areas as services, intellectual property rights, and dispute settlement. The issue of a new World Trade Organization had come up first in a Quad meeting in October 1989, but serious discussion of the specific provisions only began after the Brussels meeting, and the final result was shaped largely in a series of Quad meetings prior to broader-based negotiations in Geneva.

Tariff cuts on manufactured products also received belated attention and were addressed principally among Quad members. The United States had placed low priority on the issue through the Brussels meeting in 1990, and the U.S. approach of item-by-item request and offer lists appeared less likely to achieve the one-third average reduction target agreed upon at Montreal than the formula approach proposed by others. The specific U.S. offer list first put forward in October 1989, however, did include tariff elimination in certain sectors conditional on like action by others.[8] U.S. negotiators, in fact, deferred to their industry advisers in this area, and as private-sector interest grew for tariff elimination by sector, the "zero-for-zero" approach became more prominent. The U.S. pharmaceutical sector was the first to consult with European and Japanese counterparts and to reach a consensus that duty elimination by all was desirable. Momentum grew in 1991 and 1992 to consider other sectors—construction and agricultural machinery, toys, furniture, nonferrous metals, and forest products—and linkages began to develop toward a balanced overall package. The EC and others still officially supported the formula approach, but attention focused more and more on sectors ripe for reciprocal duty elimination. The appealing concept, from both a policy and business perspective, caught on and produced a surprisingly large end result, as well as a precedent for future negotiations.

As early as the summer of 1991, these various negotiating groups, at Geneva and within the Quad, began making progress while U.S. and EC political leaders remained at an impasse over agriculture. Even in the agricultural sector, however, Arthur Dunkel's negotiating group made headway on the "technical" question of how to define and measure commitments to liberalize trade. For domestic support, the Aggregate Measure of Support (AMS), developed earlier in the OECD, was further refined to distinguish "green box" income-support policies that would be exempt from reduction on the grounds that they would not impact on prices and levels of production. As a general approach to market access, all forms of import barriers were to be converted to fixed tariffs, a process of "tariffication." Discussion of export subsidies, as usual, was the most contentious, involving the specific practices that would be classified as subsidies, and whether cuts would be made in terms of budget outlays, export volumes, or some combination thereof. All of this technical work dealing with "instruments" set the stage for later decisions on the "numbers" (i.e., the percentage cuts in support) to be taken at the political level.

Other significant summer developments included agreement at the end of July to extend the Multifiber Agreement on textiles in existing form for only seventeen months, thus linking its expiration to the anticipated final Uruguay Round agreement. Brazil announced in July that it would no longer utilize Article XVIII-B, the balance-of-payments clause, for selective import restrictions, except in the informatics sector, a positive step toward achieving Uruguay Round agreement to rein in discretionary quota restrictions by all countries. In late August, India indicated it was prepared to support an international agreement on services under certain conditions. Though a guarded statement, it acknowledged that India had export interests in a wide range of service industries, including financial, engineering, and computer services.[9]

Extended Agricultural Impasse

Events elsewhere again disrupted August holidays in 1991, this time the failed coup attempt against President Gorbachev, the demise of the Communist party in the "former" Soviet Union, and the dramatic rise of Russian President Boris Yeltsin. Political attention, particularly among Europeans, became even more riveted on the future of Europe. Pressing initiatives for a new Europe inundated the European Community decision-making structure. Economic aid for East European countries and the Soviet Union became a multifaceted undertaking. Negotiations over European Monetary Union were reaching a crescendo, with a final agreement scheduled for December. A comprehensive free-trade agreement with the EFTA countries to create a "European economic area," which would incorporate much of the EC-92 market unification program, was finally completed in November.

A striking example of how the European Community put regional interests above the GATT multilateral system was the bilateral agreement with Japan for automobiles concluded in July. The agreement consolidated automobile import quotas in some member states into a Community-wide quota consistent with the EC-92 program, and the result was agreement to limit imports at the existing level for seven years, with no growth, and to include informal targets for the output of Japanese plants in the Community as well. This agreement, outside the GATT, conflicted with the tenuous negotiations in the Uruguay Round for a revised Article-XIX safeguards clause based on a draft that would limit "temporary" quotas to perhaps three years, include a minimum rate of growth for imports, and certainly not extend in any way to foreign direct investment.[10] The bilateral auto pact became known as the new CAP—Common Automobile Policy—and quickly gained popularity within the U.S. auto industry as a model for the automotive sector in a North American free-trade agreement.

As summer moved toward autumn, pessimism grew about concluding the round by year's end or early 1992, the necessary time frame to get the final agreement through the U.S. Congress before the presidential elections in 1992.[11] If final agreement were delayed beyond election day in November, there would be only a short period for negotiation in early 1993, up to March 1, when the extended fast-track authority expired. Such a contingency would be complicated by the fact that the EC Commission term would run out at the end of 1992, and a new Commission might not be able to resolve the agricultural reform issue, in particular, in such a brief time. One contingency that would greatly influence the final Uruguay Round outcome was not given any serious consideration, namely that George Bush would lose the elections in 1992. His popularity was soaring in mid-1991, following the Gulf War victory the previous January, and few of the Geneva negotiators had ever heard of Bill Clinton.

The increasing attention to timing was made more explicit in July when Trade Representative Carla Hills stated it would take four to six months to conclude the overall negotiations "after we see movement in agriculture."[12] Arthur Dunkel took the bull by the horns on September 20, 1991, by laying down an ultimatum. He announced that he would put forward a complete draft package agreement by early November, "on a take-it-or-leave-it basis. . . . This is it—whether we are going forward or quitting!"[13]

A showdown within Europe over agricultural reform and the Uruguay Round was shaping up—predominantly as a Franco-German confrontation thus far avoided. In July the EC Commission had approved a basic reform of the Community farm policy, involving a partial shift from unlimited price supports to direct payments to farmers linked to acreage restrictions. In concept, this would permit an Uruguay Round agreement based on reduced internal price supports and export subsidies, but France still strongly opposed binding international commitments, especially on export subsidies. If Germany continued to support such French intransigence, the Uruguay Round would almost surely fail, while a shift in the German position in favor of firm international commitments would swing the internal EC balance against France. Only Ireland could be expected to stand firm with the French, and its support was insufficient for a blocking vote.[14]

Within France, President Mitterand's policy direction was weakening. He had misjudged the August Moscow coup, initially indicating he could deal with the hard-line perpetrators who quickly lost out to Gorbachev and Yeltsin. His protégée prime minister, Edith Cresson, outspokenly protectionist and given to racist comments about Japan, proved to be divisive and unpopular. Farmers, angry over falling prices, grew fearful of cuts in EC support programs. In late September, two hundred thousand farmers took to the streets in protest, and government buildings were set afire.

The internal German debate was even more complex. Chancellor Kohl's coalition partner, the Free Democratic party, strongly supported free trade and, in particular, agricultural reform to achieve a successful Uruguay Round, which in turn would benefit German industry. Farm groups opposed reductions in government support, but the rising budget costs of the CAP was an offsetting concern. Kohl had commented in May that the EC farm policy "made no economic sense," and in September, during a visit to Washington, he became more explicit on its impact on developing countries: "It is absurd not to allow these mainly agricultural countries to sell to our markets."[15] The chancellor had, in fact, made a commitment to his Free Democrat partners that he would take on the French and break the agricultural impasse. A cabinet meeting on October 10 was designed to override Agricultural Minister Ignaz Kiechle, and Minister of Economics Jurgen Mollemann, a free trader and Free Democrat, played the leading role in doing so. On October 16 in Brussels, a triumphant Minister Mollemann announced: "There has to be a change in the EC's position on agriculture, including export subsidies."[16]

Minister Kiechle angrily disputed the Mollemann-announced change in the EC negotiating position, but in fact a critical step had been taken.[17] EC negotiators were now willing not only to consider deeper cuts in domestic support levels for farmers, but also, for the first time, to negotiate specific commitments to limit export subsidies. This changed position led to two months of intensive U.S.-EC negotiations to reach agreement on a comprehensive agricultural package. George Bush, deeply committed to a successful conclusion of the Uruguay Round, quickly took the initiative with counterpart European leaders. He met on November 10 in the Hague with Dutch Prime

Minister Ruud Lubbers, then president of the EC Council of Ministers, and EC Commission President Jacques Delors. As a step toward compromise, Bush eased the U.S. demand for a 90 percent reduction in farm export subsidies over ten years, suggesting a 30–35 percent reduction over five or six years. The Europeans responded positively, with the usually dour Delors conceding that he was, "for the first time, optimistic that we can get an agreement on the Uruguay Round."[18] The intent was to reach agreement before the Christmas break, scheduled for December 20.

Finally, after three years of impasse since the Montreal Ministerial meeting in December 1988, the United States and the EC were engaged in negotiating specific commitments for agriculture, including limits on export subsidies. In the weeks through early December, positions on the key issues were defined more precisely and gaps narrowed somewhat. A final agreement hinged on three key issues:

1. *Oilseeds.* A longstanding EC demand for "rebalancing"—whereby an overall reduction in farm supports would be balanced with a GATT-approved right to raise import duties on soybeans and other oilseeds—was dropped. This related to an ongoing U.S.-EC dispute outside the Uruguay Round over the conditions for continued access for U.S. oilseeds exports to the EC market. The linkage between the Uruguay Round agricultural package and the oilseeds dispute, however, would continue and become a key element in the final agreement.

2. *Green box domestic support.* A reduction of internal EC price supports could be compensated by direct payments to farmers as long as the form of the payments did not stimulate additional production and thus become "trade-distorting." Such payments would be exempted in a "green box," although the definition of what payments could or could not be exempted remained unsettled. Proposed EC direct support payments to farmers to offset the reduction of price support levels were considered trade-distorting by the Americans.

3. *Export subsidies.* This continued to be the most important and contentious issue. A reduction of 30–35 percent over five to six years was basically agreed, but the United States insisted that the cuts be applied to the volume of exports receiving subsidies while the EC offered cuts in the value of export subsidies. This was a critical distinction since if the EC reduced internal price supports while shifting to direct payments to farmers, a much larger volume of exports could be subsidized within a value-based limit. Another important difference was the base period from which to make the export subsidy cuts. For EC subsidized grain exports,

137

the United States sought a reduction to about 11 million tons after five years while the EC spoke in terms of a 13–15 million ton range. This compared with 13–14 million tons of actual EC-subsidized grain exports in 1986, when the Uruguay Round began, and 17 million tons in 1990.[19] Nevertheless, the difference in positions, even on this difficult issue, appeared to be relatively small, and there was optimism that a deal would be struck.

In Geneva, serious negotiations gathered momentum on other key issues, in parallel with the U.S.-EC agricultural talks. The United States and the EC agreed to an accelerated liberalization of the textile sector, whereby import quotas would be phased out over ten years. The reaction of the American Textile Manufacturers Institute: "We're bitterly opposed to it."[20] In the services sector, the United States offered to extend most-favored-nation treatment to long-distance telecommunications services but continued to condition such treatment on agreement by major U.S. trading partners "to open their long distance services markets to international competition."[21] Agreement also appeared closer in the areas of antidumping and nonagricultural subsidies. Tariff cuts for manufactured goods, as described above, were taking shape through the "zero-for-zero" approach of tariff elimination by sector.

As December 20 approached, however, the final gaps in agriculture were still not bridged. At the political level, George Bush continued his characteristic "working the phones" with counterparts Kohl, Lubbers, Major, and Mitterand, but to no avail. The impact of reduced export subsidies in sectors other than grains proved to be a belated stumbling block. The United States and others insisted that the cuts apply to each broad sector of farm exports. Thus, a 30–35 percent reduction in subsidized EC dairy and oilseeds exports, for example, would affect sensitive domestic interests in several member states, including the Netherlands, which gave Prime Minister Lubbers, a key interlocutor as EC Council president, political cause to draw back.

In the end, the political will fell short once again, especially on the EC side, and the agricultural impasse continued to prevent a broader Uruguay Round agreement. On December 20, Arthur Dunkel carried through on his earlier ultimatum and produced his own draft for a final agreement. He explained: "It offers us, for the first time, a concrete idea of the scope and scale of the benefits of broad-based liberalization and strengthened multilateral rules which are within our grasp. In short, a promise given, a promise kept."[22]

The Dunkel Draft

The Dunkel Draft Final Act of the Uruguay Round was a bold initiative to bridge the numerous substantive differences in the many sectors of negotiation and to present a balanced package agreement tilted in the direction of a maximum overall result. It was not quite the "take it or leave it" final agreement promised by Arthur Dunkel two months earlier. In particular, a specified, country-by-country schedule for improved market access for goods and services had not yet been developed. Nevertheless, the 436-page document constituted a detailed compilation of commitments representing both clear benefits and difficult concessions for all major participants. The twenty-nine sections of what became known as the Dunkel Draft included not only the familiar areas of negotiation—such as agriculture, textiles, antidumping, intellectual-property rights, and trade in services—but also the more arcane subjects of rules of origin, preshipment inspection, and import licensing procedures.

The Dunkel initiative was a critical yet risky step to bring together parties in what had become, after five years of negotiation, a technically complex and politically weary impasse. As director-general of the GATT, Arthur Dunkel was a creature of the GATT membership with no designated authority to act as a mediator. Such a role for the head of an international secretariat is not uncommon, however, and the crucial factor is the judgment as to when and how to act. The parties must be brought as close together as possible on their own, exhausting all reasonable procedures for final agreement, and the level of political frustration should be sufficiently high so as to make the initiative of a neutral director-general appear to be both sensible and necessary. A precedent within the GATT context was the May 1967 "package deal" of Director-General Eric Wyndham White, which brought the Kennedy Round to a successful conclusion. But that package, which dealt principally with a U.S.-EC agreement on tariff cuts in the chemicals sector, paled by comparison to the comprehensive Dunkel Draft.[23] In effect, Arthur Dunkel had presented a highly integrated Pandora's Box of commitments. Some minor adjustments could still be negotiated, but if one participant attempted to withdraw or undermine a major component of the package, others would likely follow suit, leading to a general unraveling of the draft. The onus of political responsibility for failure would clearly rest on those who first rejected major components of the package.

The Dunkel Draft had special credibility since it incorporated compromises developed within the seven negotiating groups. Right up to December 19—while press reports centered on the continuing agricultural negotiations in Brussels between EC farm commissioner Ray MacSharry and U.S. secretary of agriculture Edward Madigan—Arthur Dunkel continued to coordinate closely with the chairmen of the negotiating groups. The final text reflected predominantly the judgment of these veteran negotiators as to what would constitute a broadly acceptable final agreement. Arthur Dunkel concentrated his efforts almost exclusively on the agricultural group under his direct chairmanship. He had consulted extensively with EC Commission and member-state officials and assessed deep divisions within the Community, even within the Agricultural Directorate of the Commission. To test his thinking on a politically feasible compromise, Dunkel spent one evening at Russin with senior secretariat advisers, playacting debate in the roles of EC, U.S., and Cairns group leaders.

The Dunkel text on agriculture split some differences between the existing U.S. and EC positions but tended toward the stronger commitments sought by the United States and the Cairns Group. Domestic support levels would be reduced by 20 percent from 1993 to 1999 while import barriers would come down by 36 percent. For export subsidies, there would be a 36 percent cut in budget outlays and a 24 percent reduction in the quantity of subsidized exports, over six years, applied to each of twenty-two categories of products. The Dunkel text was categoric on "green box" permission for direct payments to farmers: "Decoupled income support . . . shall not be related to or based on the type or volume of production undertaken . . . (or) the prices, domestic or international, applying to any production undertaken."[24] This "decoupling" of payments from production levels would exclude proposed EC payments for acreage set asides, an integral part of the recently adopted reform of the Common Agricultural Policy.

Arthur Dunkel circulated his draft to the Trade Negotiations Committee on December 20, 1991, for evaluation in capitals. He scheduled a follow-up meeting for January 13 "with a view to concluding the Uruguay Round" and made the package approach explicit: "I would not for a moment expect all participants to be fully content with all the decisions I have had to make . . . (however) the document I have tabled today forms a single package, and it is as a package that it should be judged. . . . I am confident that, if we continue to share the vision which brought us together at Punta del Este five years ago, your governments will judge the package favorably."[25]

Initial reactions by governments varied. Prime Minister Edith Cresson of France denounced the draft two days before it was circulated as "without any regard for European interests, whether in agriculture or other fields."[26] On December 23, an EC communiqué formally declared that the "so-called 'final act' . . . is not acceptable and therefore has to be modified." Japan and South Korea also opposed the draft because it would not permit them to continue to bar rice imports. The U.S. response was guardedly supportive, with reservations. Arthur Dunkel "deserves great praise for his exhaustive work in bringing the negotiations to this stage . . . (but) this document is only a *draft*. . . . Nothing in this draft is agreed until everything is agreed. . . . we will continue to be guided by our strong belief that no agreement is better than a bad agreement."[27] Australia, Canada, and most other participants were more supportive in their initial reactions, although all knew that additional hard bargaining lay ahead, at least for market access commitments and a few of the most difficult other issues.

The January 13 meeting reached agreement only on a new mid-April deadline to conclude the negotiations. In the United States, opposition to the Dunkel Draft came from several directions. Jack Valenti, president of the Motion Picture Association of America, rejected the draft as "fatally flawed" because it condoned television quotas by the European Community, and the Pharmaceutical Manufacturers Association considered it "more than unacceptable . . . it's unthinkable" given its lengthy transition period for recognition of patents on drugs.[28] Nevertheless, it was agriculture again that took center stage. The U.S.-EC agricultural impasse remained as French opposition to the Dunkel text hardened. George Bush, in a speech before U.S. farmers, warned that "sooner or later, the EC must stop hiding behind its own Iron Curtain of protectionism."[29] President Mitterand responded: "France is not ready to bow to American demands nor to submit to the interests of any other country, and will not give way."[30]

Intensive negotiations over agriculture continued through the spring and into the summer of 1992, but with little progress. The agricultural impasse came to a head at the G-7 economic summit in Munich. Chancellor Kohl, aware that pledges by the industrialized-country leaders to conclude the Uruguay Round at the previous two summit meetings had not been fulfilled, tried to keep the Uruguay Round off the Munich summit agenda, but the United States pressed ahead. Compromise proposals from the British and Germans on export subsidy commitments offered hope for agreement as the summiteers gathered in the baroque Nymphenburg castle. The moment of truth, however, came during an exchange over dinner between U.S. Secretary of State James Baker and French Foreign Minister Roland Dumas.

Baker: "Are the French ready to move?"

Dumas: "No."

Baker: "Even if you get all the concessions you are asking for?"

Dumas: "No."[31]

Failure to break the agricultural impasse at the Munich summit appeared to end hope for an Uruguay Round agreement in 1992. Other issues were crowding out any remaining political will on both sides of the Atlantic. The beleaguered EC draft Maastricht Treaty, which would establish monetary union and strengthen the political structure of the Community, faced a critical referendum in France in September, which influenced, to some extent, Minister Dumas's extraordinary performance at Munich. Multilateral discussions, parallel to the Uruguay Round, to limit subsidies on steel exports had broken down in March, and the United States was poised to release a flood of anti-dumping actions against European and other steel imports. On April 30, after five years of U.S. efforts to negotiate an end to EC oilseeds subsidies, which violated GATT commitments and caused serious harm to U.S. exports, the United States announced its intention to impose punitive tariffs against $1 billion of imports from the EC. Most important, President Bush was falling increasingly behind in the election polls as the summer progressed, undercutting his credibility to negotiate an agreement for approval by Congress in 1993.

Negotiations nevertheless continued through September and October. A breakthrough on agriculture before November 3 could help George Bush's reelection prospects, and he appeared willing to make extra concessions to the Europeans—which might not be offered later if Bill Clinton won the presidency. A market-access arrangement for oilseeds would be part of a package, along with Uruguay Round commitments for reduced domestic price supports and export subsidies along the lines of the Dunkel Draft. Some easing of "green box" restrictions for direct payments to farmers would also be part of the deal. An October 26 *Newsweek* story threatened the talks by recounting how an adviser to candidate Bill Clinton had told the EC ambassador in Washington that a trade deal would help George Bush in the elections and would therefore be viewed by Clinton as interference in U.S. politics. This played into the hands of the French and others trying to block an agricultural agreement even though Clinton disclaimed the report and the individual involved turned out to be an informal adviser with no official position in the Clinton campaign.

Negotiations broke off on October 22 when the EC backtracked on earlier positions, reflecting an internal rift between Agricultural Commissioner Ray MacSharry and the more hard-line Commission president, Jacques Delors. A lengthy phone conversation between U. K. Prime Minister Major and German Chancellor Kohl, however, resulted in a new mandate to MacSharry to resume negotiations since "the talks could not be allowed to flounder."[32] On Sunday evening, November 1, MacSharry met with U.S. Secretary of Agriculture Madigan in Chicago, and intensive negotiations continued through Monday and Tuesday morning. By the end of the day on Tuesday, Madigan announced that the Uruguay Round agricultural talks remained at an impasse, and George Bush had lost the presidential election.

Blair House Accord

Bill Clinton's electoral victory, by reasonable presumption and general expectation, meant a three-month hiatus for the Uruguay Round until a new U.S. trade negotiating team was in place, while George Bush and Carla Hills would turn their attention to memoir writing and other post-government activities. This presumption, however, turned out to be wrong, and the presidential transition period instead became an extraordinary episode in trade negotiations that finally produced an agricultural agreement and may well have saved the Uruguay Round from a fatal unraveling in early 1993. An admiring European negotiator referred to the undaunted persistence of "Bush and Hills" trade diplomacy.

When negotiations broke down on November 3, Secretary of Agriculture Madigan recommended retaliation against the EC over the longstanding oilseeds dispute. Two GATT panels had found in favor of the United States, and the failure to resolve the issue within a comprehensive Uruguay Round agreement left the United States free to pursue this dispute independently. President Bush accepted the recommendation and, on November 6, Carla Hills announced that a 200 percent tariff would be levied on $300 million of white wine and other agricultural imports from the EC, effective December 5. Total losses to U.S. oilseed exporters were assessed at $1 billion, and additional sanctions of $700 million were threatened for later.

The EC quickly warned that it would counterretaliate if the United States went ahead with its announced sanctions. The French pressed, within the Community, to draw up a list of target products, and Agricultural Minister Jean-Pierre Soisson recommended that the EC first let the Clinton administration take office, "and then we'll see how we can reach a comprehensive bilateral accord on new foundations."[33] This implied that U.S. sanctions would take effect on December 5. A trade war of proportions unprecedented since the 1930s was imminent.

The crisis drew mixed reaction from trade experts. Professor Jagdish Bhagwati, an adviser to GATT Director-General Dunkel, decried "a paucity of presidential leadership in the U.S. and France" and the failure of the United States to "face down its own (farm) lobby."[34] Professor Gary Hufbauer made a more accurate and supportive assessment: "Oilseeds are the fulcrum by which the U.S. hopes to open up [world trade talks]. . . . It's a high-stakes game of trade diplomacy."[35] Indeed, the Bush decision to retaliate was a calculated move to force the EC to an agreement on agriculture. There was serious risk of actually unleashing a trade war, but the United States held a strong tactical position.

The EC was vulnerable in the oilseeds dispute, as evident by the GATT panel findings that previous commitments to the United States had been violated. There was also disarray within the EC Commission following the November 3 breakdown in talks at Chicago. Agricultural Commissioner Ray MacSharry had been undercut as negotiator by a phone call from Commission President Jaques Delors informing him that he had exceeded his mandate. MacSharry resigned as EC agricultural negotiator on November 5, accusing Delors of favoring French interests by sabotaging the talks, a "betrayal of trust." The press reported Delors's ambition to be president of France, which he dismissed as "slander."[36] Member states were also split, with the United Kingdom and Germany displeased with the breakdown in negotiations while France and some smaller member states supported Delors.

Political momentum within the Community quickly gathered toward resumed negotiations along the lines pursued by MacSharry. There was no support for quick counterretaliation, and the prospect of addressing the crisis with a newly installed President Clinton, who had campaigned on a tough stand in support of U.S. export interests, was not appealing. Meanwhile, European white wine exporters would suffer. An emergency GATT session on November 9 called for renewed negotiations and Director-General Dunkel was instructed to intervene and to bring the parties together. President François Mitterand backed off, stating on French television that the EC might make new concessions in the GATT since "it would be very dangerous for France to become isolated."[37] On November 10, MacSharry withdrew his resignation on the understanding that his interpretation of the negotiating mandate would prevail. A chastised Delors expressed support. The Bush and Hills strategy was working.

Negotiations resumed in Washington on November 18 at the Blair House presidential guest quarters. U.S. Trade Representative Hills and Agriculture Secretary Madigan met with EC Commissioners Andriessen and MacSharry for two days of intensive talks that led to a joint announcement on November 20: "In agriculture we have resolved our differences on the main elements concerning domestic support, export subsidies and market access."[38]

They had reached a comprehensive agreement covering both Uruguay Round issues and the oilseeds dispute. The two critical commitments concerned export subsidies and access to the EC market for oilseeds. For export subsidies, the key U.S. objective had been the Dunkel Draft proposal of a 24-percent reduction, over six years, in the quantity of exports receiving subsidies. The EC had offered 18 percent, and the final agreement specified 21 percent. However, the use of an extended base period of 1986–90 brought the subsidy reduction from the 1991–92 level up to 24 percent. The United States was less successful concerning oilseeds, for which it had consistently pressed for a reduced quantitative limit on EC domestic production to 8–9 million metric tons compared to 12.8 million tons of production in 1991. The EC insisted that a quantitative production limit went beyond the mandate for internal EC agricultural reform, which was limited to reduction in acreage, and the final agreement called for a 10–15 percent acreage reduction. Secretary Madigan projected that this would lead to a reduction in output to 8.5–9.7 million metric tons, but more intensive farming and higher yields would likely result in production levels at the high end of the range or higher.

In any event, the Blair House Accord marked the definitive breakthrough in the agricultural sector that had eluded negotiators and summit leaders for four years. Final approval by EC governments was not assured, and French Agricultural Minister Soisson quickly stated that he could not accept the agreement. But the French government admitted it did not have veto power over the agricultural package alone and could only seek to veto the overall Uruguay Round agreement, which would be very difficult if other outstanding issues were resolved.

With the Blair House agricultural package in hand, U.S. and EC negotiators turned quickly to other outstanding issues in an attempt to agree on the basic elements of an overall Uruguay Round accord by December 23, before the Christmas holidays. This would allow the drafting of a full and final agreement by March 3, 1993, when the extended U.S. fast-track negotiating authority effectively expired. The French socialist government, opposed to the agricultural accord and facing an uphill struggle in parliamentary elections scheduled for March, utilized every means to slow down and postpone a final Uruguay Round agreement. The EC Commission, however, with firm support from the other principal member states, held together in pressing the Americans for additional concessions, principally reductions in very high textile tariffs and limits on future unilateral actions under Section 301.

The U.S. negotiating team, generally lauded for achieving the agricultural breakthrough, faced wide-ranging resistance to a quick resolution of other issues on the grounds that U.S. interests might be sold short in the rush to conclude an agreement before President Bush left office on January 20. Intel Corporation lobbied for delay in order to achieve deeper cuts in the EC 14-percent tariff on semiconductors. The pharmaceutical industry continued to oppose the lengthy transition contained in the draft agreement on intellectual-property rights, while the Motion Picture Association of America did likewise with respect to European quotas on U.S. films. The textile industry strongly opposed the draft agreement to phase out import quotas, not to mention deep tariffs cuts. A range of industries wanted substantial changes in the antidumping text, and environmental groups pressed for changes in several sections of the agreement.

On the political front, Senator Max Baucus, chairman of the Trade Subcommittee of the Senate Finance Committee, and House Majority Leader Richard Gephardt called for delay so that the incoming Democratic president would not be stuck with a faulty agreement that he would then have to sell to the Congress. The transition team drew up an options paper on how the president-elect should respond. A statement by Bill Clinton to hold off would end any further negotiations by the Bush negotiating team, but Clinton chose not to do so. He was busy developing his domestic economic program, and his treasury secretary–designate, Chairman Lloyd Bentsen of the Senate Finance Committee, had tacitly supported an early agreement by judging it unlikely that the Congress would grant another extension of fast-track negotiating authority in 1993.[39]

And so the Bush and Hills team continued to press for a final agreement. The December 23 deadline passed, but President Bush and Prime Minister Major, in private talks, agreed to make one last try in early January. On January 1, 1993, Sir Leon Brittan became the new EC commissioner for external relations, succeeding Frans Andriessen as principal Uruguay Round negotiator. Carla Hills flew to London to meet with Brittan on January 2, which led to intensive further negotiations, particularly over reductions in industrial tariffs. The talks continued on expanded market-access commitments, namely deeper cuts in textile tariffs by the United States and corresponding EC reductions for semiconductors, aluminum, and wood and paper. Carla Hills, in the face of strong opposition from U.S. industry, offered 50 percent cuts for 250 textile products as requested by the Community. Sir Leon, however, was unable to obtain support from the Brussels trade bureaucracy for substantial further movement on the EC side.[40] A meeting in Geneva of principal GATT negotiators was scheduled for January 19, the day before Bill Clinton's inauguration, but by January 15 it became apparent that the final gaps could not be bridged.

The Uruguay Round thus was left once more in limbo, with negotiating authority about to expire for a newly inaugurated U.S. president. The content of the agreement, however, had been largely determined and the remaining differences, while important, were narrowly drawn. In any event, it would be extremely difficult to reopen major elements of the overall draft agreement without unraveling the complex balance of interests contained in it. Arthur Dunkel had put forward his Pandora's Box through the comprehensive draft agreement of December 1991 and George Bush had forced the EC into an agricultural accord within the Dunkel framework. In effect, there was now a Pandora's Box within a Pandora's Box, a formidable tactical advantage for supporters of a comprehensive final agreement. It was largely the work of two individuals with deep and dogged personal commitments to free trade. Unfortunately, neither George Bush nor Arthur Dunkel remained in office to see the Uruguay Round through the final year to its ultimate successful conclusion.

TOPICAL ADDENDUM: TRADE AND THE ENVIRONMENT

In the midst of the U.S.-EC agricultural dispute at the Brussels ministerial meeting in December 1990, a one-page flyer circulated through the crowded press working areas entitled, "The GATT Secretariat Censors Information." The complaint came from GATTastrophe, a group of environmental activists deeply concerned about the impact of the draft Uruguay Round agreement on environmental interests. The flyer accurately explained that press releases delivered by GATTastrophe at the entrance of the press area had been systematically removed by the GATT secretariat. In response, the Belgian minister of foreign trade and the GATT secretariat first accused each other of fostering such censorship before agreeing that no further obstacles would be placed on press-release distribution. While protesting European farmers were cordoned off by police far from the Heysel conference facilities, GATTastrophe convened a press conference at a hotel only a few hundred feet away on the subject of GATT and the environment. The environmentalists had arrived on the trade policy scene.

Environmentalist opposition to certain Uruguay Round objectives had, in fact, been launched months earlier, on May 15, 1990, when a coalition of U.S. groups, the Ad-Hoc Working Group on Trade and Environmentally Sustainable Development, held a press conference in Washington to support a congressional resolution on GATT and the environment introduced by Congressman James Scheuer. The initial demands of the environmentalists, as expressed in the press statements handed out at Brussels, were limited primarily to specific provisions of the draft Uruguay Round text, in particular:

1. *Sanitary and phytosanitary measures.* One highly technical part of the agricultural negotiations that had moved forward with little publicity was the attempt to harmonize international food-safety standards under the

147

rubric of sanitary and phytosanitary measures. The intent was to eliminate standards undertaken principally for protectionist reasons rather
than to achieve a scientifically based food-safety standard. The establishment of harmonized standards by relevant international organizations
was encouraged "on as wide a basis as possible," and higher or nonharmo-
nized standards would require scientific justification, taking into account
"the objective of minimizing negative trade effects." The environmentalists worried that harmonized international standards would be set too low
and that the United States might not be able to establish and maintain
higher standards without violating the governing GATT criteria. In particular, they feared that the Uruguay Round agreement could lead to a weakening of the Delaney Clause in U.S. legislation, which prohibited carcin-
ogens.

2. *Technical standards.* More broadly, and with specific reference to environmental standards, the section of the Dunkel text on "Technical Barriers to
Trade" established more rigorous criteria and procedures to prevent technical standards from being used for protectionist purposes. A key provision was "that technical regulations are not proposed, adopted, or applied
with a view to *or with the effect of* creating unnecessary obstacles to trade"
(emphasis added). The italicized phrase had been added to the existing
GATT standards code negotiated in the Tokyo Round. Environmentalists
opposed it on the grounds that it could restrict nonprotectionist moti-
vated environmental measures.

3. *Intellectual-property rights.* The particular target in this area was pharmaceutical products. The environmentalists generally supported India and
other developing countries in opposing strengthened patent rights. Such
patent protection would enable pharmaceutical, biotechnology, and agro-
industrial firms to extract "the biological resources of the South without
recognizing any of the value inherent in those resources." Moreover,
these firms fail "to consider the *positive* environmental benefits that
would be gained if the potential trade value of these biological resources
was recognized."[41]

4. *Elimination of trade barriers.* A GATT commitment to free trade could, in
the environmentalists' view, curtail the right to restrain exports or imports that compromised national conservation policy. The examples
given, however, were related to export controls for conservation, such as
those on tropical timber. The more fundamental issue for the GATT trading system—import restrictions based on the production process in the
exporting countries (elaborated below in the context of the tuna/dolphin

dispute)—was not raised prominently at the time of the Brussels meeting.

The environmental assault at Brussels was, in any event, a belated attempt to influence an agreement scheduled to be concluded at the heralded ministerial meeting. When the Brussels meeting ended in stalemate, the environmentalists were able to regroup and intensify pressure for GATT reforms with explicitly environmental objectives. One immediate goal was to breathe life into the GATT Working Group on Environmental Measures and International Trade, which had been established in 1971 but had never met. At the Brussels meeting, the EFTA delegations, with strong support from the United States, requested that the group be convened at an early date.

The mood among GATT representatives during 1991 nevertheless remained cautious if not hostile toward integrating environmental commitments within the GATT. EC representative Paul Tran warned that the GATT neither could nor should be turned into a forum for the harmonization and development of global environmental policy.[42] Developing countries, especially cautious, called for a go-slow, step-by-step approach, concerned that strict environmental standards applied in the industrialized countries could be used as a form of "eco-imperialism" to restrict imports from developing-countries. This concern was confirmed by a September 1991 proposal by Senator Max Baucus to establish an environmental code in the GATT, whereby each nation would be allowed to set its own environmental standards and failure by others to meet such standards could result in punitive duties.[43] The GATT group on the environment and trade finally met for the first time in November 1991 after months of consultation to overcome resistance by developing countries.

A defining issue in the trade/environment debate involved the U.S-Mexican dispute over tuna fish and dolphins. The United States had unilaterally banned tuna imports from Mexico because a large number of dolphins were incidentally killed by Mexican tuna fishermen. The sanction was specified in the U.S. Marine Mammal Protection Act, which established a strict standard for minimal harm to dolphins. Dolphins were never an endangered species but were protected under the act as a value judgment. Mexico protested, and in August 1991, a GATT dispute-settlement panel found in favor of Mexico. GATT Article XX provides for exceptions to GATT market access commitments for measures to protect animal life or health, and to conserve exhaustible natural resources, which was the basis for the U.S. case before the GATT. The GATT panel, however, interpreted such U.S. rights as pertaining only to its territorial waters and not to the entire world.

The tuna dispute raised for the first time in the GATT the imposition of trade sanctions based not on health or environmental standards embodied in the product traded—as was the case for sanitary and phytosanitary measures—but on the production process of the exporting country, in this case a process of tuna fishing that also killed dolphins. The GATT would not accept this, at least not when imposed unilaterally. Senator Baucus responded that the "panel's decision may accurately reflect the current provisions of the GATT, but this is an argument for changing the GATT, not for ending our efforts to protect dolphins."[44]

The GATT Council scheduled consideration of the panel finding for late 1991, but in the interim the United States and Mexico reached a compromise whereby Mexico issued a detailed plan to reduce dolphin kills and the United States pledged to seek to amend its legislation to accommodate the revised Mexican fishing practices. Mexico then deferred further action in the GATT so that both countries could redirect their energies to the overriding mutual objective of concluding the NAFTA. Nevertheless, the tuna dispute continued to cloud the final phase of the Uruguay Round negotiations. By mid-1993 Mexico had reduced the dolphin kill rate by over 80 percent. The U.S. law, however, stipulated that Mexican boats had to reach standards achieved by U.S. boats, which had shifted to other, dolphin-free waters with a near zero kill rate. Meanwhile, the U.S. fishing industry continued to receive full protection from Mexican import competition.

The broader question of how the GATT trading system and environmental standards do or should interact was addressed in a candid thirty-five-page report by the GATT secretariat in February 1992.[45] Positive environmental aspects of liberal trade were emphasized. For example, highly protected agriculture in the EC and the United States results in far greater usage of chemical fertilizer than in unprotected Argentina, Australia, and Thailand. Also, trade barriers that frustrate developing countries' ability to improve living standards will at the same time frustrate efforts to raise environmental standards. As for policy prescription, countries with large forest areas that provide "carbon absorption services" should be paid for such services rather than suffer trade sanctions imposed against their exports. The report went on to state that GATT rules and dispute-settlement procedures could provide the working framework for achieving multilateral agreements on improved environmental standards, but it took a firm stand against "vigilante" actions by one country against another: "To allow each contracting party unilaterally to impose special duties against whatever it objects to among the domestic policies of other contracting parties would risk an eventual descent into chaotic trade conditions similar to those that plagued the 1930s." Director-General Dunkel was even more blunt, stating that the GATT "must protect against the risk of the environment being kidnapped by trade protectionist interests."[46]

The GATT report was a milestone in that it presented an integrated assessment of trade and environmental interests, unthinkable in the trade organization only a couple years earlier. However, the environmentalist groups, particularly in the United States, were not pleased with the conclusions of the report and continued their attacks on the terrible "GATTzilla," an allusion to the fabled Japanese monster Godzilla. Lines also became more clearly drawn between the United States and almost all other countries on the issue of unilateral trade sanctions against exporters with lower environmental standards, as in the tuna dispute. This issue came to a head at the environmental summit meeting in Rio de Janeiro in June, 1992, when the consensus declaration in the chapter on trade overrode U.S. resistance and asked that countries avoid acting unilaterally to deal with environmental challenges outside their jurisdiction.[47] Developing countries, strongly supported by the EC, later pressed within the GATT to adopt the same language, or reference to it, as a principle for the GATT approach to trade sanctions and the environment. U.S. representatives were on the defensive, but they also conveyed clearly the growing momentum of environmentalist pressures at home, which enjoyed strong congressional support, further dimming the prospects for a successful conclusion of the Uruguay Round.

By the summer of 1993, as Uruguay Round participants regrouped for the final phase of negotiations, the trade-environmental interface had still not been resolved. The GATT Group on Environmental Measures and International Trade had met about ten times, but most of the deliberations had focused on technical matters, such as the transparency of trade-related environmental measures and possible trade effects of packaging and labeling.[48] On the central issue of trade sanctions, attention focused on how the GATT should respond to multilateral environmental agreements elsewhere, which included trade sanctions as enforcement mechanisms related to the production process in the exporting country. The EC, with broad support, advocated a reinterpretation of GATT Article XX to provide exceptions to GATT rules based on certain criteria. Canada proposed a narrower, case-by-case assessment under the Article XXV waiver procedure. The United States, still concerned about its flexibility to act unilaterally, remained uncommitted.

Time overtook a definitive resolution of the GATT trade-environment relationship within the Uruguay Round framework. In October 1993, the GATT group agreed to postpone further work pending the conclusion of the Uruguay

Round. A final paper presented by Austria stated: "There is broad consensus within this Group that transboundary environmental problems should be tackled and resolved through internationally agreed measures."[49] This statement stretched normal GATT usage of consensus since it excluded the single largest trading nation.

The final Uruguay Round agreement does include significant environment-related provisions concerning definition of standards, transparency, and dispute-settlement procedures. More important, the trade-environment interface was given high priority in the new World Trade Organization through agreement on a Committee on Trade and Environment at the Marrakesh meeting in April 1994 with a specified agenda and schedule for reporting back to ministers. The most important result of the 1990–93 experience, as recounted here, however, was the fundamental change in mind-set among both trade-policy officials and environmentalists. The almost total communications disconnect between the two groups through 1990 had evolved, by 1993, into a serious, engaged debate, however disparate the points of view.

SEVEN

Diplomatic and Political Endgames, 1993–1994

The tantalizing "almost agreement" of mid-January 1993 raised hopes that a final accord could be reached by the new Clinton administration before the March 1 expiration of negotiating authority. Arthur Dunkel announced that "the Uruguay Round can, and must be, concluded quickly," and Leon Brittan called for new initiatives before the U.S. negotiating authority expired.[1] But such hopes quickly proved illusory. The Clinton trade-policy team would need time to organize its negotiating strategy. In any event, the president's immediate priorities were domestic, fiscal deficit reduction and national health care. Even in the field of trade policy, initial attention focused on what to do with the NAFTA, signed in December by President Bush but still subject to congressional approval, and on how to formulate a bilateral trade initiative with Japan based on the tough rhetoric of the election campaign. The new and mercurial chairman of the Senate Finance Committee, Patrick Moynihan, suggested that the president request a leisurely two-year extension of the Uruguay Round negotiating authority, which sent shudders through the weary negotiators in Geneva.[2]

The general frustration was widely articulated during the annual economic gathering at Davos, Switzerland, in late February. Fred Bergsten, director of the Washington-based Institute for International Economics, called for early agreement on a "mini-package" for the Uruguay Round coupled with the launching of a new GATT round. What would be left in the mini-package remained unclear. Argentine President Carlos Saul Menem, whose government had played a constructive and active role throughout the round, tended cataclysmic: Latin America could return to "a dark age of disruption and instability" if there were no Uruguay Round agreement, and "the course of events against a background of world recession would lead us to the errors of the past, the consequences of which would be tragic for the world."[3]

The frustration was, of course, directed at the two principal participants in the world trading system, the United States and the EC. The Uruguay Round had been launched at strong U.S. initiative, with a far broader sweep of issues and country participation than any previous negotiation. But now, more than six years later, and after others had done their part, the two principals proved incapable of bridging the final gaps for a comprehensive agreement, ostensibly over relatively modest tariff reductions in a few sectors. Moreover, the political will in Washington and Brussels to regroup and conclude the affair was open to disturbing new question. The half-century commitment to evermore-open trade and investment was being challenged, although for very different reasons, on each side of the Atlantic.

In the United States, two interacting developments cast a shadow over a continued liberal trade policy. First, public concern continued that the United States was losing industrial competitiveness in world markets, particularly vis-à-vis Japan. The cause was largely attributed to intervention, or "industrial policy," by the Japanese and other governments while the U.S. government was constrained by its free-trade principles. This argument had been building since the mid-1980s and crystallized in a book by Laura D'Andrea Tyson, *Who's Bashing Whom? Trade Conflict in High-Technology Industries*. Tyson viewed the multilateral GATT system as "largely irrelevant . . . for the foreseeable future" and recommended a U.S. policy response of "aggressive unilateralism" through bilateral sector-specific negotiations.[4] The study was published in November 1992, and President-elect Clinton praised the book and chose its author as chairperson of his Council of Economic Advisers the following month.

The second development was an unholy political alliance against congressional approval of the NAFTA, anticipated to come to a vote in the fall of 1993. Organized labor under the AFL-CIO, the Congressional Black Caucus, populist presidential candidate Ross Perot, conservative Republican Patrick Buchanan, consumer advocate Ralph Nader, and some environmentalist groups constituted the emotionally charged leadership of the anti-NAFTA campaign. Facts and figures were treated cavalierly, and the debate turned into a frontal assault on comparative advantage: Wages were lower in Mexico and thus free trade with Mexico was not in the U.S. interest.

Underlying both these developments was widespread anxiety and fear about job security in a period of slow growth and structural change in the U.S. economy. Sharp cutbacks were under way in defense industries. Restructuring in a wide range of manufacturing and service sectors resulted in highly publicized job cuts, particularly in prominent companies such as IBM and General Motors. Relatively little of this labor restructuring related to trade, but that did not inhibit the "Japan bashers" and NAFTA opponents. Pro-NAFTA former president Jimmy Carter hit the mark in referring to Ross Perot as a demagogue "preying on the fears and uncertainties of the American public."[5]

Ironically, U.S. trade competitiveness had strengthened greatly in the five years up to 1993, especially in high-technology industries. The semiconductor, computer, telecommunications-equipment and related service sectors had reaffirmed a U.S. technological lead. American automakers recovered U.S. market shares from Japanese companies. The U.S. trade surplus for high-technology industries increased from $16 billion in 1986 to $33 billion in 1992, with an implied net increase in jobs of 250,000.[6] But these positive trends were not widely perceived or appreciated in early 1993. The Tyson book opened with the rhetorical pronouncement that "in the full flush of geopolitical triumph, we are teetering over the abyss of economic decline."[7] The five-decade U.S. leadership for multilateral free trade was viewed as a principal contributor to such a decline and possible fall.

Two interacting developments also buffeted the EC commitment to free trade, but they were more familiar and longer-standing. One was a downward turn in the cycle of Euro-pessimism and -optimism that had prevailed throughout the 1980s. The EC-92 program of market unification had been largely implemented but with little apparent impact on economic growth and efficiency. German reunification was proving to be extremely costly while slowing down the West German economy. European monetary union as expressed in the Maastricht treaty had turned out to be premature and politically divisive. Average unemployment in the EC reached 11 percent by mid-1993 and was predicted to drift even higher in the face of deeply entrenched fiscal deficits and job-inhibiting social programs. As a result of all of the above, European trade competitiveness appeared to be weakening. The *Défi Americain*, or American challenge of the 1960s, was turning into an even more threatening Asian-American challenge of the 1990s.

The second European development was renewed French opposition to basic reform of the Common Agricultural Policy, which would be required by the Blair House Accord of November 1992. French criticism of the accord was initially muted while the United States threatened to retaliate against European white wine. However, once this threat was rescinded, the French attack intensified. The key export subsidy commitment would only reduce existing export levels moderately, phased in over six years, but French leaders described the accord in terms of strangulation and ruin for the farm community. The decisive victory of conservative parties in the March parliamentary elections did not change the momentum of opposition. The new prime minister, Edouard Balladur, while a liberal trader, was under severe constraint from his former mentor and possible future rival for the presidency, Mayor Jacques Chirac of Paris, who was especially hostile to farm-trade liberalization in the

Uruguay Round. The German liberal trade counterweight within the Community appeared hesitant at best. Chancellor Kohl had made it clear that if he were forced to choose between farm reform to save the Uruguay Round and preservation of a positive Franco-German political relationship, he would opt for the latter.

The case for multilateral free trade, in sum, was losing steam on both sides of the Atlantic. Some of the anti–free-trade issues were short-term in nature, but a fundamental rethinking and political realignment about trade policy was also taking place. As at past critical junctures for the world trading system, the pivotal factor was U.S. leadership, which now rested on the untested shoulders of President Bill Clinton.

New Dramatis Personae

The new Clinton administration got off to a slow and ambiguous start in confronting the Uruguay Round stalemate. Initial U.S.-EC trade skirmishing in the early months of 1993 was conflictive. The United States imposed preliminary antidumping penalties on imports of European steel and threatened retaliation over EC public-procurement policy in the telecommunications sector. President Clinton, in a speech at the Boeing facilities in Seattle, appeared to reopen the previous year's bilateral agreement to limit subsidies for European Airbus development. Surprisingly, the tenor of U.S. trade policy was more harsh toward the EC than Japan.

The character of the U.S.-EC relationship would be influenced greatly by the new *dramatis personae* at the trade negotiating table, consisting of a "fixer" and an ideologue. The fixer was the new U.S. trade representative, Mickey Kantor, a California lawyer/lobbyist and candidate Clinton's campaign chairman. He had no previous trade-policy experience, and his initial statements indicated a pragmatist with leanings toward the protectionist attitudes of organized labor. During the campaign, he had sided with advisers more critical of the NAFTA agreement. Shortly after confirmation, when a Japanese trade official warned him that a threatened increase in U.S. tariffs on minivans would violate GATT rules, Kantor replied, "I'm not interested in theology."[8] Kantor's long-standing work in California politics, however, had earned him his fixer reputation as a person who could negotiate a deal for complicated and highly politicized problems. This is what President Clinton needed and got in his choice for trade representative.

The ideologue was the new EC commissioner for external relations and principal Uruguay Round negotiator, Leon Brittan. An urbane, conservative former member of the government of Margaret Thatcher, Sir Leon believed in free trade and was determined to see the Uruguay Round through to a successful conclusion. Far more assertive and outspoken than his predecessor, Frans Andriessen, he quickly assumed a strong leadership role within the normally fractious Commission. His initial negotiating efforts in January with lame-duck Trade Representative Carla Hills had produced significant results, although falling short of full agreement, and the momentum of his positive thinking quickly resumed in his initial contacts with the Clinton administration. Kantor and Brittan were a contrast in appearance, character, and intellectual orientation. The lean, reserved, pragmatic lawyer versus the portly, outspoken, philosophically committed politician. It was to be a mutually reinforcing contrast that would produce sorely needed synergy at the bargaining table during the final months of the Uruguay Round.

The first concrete test of the Brittan/Kantor negotiating relationship came over a telecommunications public procurement dispute. An EC utilities directive entered into force on January 1, 1993, giving EC companies a 3 percent preference in bidding over foreign companies and allowing EC public entities to ignore a foreign bidder entirely if there were less than 50 percent European content in the offer. In response, the United States threatened $45 million in sanctions, which would block EC firms from competing for federal contracts in the United States. The EC protested on the grounds that the United States had similar longstanding preferences for public procurement. During Mickey Kantor's first visit to Brussels in late March, the two men worked out the framework for a compromise resolution of the problem and the details were adopted on April 22. Sir Leon agreed to waive the new EC directive for heavy electrical equipment, and Kantor announced the removal of preferential restrictions on EC bids for five publicly owned federal facilities and the Tennessee Valley Authority (TVA). Follow-up bilateral discussions would seek a broader opening of public procurement, including at the state and municipal levels in the United States. Finally, the United States scaled back its sanctions to about $20 million. Both sides had made significant concessions, the direction of change shifted toward more open markets, and a heated bilateral dispute had been cleared away so as to concentrate attention on conclusion of the Uruguay Round.

The Clinton/Kantor Uruguay Round strategy, meanwhile, lingered in limbo through March. A lengthy speech on trade policy by the president at American University on February 26 combined general support for open markets with wide-ranging qualifications. Only one sentence referred to "a prompt and successful completion of the Uruguay Round of the GATT talks." The *Journal of Commerce* lamented: "Mr. Clinton has been in office nearly two months yet we know scarcely more about his trade policy than we did during the election campaign. . . . yet while the Clinton team has offered no opinion on the Dunkel text, legions of Washington special interests have been urging them to pick it apart."[9]

Mickey Kantor, during his March visit to Brussels, talked tough about U.S. interests and appeared receptive to Washington apart-pickers. He called for significant changes in the draft Uruguay Round agreement, including antidumping provisions, copyright protection, and greater attention to environmental issues. The European press claimed that U.S. trade policy continued to be "incomplete" and "contradictory" as to whether the United States was following a liberal trade strategy or a protectionist course. The *Guardian* of London observed succinctly that "Mr. Kantor came to Europe to kick ass." French observers stressed the need for Europe to remain united in the face of U.S. trade pressures.[10]

President Clinton's request to the Congress for renewed fast-track negotiating authority became the immediate Uruguay Round issue. He had stated his intent to seek the extension, and Congress was disposed to grant it, giving the new president one more chance to conclude the round, but the duration of the new authority was crucial since it would establish the deadline for the negotiations. Mickey Kantor leaned in favor of a lengthy extension of a year or more so as to avoid overlap between the final phase of Uruguay Round negotiations and the congressional vote on NAFTA. Sir Leon, in contrast, pressed for an early date in order to mobilize political support against the gathering forces seeking to undermine the agreement, and his view prevailed. On April 9, President Clinton requested legislation that would renew his authority to sign an Uruguay Round agreement no later than April 15, 1994. However, the agreement would effectively have to be completed by December 15, 1993, to allow a revised 120-day consultation period with the Congress prior to formal signing. The die was thus cast for what was the last and most credible deadline for the Uruguay Round.

The final phase of the Uruguay Round would also be influenced by a third key change in the *dramatis personae,* and a second free trade ideologue. GATT Director-General Arthur Dunkel's tour had twice been extended, but when he announced his intent to retire on schedule at the end of June, there was no attempt to persuade him to continue on. Instead, attention turned to Peter Sutherland as his successor. Sutherland had demonstrated great energy, political skill, and a deep commitment to free trade as EC commissioner for competition policy during the 1980s. He returned to his native Ireland to assume the chairmanship of Allied Irish Banks PLC, and was at first reluctant to take on the Geneva post in view of the uncertain prospects for the Uruguay Round. He was persuaded to do so at European and American urging, and after two competing Latin American candidates withdrew, he was approved by acclamation to begin his new job on July 1.

Sutherland lost no time in adopting a more outspoken and pro-active public role for the GATT director-generalship. On his first day in office, he accused the industrialized country leaders of "obfuscation and paralysis" and warned that if the upcoming economic summit meeting in Tokyo failed to adopt a detailed communiqué for concluding the round, the round would be a "pipe dream. . . . It is simply not good enough for the G-7 to make general protestations in favor of trade reform, as they have for the past five summits. If the outcome is unclear, it is negative."[11]

The Uruguay Round diplomatic endgame was thus taking shape as the July Tokyo submit meeting approached. The substantive priorities were reasonably clear as they had been over the past two and half years of U.S.-EC impasse. One difference at this junction was that the summit leaders knew that this was the last chance for striking a deal to reinvigorate the multilateral trading system. If the Blair House agricultural package came apart or the remaining tariff and other issues went unresolved, there would be little reason for President Clinton to seek renewed authority yet again nor much disposition on the part of the Congress to grant it. Another difference was the new element of leadership, driven by the three principal players at Geneva: Brittan, Kantor, and Sutherland.

There was also a sadder, personal note to this changing of the diplomatic guard. Arthur Dunkel deserved better than the cursory farewell he received. He had provided a firm helm and intellectual depth for the negotiations from the preparatory phase of the early 1980s through his initiative to place a comprehensive draft agreement before recalcitrant governments in December 1991. The lanky, chain-smoking Swiss diplomat preferred quiet talk in closed negotiating rooms to posturing on the political podium, an attribute that was criticized as the Uruguay Round languished. The United States considered him too soft on the developing countries and not assertive enough with European governments.[12] The French never forgave him for the take-it-or-leave-it manner in which he put forward his draft agreement, including specific commitments for agriculture that largely prevailed in the later Blair House Accord. There was good reason to seek a new director general with greater political visibility who would preside over the conclusion of the Uruguay Round and then go on to lead a newly created World Trade Organization. But somehow Arthur Dunkel should have been able to share in the final six months of triumph after thirteen years of painstaking dedication to the quest. He was there in name, of course, because until the final days, the 436-page document under negotiation continued to be referred to as the Dunkel Draft.

Relaunching the Round

The specific Uruguay Round objective the industrialized country leaders had adopted for the July 7–9 meeting in Tokyo was a "market access" agreement on tariff cuts for industrialized sectors. Some sectors would be subject to the "zero-for-zero" total elimination of tariffs on a reciprocal basis, others for up to 50-percent reductions and still others for a minimum one-third reduction. In effect, this picked up where the Brittan/Hills negotiations had broken off in January. The idea was to achieve a breakthrough in Tokyo with a package deal in which each participant would offer additional tariff cuts. The Quad trade ministers met three times in May and June to set the stage for such a breakthrough.

As leaders arrived in Tokyo, however, agreement had still not been achieved, and considerable pessimism prevailed. U.S. press briefings attempted to "downplay expectations." In particular, the United States did not intend to offer further cuts in high tariffs on textiles and apparel of interest to European exporters, and the EC continued to resist deep cuts in semiconductors and other electronics products. The Sutherland warning that an unclear outcome would be a negative one was nevertheless understood. Trade representatives continued a six-hour negotiating session until 3 A.M. on July 7 and finally came up with a package agreement that extended significantly market-access commitments. The critical move came from Japan, who surprisingly agreed to zero duties for "colored" distilled spirits, including scotch and bourbon. This triggered responses by Canada to eliminate duties on beer and furniture, and by the EC, who had been pressing Canada on furniture, to eliminate duties on farm equipment. The overall agreement involved duty elimination in eight sectors, harmonization of tariffs at low levels for the chemicals sector, minimum average cuts of one-third for four other sectors, and tariff cuts of up to 50 percent for high tariffs in the ceramics, glass, textiles, and apparel sectors.

Official and press reactions to the announced agreement varied greatly. President Clinton announced, "We have recaptured the momentum," and Mickey Kantor referred to the agreement as "truly a breakthrough" that would achieve the biggest tariff cuts in history. Prime Minister John Major of the United Kingdom went further, calling it "infinitely bigger than anything we have seen before." Foreign Minister Alain Juppé of France, in contrast, referred to "a rapport, not an accord . . . a direction and not a result."[13] The press initially tended to view the agreement as a breakthrough but then tempered its assessment when it became clear that most of the package—for example, tariff elimination for pharmaceuticals, construction and medical equipment, and harmonization of chemical tariffs—had been agreed during the Bush administration, while the toughest issues, including textiles and electronics, remained unresolved. The United States had, in fact, backed off somewhat from the degree of textile tariff cuts offered by the Bush administration.

In any event, the Tokyo market-access package represented a concrete step forward for the Uruguay Round and provided the necessary political momentum to reactivate the stalled negotiations. Renewed activity began almost immediately at both the multilateral level in Geneva and the U.S.-EC level between Washington and Brussels.

Peter Sutherland quickly assumed charge in Geneva and convened two meetings of the Trade Negotiations Committee during July to organize the final phase of the negotiations. His forceful manner and crisp style, limiting speakers to five-minute interventions, was well received in an institution renowned for tedious deliberations. Asian and Latin American developing countries expressed concern that issues of interest to them had been largely ignored while zero-for-zero tariff elimination focused on sectors of trade dominated by the industrialized countries. Ambassador Juan Archibaldo Lanus of Argentina suggested facetiously zero-for-zero tariff elimination for bananas, wheat, and orange juice.[14] Sutherland was responsive to developing country concerns in emphasizing the need to establish proper practices for dumping and countervailing duty actions and, in a warning to the United States, noted that any change in the draft agreement in these areas would be subject to the approval of all participants.

Peter Sutherland and his senior deputies also developed a detailed negotiating strategy for the complex diplomatic endgame ahead.[15] Sutherland himself would initially remain above the day-to-day group negotiations, engaging instead in a high-visibility public campaign to keep political leaders committed to a successful outcome. He spent most of September and October traveling to capitals in industrialized and developing countries, explaining that December 15 was the final deadline for the Uruguay Round and that failure to take necessary decisions would be politically damaging to everyone. Sutherland thus reserved his own personal involvement in the negotiations to the final stage when he could intervene as the ultimate honest broker. This was in contrast to Arthur Dunkel's earlier role as chairman of the contentious agriculture and textile negotiating groups.

The leadership team consisted of Sutherland, his three deputy directors-general, and four "Friends of the Chair." The three deputies were all former senior Uruguay Round negotiators. The American, Warren Lavorel, had been involved continuously in the Uruguay Round process since the 1982 GATT ministerial meeting, rising to the position of Uruguay Round coordinator in the office of the U.S. trade representative. Anwarul Hoda had been a senior official in the Indian Ministry of Commerce, and Jesús Seade had previously served as Mexican Geneva representative to the GATT. The four "Friends" were also experienced negotiators selected to chair key negotiating groups. The Canadian, Germain Denis, who had been chairing the market access group, received an expanded mandate for agriculture and textiles. David Hawes of Australia was also already on the scene chairing the services group. Julio Lacarte-Muro returned from retirement in Uruguay to resume his earlier charge of institutional matters, including the MTO and dispute settlement. Michael Cartland was similarly recalled temporarily from his ministerial position in Hong Kong—at Sutherland's personal request to the governor general—to handle antidumping and subsidies. This leadership team, together with a few other senior members of the GATT secretariat, conferred regularly—toward the end, almost daily—to review progress and map out negotiating strategy.

Finally, the negotiating strategy called for a staggered agenda in the respective groups, beginning in September, rather than a "global" approach of negotiating tradeoffs within a comprehensive draft agreement, which could delay difficult decisions in all areas. Sutherland warned, "Playing a waiting game over negotiating offers could plunge the round back into the perilous position it faced before the Tokyo breakthrough."[16]

The U.S.-EC bilateral talks got off to an equally brisk new start and soon eclipsed the multilateral forum in Geneva. The market-access accord still left unresolved tariff cuts for textiles and semiconductors, both represented by influential private-sector constituencies. The United States was turning up the heat for reducing European quotas on U.S. films and other audio-visual services, as well as French film industry subsidies. The U.S.-EC agreement of the previous year on subsidies for commercial aircraft production was related to a draft multilateral agreement for this sector. The EC continued to press the United States for inclusion of maritime services within the new framework agreement for trade in services, and was particularly incensed about U.S. antidumping duties on European steel just as a sectoral agreement was being pursued within the Uruguay Round to eliminate steel tariffs and control subsidies. French Prime Minister Balladur had stated prior to the Tokyo summit that there would be no trade agreement "if the [U.S.] sanctions on imported steel, particularly French steel, are not lifted. . . . There is no question of our negotiating or of our accepting any agreement whatsoever while submitting to a national law that does not conform to international rules."[17]

The central unresolved issue between the United States and the EC, however, remained agriculture. France had acceded to moving ahead in Tokyo on market access commitments for industrial sectors, but there was no question that the Blair House Accord was unacceptable to French interests. During the spring, Prime Minister Balladur had been qualified in his rejection of the accord, calling for limited modifications: "We are looking for solutions without provoking a crisis. . . . We don't want to destroy the GATT, which is important."[18] On June 8, France agreed to implement the part of the Blair House Accord dealing with EC oilseed imports, where the United States had been most forthcoming and which was the basis for threatened U.S. retaliation. Then, as the Tokyo summit approached, the French position hardened and continued to build in intensity during the summer. The same Prime Minister Balladur now warned: "There should be no ambiguity about the position of the French government. We do not agree with Blair House. We do not accept it, in substance or form."[19]

The agricultural issue came to a head within the Community on August 28, when Prime Minister Balladur met with German Chancellor Helmut Kohl. After the meeting, Kohl said he sympathized with France's need for compromise and that Germany also had severe problems with the agricultural part of the Uruguay Round: "We want a balanced compromise in all areas of the GATT negotiation. A position of all or nothing is not moving forward."[20] This change from Germany's previous commitment of support for the Blair House agreement took other German officials by surprise, and Foreign Minister Klaus Kinkel of the coalition party Free Democrats tried to play down the chancellor's remarks by saying that Germany had no intention of seeking to reopen the farm agreement. But the shift in the internal EC political ranks was evident.

The next significant event was a September 20 "Jumbo Council" of EC foreign and agricultural ministers. French insistence on basic change in the agricultural accord was finessed into a mandate whereby Commissioner Brittan would raise a list of French objections with the United States while not formally requesting a reopening of the Blair House Accord. U. K. Foreign Minister Douglas Hurd called the twelve-hour marathon council meeting "a draw," but instructions for Sir Leon to ask for "amplifications or additions" constituted a victory for France, supported by Germany.[21] The question was how far the amplifications and additions would have to go, and the answer was unclear.

The U.S. answer to reopening the agricultural agreement was categoric. Mickey Kantor issued a statement on September 21 that the United States would not reopen the Blair House Accord "either directly or indirectly."[22] The Cairns group of agricultural exporters added their support to a firm stand against the French, threatening a walkout from the negotiations. The apparent new stalemate over agriculture was becoming overshadowed, however, by a competing Washington priority that would take precedence over the Uruguay Round through mid-November—namely, the showdown congressional vote on the NAFTA.

Candidate Clinton had supported the NAFTA on condition that parallel side agreements on environmental and labor standards could be negotiated with Mexico. These negotiations got off to a slow start in the spring of 1993 and were not concluded until mid-August. Meanwhile, political momentum rested with the anti-NAFTA forces, bolstered by members of Congress who had committed to a no vote on NAFTA in exchange for organized-labor support during the 1992 campaign. The Democratic House majority leader, Richard Gephardt, quickly assessed the side agreements as inadequate and opposed the overall agreement, joining House Majority Whip David Bonior in opposition. President Clinton finally launched his campaign in support of NAFTA on September 14 in a joint White House presentation with former presidents Bush, Carter, and Ford, but by then the preliminary vote count, particularly in the House of Representatives, was running heavily against the NAFTA. By the end of October, with the outlook equally bleak, the president pressed ahead for a House vote on November 17, just before Congress was to recess until the following year. A defeat for NAFTA would have been a triumph for wide-ranging protectionist forces, especially in the president's own party, and the likely prospect cast gloom over the Geneva GATT negotiations.

Then, during the final two weeks before the critical vote, President Clinton discarded all previous hesitancy and hedging about free trade and led a vigorous no-holds-barred campaign for NAFTA approval. He brought to bear intensive pressures on individual members of the Congress and granted political concessions, including a presidential letter to textiles district members pledging to seek an extension from ten to fifteen years for the Uruguay Round textile-quota phaseout.[23] Vice President Al Gore debated Ross Perot on television, essentially on U.S. interests in open trade, and won. Strong bipartisan support from the Republican leadership was a crucial factor, and in the final days the momentum shifted decisively toward the president. The House voted

234-200 in favor of NAFTA followed by a 61–38 favorable vote in the Senate.[24]

The remarkable NAFTA victory strongly bolstered President Clinton, and he immediately flew to Seattle to host a meeting of Asian-Pacific leaders within the Asia-Pacific Economic Cooperation forum (APEC). Clinton again appealed for a more open trading system, with a veiled warning that if the Europeans blocked a successful Uruguay Round, the dynamic Pacific Basin trading partners would move ahead on their own.[25] Mickey Kantor got his marching orders to make an all-out effort to conclude the Uruguay Round in the four weeks before December 15, and he now held a much stronger bargaining position to do so.

Final Agreement

European and other leaders applauded President Clinton's NAFTA victory as a sign that he would not succumb to protectionism and that the way was now open to conclude the Uruguay Round. Farm talks, in fact, resumed in Brussels two days after the House NAFTA vote. Another wrenching change for observers of the trade scene, however, was that the EC, more or less, had ceased to exist. The Maastricht Treaty came into effect on November 1, creating a new European Union (EU). The new Union consisted of the old Community plus the means for a common foreign policy and cooperation in justice and police matters. It did not have legal powers—for example, authority to conclude international agreements—and it was not initially clear what to call the GATT negotiators representing the twelve member states. The Brussels Commission rebaptized itself the European Commission, and the European Court in Luxembourg decided to remain The Court of Justice of the European Communities. Nevertheless, one by one, newspapers and news magazines adopted the transitional phrase "The EU (formerly the EC)," and so it will be for the remainder of this account.

U.S. officials, despite the public stance against reopening the Blair House Accord, had been exploring internally possible adjustments to appease the French without undermining the basic commitment to cut back subsidized farm exports. The 21 percent reduction from the 1986–90 base level was heavily "front-loaded," requiring the largest cut in the first year because EU (formerly EC) grain exports, in particular, were already well above the base level by 1993. Evening out the reductions was reasonable. Adjusting the base period and making special provisions for recently accumulated wheat stocks represented other possible elements of compromise. The U.S. senior agricultural negotiator, Joseph O'Mara, met with his EU counterpart Guy Legras for closely held private discussions in Brussels on November 20–21. They covered these issues as well as enhanced access for U.S. agricultural products in the European market. The negotiations then shifted to Washington, where Mickey Kantor and Leon Brittan met for lengthy sessions on November 22–23. They reported a narrowing of differences and it became clear that the range of issues under negotiation had broadened to include market access for industrial goods, trade in services, antidumping, and subsidies for steel and aircraft. Brittan and Kantor planned a follow-up session in Brussels to begin on December 1. It would clearly be the final and decisive showdown, at least for agriculture.

A last round of trans-Atlantic political posturing ensued as December 1 approached. French President François Mitterand delivered a stinging attack on what he said were bullying U.S. tactics following the NAFTA victory. Prime Minister Balladur declared, "We have obtained nothing . . . of what we have asked" at the Washington talks and rejected calls for greater French leadership to bring the round to a successful conclusion. An Anglo-German summit in Bonn on November 25 between Prime Minister Major and Chancellor Kohl concluded that failure to reach an Uruguay Round agreement would have "intolerable" consequences, and Major went on to warn that several countries had to show more "flexibility," without naming them. A Franco-German summit on the eve of the Brussels meeting, including both President Mitterand and Prime Minister Balladur, failed to resolve U.S.-French differences over agriculture, and Chancellor Kohl, ever reluctant to disagree publicly, explained, "We should not create the impression in Europe and elsewhere that our French friends are being manoeuvered into a corner in these negotiations." In private, however, he had conveyed to his French interlocutors the vital German interest in a successful outcome for the round. On December 1, Secretary of State Warren Christopher arrived in Brussels, along with Trade Representative Kantor and Secretary of Agriculture Mike Espy, to stress the political stakes involved. Economic security was a cornerstone of U.S. foreign policy, Christopher explained, and failure of the Uruguay Round "will threaten economic recession in Europe, the United States, and indeed the world as a whole."[26]

Beneath the rhetorical surface, however, all sides were prepared for compromise, and the protracted Brussels discussions of December 1–3, led by Brittan and Kantor, did indeed produce the decisive breakthrough that finally assured a successful conclusion to the Uruguay Round. Agriculture, of course, remained at center stage, and the Americans made very significant concessions that altered the Blair House commitments to the advantage of European—especially French—farmers. The 21 percent reduction in subsidized exports was spread evenly over the six-year implementation period and, more importantly, the base period from which to measure the reduction was moved up from 1986–90 to 1991–92, thus allowing a higher level of subsidized exports throughout.[27] The French wheat farmers gained in the order of 8 million tons over six years. A formula was also included for the EU to dispose on world markets its 25 million tons of grain stocks. Another U.S. concession extended from six to eight years the period of the so-called peace accord, an anomalous commitment whereby the United States agreed not to challenge the EU farm policy in the GATT. In sum the French had achieved a significant watering down of the agreement made by the EC negotiators a year earlier, while the basic framework for reversing the upward trend of subsidized exports and cutting them back by about a fifth over six years was maintained.

The United States in return received significant market-access commitments for its farm exports to Europe, including for almonds, citrus and other fresh fruit, pork, and turkey products. Continued U.S. sales of corn and sorghum to Spain and Portugal, the lingering problem from the earlier accession of these countries to the EC, was assured. Agreement on nonagricultural issues was less noteworthy. Some further progress was made in tariff reductions in industrial sectors, including tariff elimination for most wood, paper, and toys. For steel, zero-for-zero tariff elimination prevailed but resolution of the more important subsidy/dumping dispute was abandoned until after the Uruguay Round. The United States initially offered to include maritime services partially within the services framework agreement, and a more concerted approach was adopted for dealing with the textiles and antidumping sectors. There remained U.S.-EU disagreement on only two highly contentious issues, subsidies for commercial aircraft production and European protection of its film industry.

The U.S.-EU agreement was not made public while intensive review and approval within the EU went forward. The final concession to France came during a breakfast meeting at the French ambassador's residence in Brussels on December 11, when Chancellor Kohl agreed on a formula proposed by President Mitterand that would enable French farmers to receive compensation from the EU budget if the GATT agreement on agriculture resulted in excessive harm to them.[28] The key provisions of the U.S.-EU agreement immediately leaked out, however, and with the understanding that basic agreement on agriculture had finally been achieved, attention shifted to Geneva, where Director-General Sutherland's carefully orchestrated strategy was paying dividends. Considerable quiet progress had been made in a number of areas, including services, agriculture, intellectual-property rights, dispute settlement and the new trade organization. Revised texts for almost all sections of the full agreement were distributed on December 6. The final critical pieces now quickly began to fall into place.

Sutherland's principal procedural vehicle at this point was his chairmanship of a plenary group of delegation heads, which had been meeting regularly and as of December 10 went into continuous session. Many participants questioned the plenary-group approach as unwieldy compared to the more-limited participation "green room" deliberations of the Dunkel years. But Sutherland believed in openness and made it work through a heavy-handed approach of reviewing portions of the agreement text and then "gavelling" them through as final and approved. Delegates grumbled and joked about Peter's quick gavel, but they realized that it was working and accepted it. They placed "reserves" on particular points in the text and made statements "for the record," even though no records were being kept of these meetings.

Several major issues, however, required special treatment. For agriculture, Chairman Denis moved the agreement forward at the multilateral level even while the United States and the EU continued negotiating revisions bilaterally in the Blair House text. Two central objectives were expansion of the country lists of offers to liberalize imports and "tariffication"—the conversion of quantitative and other import barriers to a single fixed tariff. As of mid-September, only forty-three participants had tabled offer lists, in some cases of very limited scope. Subsequent intensive bilateral and small-group negotiations increased this number to eighty-four by December 15, and product coverage had broadened considerably. Tariffication posed a problem for thirteen participants, including Canada, Indonesia, Korea, Mexico, Norway, Japan, Switzerland, and Venezuela. One by one, most of these countries were persuaded to accept tariffication, with negotiated offsetting concessions, although some, including Canada, Mexico, and Norway, did not accept comprehensive tariffication until December 14.

The two most difficult and important countries for tariffication in the agricultural sector were Japan and Korea. In each case, the final deal accepted a six-year delay in full tariffication in return for an immediate commitment on market access for imports—particularly for rice, which was currently banned. Japan accepted immediate rice imports of 4 percent of consumption, rising to 8 percent over six years. Korea, far more resistant, would go no further than 1 percent immediately, rising to 4 percent. The process for arriving at these agreements consisted of a combination of strong U.S. bilateral pressures and intensive multilateral negotiations in Geneva.

The political repercussions to the final outcome for rice were very different in Tokyo and Seoul. Japanese Prime Minister Morihiro Hosokawa announced on December 7 that his country would open its market to rice imports because it benefited from the world's free-trade system and thus needed to bear a proportional burden for successful conclusion of the Uruguay Round. The news of this pending commitment had been rumored for a couple of weeks, and the Japanese public reacted relatively mildly despite the political sensitivity accorded rice farmers. In contrast, on December 9, South Korean President Kim Young-Sam announced the undertaking to liberalize rice imports and apologized publicly for breaking his presidential campaign pledge not to do so. He posed the question: "Are we to live as an orphan by rejecting the GATT system, or lead our country toward globalization and internationalization by accepting the GATT framework?"[29] The Korean people, taken more by surprise, were not prepared for such a display of international leadership, and rioting broke out in the streets, much of it anti-American.

One of the most contentious final areas was textiles and apparel, especially because of President Clinton's written pledge to members of the Congress related to the NAFTA vote. The United States pressed to extend the phaseout of import quotas from ten to fifteen years but ran into total opposition from both industrialized and developing countries, and it had to back down. The other major U.S. objective was to get textile-exporting nations, particularly the large Asian economies, to open their markets in this sector on a reciprocal basis. Asian exporters were highly competitive for most textile and apparel products but maintained ironclad restrictions on their own markets, while the United States, the EU, and other industrialized countries were potential exporters of textile fabrics and some quality lines of apparel. The United States and the EU developed a joint proposal that Mickey Kantor presented to Ambassadors Balkrishan Zutshi of India and Ahmad Kamal of Pakistan. It stated that any nation failing to provide "effective access for textiles and clothing" would be excluded from the ten-year quota phaseout. The South Asians rejected the proposal and tensions rose. Director-General Sutherland, exercising his delayed mediator role, convened a stormy session in his office that went long into the night of December 14. Finally, at 3:30 A.M. on December 15, Rufus Yerxa, chief deputy to Mickey Kantor, made a last effort by proposing to change the existing phrase "promote improved access" to "achieve improved access." The South Asians remained silent and Sutherland declared the issue resolved.[30]

The United States had been forced to back down almost entirely in the textiles sector, but was not prepared to do so with respect to the proposed antidumping code. The draft code attempted to place restraints on the unilateral application of antidumping duties, which was subject to protectionist abuse, particularly in the United States. U.S. negotiators had presented eleven key changes to the draft code that would effectively maintain existing U.S. freedom of action in this area. Jeffrey Garten, Department of Commerce undersecretary and senior U.S. negotiator, arrived in Geneva insisting that all eleven changes be accepted. He was credibly supported by an avalanche of congressional and private-sector leaders with antidumping as their top priority. Senate Finance Committee Chairman Patrick Moynihan and senior committee member Jay Rockefeller held a series of meetings with an ultimatum warning about committee support for the Uruguay Round agreement. Senate Minority Leader Robert Dole and House Majority Leader Richard Gephardt led a group of eleven corporate leaders, representing steel, semiconductor, automobile, and other sectors who delivered a similar message. Various other members of the Congress, including Chairman Dan Rostenkowski of the House Ways and Means Committee and countless industry representatives, added to the antidumping blitz. The peremptory manner of the U.S. lobbying irritated others, but they also accepted political realty and were prepared to make limited further concessions.

On Sunday morning, December 12, plenary heads of delegation found themselves at an impasse on the antidumping text, and Peter Sutherland convened his first and only restricted "green room" meeting of about 20 key delegates. It would also be the last "green room" meeting, since shortly after the conclusion of the round this renown negotiating venue would be painted a more neutral color. The two most difficult issues were the "standards of review," which delineated the scope of enquiry for dispute panels and "anticircumvention" actions against indirect dumping through third countries. The standards-of-review issue was resolved first, essentially continuing existing GATT practice of not challenging the standards applied by importing countries. Other U.S.-requested changes were negotiated one-by-one during the long day session that extended into the evening. Finally, only anticircumvention remained. After a break for consultation, U.S. Deputy Trade Representative Rufus Yerxa returned without his Department of Commerce colleague Garten to announce a preference to expunge all references to permissible anticircumvention action, thus again maintaining the status quo, which does not explicitly accept or challenge such actions. Agreement was thus achieved, with the United States publicly claiming that it had obtained eight out the eleven proposed changes and others quietly reporting home that the score was more even.

Almost all other issues had been agreed during the previous weeks of intense negotiations or with relatively minor final changes, including framework agreements for trade in services and intellectual property rights, a revised dispute-settlement mechanism, trade-related investment measures, safeguards, and phytosanitary measures. For the subsidies code, the United States, which had always pressed to minimize GATT-sanctioned "green light" subsidies, reversed its position and insisted that the degree of subsidy permitted for research and development be increased from the 50- and 25-percent levels for "industrial research" and "precompetitive development activity," respectively—as in the Dunkel Draft—to 75 and 50 percent, a reflection of the Clinton administration policy to subsidize commercially promising new technologies.[31] Market-access commitments for traded goods were broadened as more countries put forward offers, and further commitments were expected even after the December 15 deadline.

Market access for trade in services ended up more limited in scope than many had hoped, and key sectors were left for post–Uruguay Round negotiation. For maritime services, the United States had offered to liberalize port and ancillary facilities but not ocean shipping, while the EU, pressed by Danish and Greek shipping interests, insisted on all or nothing, and the final result was nothing. For financial services, the Untied States had proposed in November a two-tiered system providing future market liberalization on a conditional MFN basis. This derogation from the GATT-sacrosanct MFN principle brought howls of protest from others, and Peter Sutherland had to call U.S. Treasury Secretary Lloyd Bentsen to seek a solution. In the end, negotiations on an MFN commitment for financial services, as well as for basic telecommunications services, were left to continue on beyond the conclusion of the round.

As December 15 loomed, the focus of final negotiations reverted back from the multilateral arena to a U.S.-EU bilateral context. The two major bilateral issues remained, government support for commercial aircraft production and European restrictions on U.S. audiovisual services. Negotiators settled the aircraft issue by stretching out the negotiation of a multilateral accord into the post–Uruguay Round period, but the audiovisual dispute proved far more difficult and politically charged. In effect, it pitted deeply felt French cultural identity against Hollywood.

The French film industry, like other European filmmakers, faced devastating American competition in a new era of mass communications and technological innovation. But while others tended to seek joint ventures with Hollywood, the French government steadfastly supported an independent film industry through large subsidies and the recently adopted EU directive that permitted member governments to limit non-European television programs to 49 percent of viewing time. The U.S. negotiating priority to reduce these restrictions, in turn, reflected far more than the fact that films and television programs constituted a major U.S. export industry. California was suffering a severe recession after decades of buoyant growth and would likely be a decisive state for the 1996 presidential elections. Defense cutbacks, accelerated by the Clinton administration, were a major cause of the recession, and President Clinton's personal commitment to open the European market for U.S. audiovisual services in the Uruguay Round could be a positive offset. The Clintons enjoyed socializing with the predominantly liberal Hollywood social set, and the film industry had organized lucrative political fund-raisers for the president. Californian Mickey Kantor's personal contacts with film-industry interests added a personal touch to the negotiating drama. It was hard to conceive that the Uruguay Round would fail over the issue of American films on Parisian prime time television when all other issues, including agriculture, had been settled, but that specter continued to capture press headlines on the morning of December 14.

Mickey Kantor and Leon Brittan labored throughout December 13 and on into the night at the U.S. trade mission in Geneva. At 6:00 A.M. on December 14, the most that Sir Leon could offer his American counterpart was a binding commitment that the existing 49 percent limit on non-European television programs would not be reduced further, and that negotiations to change the French levies on box office tickets and blank audio and video cassettes, used to subsidize French filmmakers, would begin "as soon as possible." A weary Kantor called President Clinton to report the situation, and shortly after the president called back to say the offer was not good enough. Kantor then informed Brittan, "We're backing away from the table." In other words, the dispute would continue on beyond the Uruguay Round. The two men took a break for a shower and a change of clothes before holding a mid-morning joint press conference to announce the failure of the audio-visual services negotiations, agreement on other outstanding issues, and a now virtually certain overall successful conclusion of the Uruguay Round, characterized by Kantor as "a truly historic trade agreement."[32]

The very last major issue to be resolved was adoption of the proposed new Multilateral Trade Organization to succeed the GATT and incorporate all facets of the Uruguay Round agreement.[33] The United States had resisted the creation of such a permanent new organization for more than a year, concerned that it could restrict U.S. freedom of action on trade matters and perhaps change the heretofore pragmatic GATT trade forum into a more politicized UN-type body. Concessions had earlier been made to the United States, particularly with respect to voting procedures and, like another dog that didn't bark, the absence of press reporting on this issue was an indication that the United States was prepared to accept the new institution once all other substantive issues were resolved. On the morning of December 15, the MTO draft text had still not been adopted and had become linked to other unresolved issues in the intellectual-property rights and subsidies agreements.[34] The United States then offered to accept the MTO text provided the other issues were resolved to its satisfaction and that the name of the new organization be changed from the Multilateral Trade Organization to the World Trade Organization (WTO). Mickey Kantor considered the former too bureaucratic while the latter had more "pop" and political appeal.[35] Other weary delegates accepted the last-minute name change with good grace even while the final text was being circulated to the press with the MTO appellation still prominently intact. The fact that World Trade Organization was the original name proposed by Canada almost four years earlier was politely ignored.

The final symbolic act by Director-General Sutherland to conclude the Uruguay Round negotiations on December 15, like so many previous negotiating deadlines, appropriately fell behind schedule. Delegates went on for 90 minutes of unscheduled speeches while the press and television crews fretted and the celebratory champagne grew warm. Finally, Peter Sutherland's turn came for brief remarks, after which, with one resounding blow of the gavel, he solemnly declared the Uruguay Round negotiations concluded. Then, as applause and cheers within the crowded hall built toward a crescendo, Sutherland lifted his gavel high in the air and, with a broad Irish smile, conveyed to all the world—live via CNN—that a very far-reaching and historic trade accord had been achieved.

Press and Public Reactions

Press reactions in industrialized countries to the December 15 agreement were overwhelmingly favorable, but to a large extent reactions were more expressions of relief than of euphoria. There was general agreement that the new accord symbolized a strengthened commitment to free trade and a more equitable trading system. At the same time, however, some trade disputes remained unresolved and prevalent protectionist forces continued to pose a threat to open markets. Broad-based credit was given to President Clinton and Mickey Kantor for their leadership. The French press predictably hailed the victory of French diplomacy. A sampling of commentary[36]:

> The war of nerves has come to an end, and everybody can sigh with relief: the states, their economies and the consumers. . . .

The conclusion of the agreement, even though it is not perfect, will influence the global economy like a warm April shower.

Frankfurter Allgemeine, Germany, December 16.

The agreement will force member nations to make painful industrial adjustments in a short period. Nevertheless, the GATT deals will allow them to expand their export opportunities and increase the incomes of their people. The Round agreements will also serve to help overcome the slumping global economy.

Yomiuri, Japan, December 16.

With the GATT round wrapped up, the Clinton Administration has countered its critics and established its pragmatic free trade credentials. . . . For the United States has shown that it can and will, at virtually the same time, pursue a multilateral GATT deal and use bilateral trade muscle—such as against Japan—in the interests of levering open foreign markets to American exports.

Australian Financial Review, Australia, December 16.

We have a global trade deal . . . because the United States and Europe finally got their wheels down on agriculture and some, but not all, of the other crucial areas that divided them. . . . the result is a partial deal that is better than no deal but far short of what could have been achieved.

Toronto Globe & Mail, Canada, December 16.

The happy ending of the Uruguay Round is good news for world trade. But all differences have not been totally resolved. . . . a positive conclusion of the round does not definitively push away the specter of an America continuing to defend itself with unilateral weapons. . . . The Geneva compromise is first an important, positive political result for France . . . and even more for Europe which . . . managed to show its cohesion.

Le Monde, France, December 16.

The Clinton Administration has shown itself, in the crunch, willing to cut a deal, even when it said it would not, in the pursuit of the broader goal. . . . Much of the individual credit on the U.S. side must lie with Mr. Mickey Kantor . . . who can never again be accused by sniffy Europeans and Washington trade experts of not knowing his brief. But he takes his instructions from his President—and, on both NAFTA and the round, Bill Clinton was intimately involved in much of the fine print.

Financial Times, United Kingdom, December 16.

The trade agreement is good for the U.S. and good for the world. Its real importance lies less in its individual provisions than in its vibrant message; the world's trading partners have now pledged to keep marching relentlessly toward liberalized trade. And that, in turn, will bring higher living standards than any government policy will.

New York Times, United States, December 16.

Developing-country press reactions were mixed. They broadly recognized that more open trade and a strengthened multilateral trading system was in the interest of developing countries. The ideological attacks on the GATT of a decade earlier were largely—but not entirely—absent. Wider-ranging criticism of the agreement, however, focused on the lower priority afforded specific trading interests of the poorer countries and on the fact that they were excluded from bargaining sessions dominated by the large industrialized powers. A sampling of commentary:

> If the Uruguay Round of trade negotiations has become one of the more controversial GATT rounds it is because of the intransigence of the developed economies, especially the United States and the European Community, and the selfish manner in which they have defended their economic interests at the cost of the developing world. However, despite this regrettable lack of balance in the final outcome, it is extremely important for India to remain a part of the multilateral trading system.
>
> *Times of India,* India, December 16.

> What is important is that the victory of agreement over divergence between countries shows that the developed world shows a system of mutually recognized and accepted rules to the individualist protectionism, which had been growing in international relations in the 1990s. . . . The accord, which evidently does not resolve all problems but is a large step toward disciplining international trade . . . also serves to strengthen international recognition that protectionism was and is backwardness in terms of governmental policy and administrative practice.
>
> *Jornal da Tarde,* Brazil, December 16.

> The success of the final stage of the GATT talks reflects the recognition by world leaders from both the industrialized and developing nations that global free trade is beneficial . . . (and) that short term risks are worth taking to obtain long term benefits.
>
> *Analisa,* Indonesia, December 15.

> If the treaty does the work intended, which is to keep markets open by statute, it will be a wondrous new world that the 21st

century opens to. . . . But let no one be under the illusion that
GATT makes for a perfect market mechanism. It would be foolish
to assume that protectionist instincts have been deadened just because 117 signatory nations say they wish to trade with one another.

Straits Times, Singapore, December 17.

The accord . . . took a significant step toward the removal of
myopic restrictions in the interchange of goods and services
among the countries around the globe. The treaty . . . will increase global income by some $300 billion dollars yearly . . . and
while it will not benefit all countries equally, it allowed the con-
spicuous spokesmen to say that no one there had left a loser. All
had won.

La Prensa, Argentina, December 22.

As far as the whole world is concerned, free trade favors Europe and the United States, which hold strong economic power;
the countries who suffer the losses are developing countries in
the Third World. . . . The compromises made by Europe and the
United States are temporary, not a permanent peace. During the
negotiations, France won "complete victory" on the issues of agriculture, audio-visual, world trade organization and means of protecting trade. This has greatly strengthened the position of French
hardliners, such as Prime Minister Balladur, against the United
States, which will affect future relations between France and the
United States, and between Europe and the United States.

Guang Ming Daily, China, December 20.

The agreement . . . was in truth an accord between the United
States and the European Union. For all the drama that the world
was endangered if the seven-year old GATT talks were allowed to
collapse, the under-developed world was accurately absent at the
talks. . . . The new GATT agreements are merely a conspiracy between the United States and Europe to divide the trade and wealth
of the world among themselves. It is not the GATT of the whole
world but that of the rich and powerful.

Vanguard, Nigeria, December 22.

Governments were understandably more upbeat in claiming victory for
the final agreement since, among other things, they were now faced with
securing treaty ratification. Even developing country governments, while
more qualified in their support of the agreement, could not, as they did at the

conclusion of the Tokyo Round, decry the results and boycott the final ceremony. This time, membership in the new World Trade Organization depended on ratification of almost the entire set of Uruguay Round agreements.[37] Beyond these political realities, however, there was near unanimous recognition that the final Uruguay Round result was a major achievement and certainly far superior to the collapse or unraveling process that had constantly threatened the negotiations.

On a personal note, President Clinton's approval rating rose from 50 percent in November to 58 percent in December, largely as a result of his strong leadership in support of open trade. Protectionist interests were muted in their criticism, and even the motion picture industry tempered its disappointment and avoided personal rebuke of the president. Leon Brittan also received wide credit for protecting European interests while achieving a substantial agreement, and speculation rose about his long shot candidacy to succeed Jacques Delors as president of the European Commission. Prime Minister Balladur received a 58 percent public-approval rating for his defense of French interests, versus only 31 percent negative ratings, boosting his future presidential prospects within France. The positive French public reaction was only slightly tarnished by Foreign Minister Juppé's widely quoted quip, "I never want to hear about GATT again."[38] Prime Minister Hosokawa of Japan also received generally favorable ratings for handling the difficult rice-import issue in the context of broader Japanese trade interests. The only immediate casualty from the Uruguay Round agreement was South Korean Prime Minister Hwang In-Sung, who was forced to resign on December 16 in the aftermath of the riots triggered by the last-minute decision to permit some rice imports.

December 15, however, was not the end of the Uruguay Round. It was the point of final agreement on all major issues of negotiation, but many loose ends remained. Final offers on market access for goods were left open for additions until February 15, 1994. The "positive lists" for sectoral inclusion in the services agreement also needed clarification and amplification. In any event, the date for signing the final agreement was set for April 15, the last day of President Clinton's legal authority to do so, which would take place at a ministerial-level meeting in Marrakesh, Morocco. The accompanying ministerial decisions would have to address preparations and perhaps substantive objectives for the new World Trade Organization, which would become a subject of intense negotiation. The weary Uruguay Round negotiators deserved a year-end holiday respite, but they faced a busy home-stretch schedule through April 15.

Marrakesh Decisions

The substantive loose ends of the Uruguay Round agreement were time-consuming for the GATT secretariat and member missions in Geneva from January through March 1994, but relatively uneventful. Twenty-two thousand pages of final offer lists for tariff reductions and other commitments required careful checking, which uncovered gaps from earlier "conditional" offers later withdrawn from the final lists. This provoked some acrimony about how explicit the conditions had been, but a significant unraveling of December 15 offer lists was avoided. Director-General Sutherland insisted that the December 15 lists could only be expanded, not reduced. Pressure was put on Japan, in particular, to expand its final list, although in the end no additional commitments were forthcoming. The most important development during this process was the expansion and consolidation of country market-access commitments for trade in services. Many developing countries had submitted very limited or no sectoral lists of market access for services by December 15, but as of the beginning of April, after laborious prodding by the secretariat's director, David Hartridge, in particular, more forthcoming lists arrived from seventy-seven developing countries as well as from the thirteen industrialized participants, counting the EU as one.

Principal attention during the first months of 1994 was on the launching and substantive priorities for the new WTO, to be adopted by ministers at the mid-April Marrakesh meeting. Three ministerial decisions were prepared for launching the WTO: one for acceptance of and accession to the organization, the second related to financial consequences, and the third to establish a Preparatory Committee, chaired by Peter Sutherland, to organize preparations for entry into force of the WTO on January 1, 1995.[39]

Far more controversial preparations for the ministerial meeting involved substantive objectives for the WTO. A logical course would have been for ministers to bask in the euphoria of Uruguay Round accomplishments and leave the WTO agenda for future WTO deliberations. In any event, a severe case of GATT fatigue prevailed in capitals. But the United States, true to past form, quickly took strong initiative to propose three priority new areas for negotiation within the WTO: competition policy, trade and the environment, and labor standards. Competition policy, although subject to wide-ranging definition of scope, was broadly viewed as an important and appropriate item for the WTO work program. Environmental and labor standards, in contrast, were highly contentious, although with important differences regarding their relationship to the international trading system.

The relationship between trade policy and environmental standards had been the subject of extensive discussion within the GATT since 1991, even though key questions concerning possible trade sanctions to achieve environmental objectives had not been fully confronted. Developing countries, in particular, worried that such sanctions would be used against them, and they resisted specific commitments before the WTO even came into being. There was never any doubt, however, that the trade/environment interface would be addressed in some manner by the new trade organization. The WTO preamble states, among other things, that trade relations should be conducted, among other things, "both to protect and preserve the environment," and it had earlier been agreed that the relationship between trade and environmental measures would be examined with a view toward making "appropriate recommendations on whether any modifications of the provisions of the multilateral trading system are required."[40] The United States pressed for a specified work program, and after prolonged debate, the Preparatory Committee agreed to a declaration by ministers at the Marrakesh meeting (see Appendix D). It created a WTO Committee on Trade and Environment, which was to report to the first WTO ministerial conference, anticipated for late 1996. The committee mandate included broad terms of reference and seven specific initial issues to be addressed. It was especially noteworthy that the ministers at Marrakesh adopted only four decisions beyond the December 15 agreement. Three dealt solely with organizational matters related to the launching of the WTO, and the only substantive issue singled out for a separate ministerial decision was trade and the environment.

The U.S. objective to bring labor standards within the WTO faced broader and more adamant opposition. U.S. attempts to place labor standards on the Uruguay Round agenda in 1986 had failed, and resistance by others, especially developing countries, had not abated. Labor issues were more politically sensitive at the national level, and the likelihood of labor standards being used for protectionist purposes was evident from statements emanating from the U.S. Congress. The only firm ally of the United States in pressing for labor standards was France—which further increased concerns about protectionist motives. Heated negotiations dragged out until April 7, only a week before the Marrakesh meeting, when the United States reluctantly accepted a face-saving reference to labor standards in the concluding remarks of the conference chairman as one of eleven enumerated issues raised by ministers during the course of the ministerial meeting.[41] There was no reference to labor standards in the ministerial statements.

With resolution of the labor-standards issue, the April 12–15 ministerial meeting at Marrakesh, Morocco, became a strictly ceremonial affair, with ministers graciously received by King Hassan II and chic Moroccan hostesses at the ornate Palais des Congrès. The obligatory round of ministerial speeches stressed the themes of the most ambitious trade negotiation in history and the challenge ahead for the new trade organization. The conference chairman, Foreign Minister Sergio Bonilla of Uruguay, rightly raised the issue of implementation and warned of the need to "strengthen our determination to honour the commitments which we will issue with the signature of the Final Act." Peter Sutherland added appropriate local color: "Few trading caravans can have viewed this beautiful city with as much pleasure—and as much relief—as ours does. But then very few trading caravans were on the road for more than seven years, and none carried such a precious cargo." The potentially most newsworthy speech came from Vice President Al Gore, sent by President Clinton to highlight U.S. interest in environmental and labor standards, but the vice president modulated his remarks in keeping with the ministerial outcome. A quick eleven lines denied U.S. protectionist interests in pressing for international labor standards. Fifty-three lines followed elaborating the environmental challenge and extolling the creation of the WTO Trade and Environment Committee: "As the world moves to resolve environmental problems and strengthen environmental protection, the corresponding trade implications will have to be discussed openly in the World Trade Organization."

The more than seven hundred journalists who made the trip to the popular resort city sought newsworthy copy during the first two days in side meetings between ministers. A U.S.-EU agreement was finally concluded on the long-standing issue of liberalized public procurement. Less progress was achieved on a dispute between Central American countries and the EU over access to the European market for bananas. A meeting between Japan's foreign minister and soon-to-be prime minister, Tsutomu Hata, and U.S. Trade Representative Kantor raised unrealized hopes of progress on stalled bilateral trade talks.

The four ministerial decisions were duly adopted on April 14, and a final signing ceremony in the glittering Salle Royale followed the next day. It took more than three hours for the representatives of 117 Uruguay Round participants to sign the basic agreement and several subsidiary documents. King Hassan II welcomed this "gigantic step forward towards broader and more intensive international cooperation," and the ministers adopted a statement declaring "the work of the Trade Negotiations Committee to be complete and the Uruguay Round finally concluded."[42]

Ratification of the New WTO

All that remained was ratification of the agreement, which was virtually assured for all major trading nations except the United States. Some problems arose elsewhere. Japan had to call a special session of the Diet to obtain approval before the January 1, 1995, date for WTO inauguration. A procedural wrangle within the EU over the relative ratification roles of the Commission and the European Assembly threatened to delay approval into 1995. Protests against the agreement occurred in various developing countries, most notably India, where Arthur Dunkel of the infamous Dunkel Draft became the target: "Because of Dunkel, the noose of slavery is going to tighten around our necks!" Tear gas and water canon dispersed one hundred thousand leftist protesters in New Delhi, but a parliamentary majority for approval of the agreement was assured.[43]

Only in the United States was the outcome uncertain. There Congress held constitutional authority for the regulation of trade, and it lacked anything resembling party discipline on trade policy. The political end game in Washington would prove just as harrowing as the many crises that characterized the long and troubled course of the Uruguay Round. The congressional debate began soon after the December 15 agreement and continued on through the spring and summer. Republican senators objected to the higher levels of subsidies permitted for R&D—which the U.S. negotiators had pushed through in the closing days of the negotiation—and sought a rollback of this element of the agreement. Questions arose about the loss of national sovereignty from WTO membership, and from the strengthened dispute-settlement mechanism in particular. Environmental groups, who had split over NAFTA approval, closed ranks to oppose the Uruguay Round agreement, although they had little apparent influence on congressional votes. Ross Perot, consumer advocate Ralph Nader, and conservative Republican Patrick Buchanan launched a broad attack against the agreement. The AFL-CIO, twice burned in failed efforts to defeat fast-track renewal in 1990 and the NAFTA in 1992, criticized but did not openly oppose it. Protectionist interests, sensing an ultimate positive vote, concentrated on changes in the proposed implementing legislation. They obtained more restrictive language concerning antidumping procedures and textile imports, although the legislation presumably still complied with the agreement.

Two difficult issues were not part of the agreement, but they dragged on into September and almost became fatal. One was the request by President Clinton to link renewal of fast-track authority to negotiate future free-trade agreements, particularly in the Western Hemisphere, to the Uruguay Round vote. It bogged down in partisan debate over the inclusion of environmental and labor standards in future agreements, which Republicans strongly opposed, and President Clinton finally dropped his request. The second issue involved the required budget offset, wherein revenues lost over ten years through Uruguay Round tariff reductions had to be made up elsewhere. Ultimately, a compromise was reached whereby $12 billion of lost revenues during the first five years of Uruguay Round implementation was compensated and a waiver sought for the remaining five years—which would require sixty votes in the Senate.

All issues were thus apparently resolved by late September, but the president and his congressional strategists, preoccupied with health care and other matters, had waited too long. One Democratic senator, Ernest Hollings of the textile producing state of South Carolina, exercised his right as chairman of the Commerce Committee to delay a vote for sixty days, beyond the November 8 congressional elections. The president, taken by surprise, countered with the unusual step of reconvening the lame-duck Congress after the elections solely to vote on the Uruguay Round agreement. Meanwhile, the Republicans won a sweeping electoral victory to gain control of both houses of the Congress, and opponents of the agreement had a new argument for postponing the vote until the following year when, among other things, fast-track authority would have expired and the outcome placed in grave doubt.

An international chorus, led by Peter Sutherland, warned of the consequences for U.S. leadership should the Congress fail to approve the agreement, yet Senate Finance Committee Chairman Patrick Moynihan in October claimed only twenty-six committed yes votes. The Senate Republican leader, Robert Dole, held the key and exacted his price. Certain provisions of the budget offset would be reviewed, and in a concession to Republican senators concerned about sovereignty, a panel of retired U.S. judges would independently monitor the WTO dispute panel findings. A congressional vote on U.S. withdrawal from the WTO might follow if the judges disagreed with WTO panels three times in five years.

On Wednesday, November 23, just before the Thanksgiving Day weekend, Dole and the president reached agreement, and with Dole's belated endorsement, critical Republican senators quickly fell into line and momentum grew for a large positive vote. On November 29, the House voted 288–146 in support of the implementing legislation, and on December 1 the Senate voted first, 68–32, for the budget waiver and then, 76–24, for the legislation. The substantial majorities in both parties supporting the agreement contrasted to the 1993

NAFTA vote, when a majority of Democrats voted against the agreement only to be offset by an even larger positive Republican vote. A surprisingly strong bipartisan reaffirmation of a liberal trade policy had been achieved. President Clinton signed the legislation on December 8, and the United States at last became a confident founding member of the WTO.

Others who had held back awaiting the outcome in Washington acted promptly to approve the Uruguay Round agreement, and by January 1, 1995, eighty-one nations representing more than 90 percent of world trade had ratified it. All major industrialized countries signed on, as did key developing countries such as Argentina, Brazil, India, Indonesia, Nigeria, and South Korea. The final weeks before January 1, however, also highlighted two unresolved matters that were harbingers for the difficulties facing the new World Trade Organization.

The first was the impasse over negotiations for Chinese entry into the WTO as a founding member. Intensive negotiations during previous months covered a wide range of initial commitments by China, including agriculture, financial services, currency convertibility, national treatment, and enforcement of intellectual-property laws. Underlying the negotiations was the question of whether China would participate in the WTO as a developing country, with all of the accompanying "special and differential" treatment, or as some form of transitional industrialized country. The United States took the lead in insisting on broad and specific Chinese commitments to open trade, and other industrialized countries closed ranks with the Americans in the final weeks of negotiation. China believed the United States would ultimately back down, but it didn't, and further negotiations were postponed until 1995.

The second matter was selection of a director-general for the WTO. The unanimous approval of Peter Sutherland as director-general of the GATT in June 1993 had been widely viewed as a bridging move for Sutherland to continue on as director-general of the new WTO. Shortly after Marrakesch in April 1994, however, Sutherland announced that, for personal reasons, he would not accept WTO leadership and planned to step down at the end of the year. Three candidates quickly emerged, each from a different region. Outgoing Mexican President Carlos Salinas de Gortari was the most distinguished, particularly for having led his country on a path of market reforms, trade liberalization, and free trade through NAFTA. Kim Chulsu, South Korea's minister of trade and industry, and former Italian Trade Minister Renato Ruggiero were the other two. A heated campaign quickly took shape, and support largely followed regional lines. The Western Hemisphere favored Salinas, Asia backed Chulsu, and Europe and much of Africa went for Ruggiero. This tendency toward UN-style regional candidates and vote counting by nation-states was disturbing in that it ran counter to the opening sentence of the Uruguay Round agreement on WTO decision-making: "The WTO shall continue the practice of decision-making by consensus followed under GATT 1947." The Europeans, who had always filled the top position in the GATT, were most outspoken about majority nation-state voting. Ruggiero's votes, however, consisted of fifteen EU member states, up to ten pending new EU members, and a large number of African states associated with the EU. The first major WTO decision was fast becoming the kind of sovereignty issue that had troubled the U.S. Congress. On December 21, Peter Sutherland agreed to stay on as the interim director-general through March 15, 1995, while deliberations continued over selection of a full-term director-general. Early in 1995, the Salinas candidacy collapsed in the face of the Mexican financial crisis, and Renato Ruggiero was finally and, by the United States, grudgingly selected as the first director-general of the WTO in late March.

On these unsettling notes, the WTO came into being on January 1, 1995. Peter Sutherland proclaimed the event "an important milestone in history" and, with reference to the large number of nations who had ratified the Uruguay Round agreement, he declared, "It's a marvelous start for the World Trade Organization and a very good omen for the future."[44] The event was clearly an important historical milestone, but the start was somewhat marred rather than marvelous. The new challenge of leadership in world trade, in capitals as in Geneva, and under circumstances far different from those that prevailed when the Uruguay Round began, still lay ahead.

EIGHT

The Final Agreement: An Assessment

The final agreement that emerged from the foregoing saga of international commercial diplomacy can be assessed in four somewhat overlapping dimensions. The first examines the negotiating process itself, the complex GATT "round" phenomenon, addressed here as "Anatomy of a Negotiation." The second dimension reviews major elements of the agreement with interpretive comment as to the content and relationship to original objectives. The third assesses quantitatively the impact of the agreement on world income and trade, while the fourth explores the significance of the new World Trade Organization (WTO) institutional framework.

Anatomy of a Negotiation

The previous chapters detailed what was without question the most complex and protracted multilateral trade negotiation in history. What can we deduce concerning the process, strategy, and tactics of a major international negotiation? The following conclusions have particular relevance for what should come next for the international trading system—the subject of the final two chapters of this work.

1. *The comprehensive "round" strategy.* This traditional GATT approach of setting a broad agenda so as to have a balance of interests among trading partners, and thus the basis for a "package" final agreement offsetting "concessions" and "benefits" for each participant[1] was far more ambitious in the Uruguay Round than for any previous round. The seven earlier rounds dealt primarily with tariff reductions, which lend themselves to a measured balance of benefits, and in any event, the packaging took place almost entirely among the industrialized country grouping. The Uruguay Round agreement, in sharp contrast, extended to important new areas of policy commitments and included developing countries in a major way. The industrialized countries sought commitments in the areas of trade in services, intellectual-property rights, and trade-related investment measures, while developing countries were interested in textiles, agriculture, safeguards, and antidumping. Tariff reductions, less prominent in the early phase of negotiations, became far more so toward the end. Agricul-

185

ture was, of course, central, pitting the EU—and Japan and South Korea with respect to rice—against the United States and the Cairns group of agricultural exporters. Other issues involved distinctive alignments of interests, while the significance of various commitments was influenced by the integrated dispute-settlement mechanism.

This unprecedentedly comprehensive round strategy did, in the end, work despite many misgivings throughout the negotiations that it was too ambitious and complicated. There was a weakening of the draft agreement for some issues, particularly in the final phase of negotiations, but this was to be expected. The overall result generally lived up to expectations as established at Punta del Este—and then some. In contrast, it is doubtful that such politically sensitive issues as agriculture, textiles, and intellectual-property rights, to name only a few, could have been negotiated with comparable result on an individual basis.

The success of the package approach in the Uruguay Round does not mean it is necessarily the most efficient or desirable route for future negotiations to liberalize trade. There is direct competition from more limited geographic approaches, such as regional free-trade agreements and bilateral initiatives as pursued by the United States and Japan. There may be some functional areas of policy that lend themselves to a self-contained balance of interests, perhaps the trade-environment policy relationship, for example. The most likely outcome, addressed in the next chapter, is some combination, as was, in fact, the experience during the Uruguay Round period. The most persistent criticism of the GATT round approach, however, is that it simply takes too long.

2. *Extended time framework.* The full Uruguay Round ran thirteen years, from U.S. Trade Representative William Brock's call for a comprehensive new trade initiative, as an urgent matter, in June 1981, until the signing of the final agreement in April 1994. This was about twice as long as the previous Kennedy and Tokyo Rounds, and is unanimously considered to be far too long. Particular criticism focuses on the lengthy five-year preparatory stage, from 1981 until formal negotiations were launched in September 1986, and the more-than-three-year delay in concluding the negotiations beyond the scheduled December 1990 date. As a result, there is a widely held view that the comprehensive GATT round approach has outlived its usefulness.

This negative view, nurtured in the frustrations of numerous missed Uruguay Round deadlines, is not justified. The extended delays during the preparatory phase and the prolonged final negotiating stage arose from specific circumstances during the 1980s, which will not be relevant for the period ahead. The five-year preparatory stage involved an impasse between the industrialized and developing countries stemming in part from disagreement over the final outcome of the Tokyo Round and in part from developing-country resistance to broadening the GATT mandate to include services and intellectual-property rights. The three-year extension of the final deadline was solely due to the unyielding U.S. challenge to the European Common Agricultural Policy, which had not happened in previous GATT rounds and will not be an issue again during the 1990s.

There has been considerable speculation that the end of the cold war weakened the cohesion of the industrialized democracies and that this was a major cause of the protracted, crisis-ridden Uruguay Round. A close examination of the negotiation, however, does not bear this out. A reduced U.S. commitment to NATO was a rumored threat at times during the Uruguay Round just as it was in the Kennedy Round twenty-five years earlier. In fact, the transatlantic showdown over agriculture was overwhelmingly a matter of internal American and European politics in the 1980s just as it had been in the 1960s. The difference was that in the 1980s the United States held firm against European farm export subsidies even if that meant dragging out and possibly scuttling the Uruguay Round.

This isn't to say that a new round could be negotiated more expeditiously— for example, one to two years of preparatory work leading to three to four years of formal negotiations. New circumstances could have an equally prolonging effect on such a new initiative. What is crucial is that the agenda and the underlying political basis for a multilateral, comprehensive initiative be carefully developed beforehand.

3. *Reciprocity and the free rider.* The dominant bargaining concept underlying previous GATT rounds was "reciprocity" in the sense that major participants would lower trade barriers by a comparable overall degree or percentage. For example, 50 percent tariff cuts were the norm in the Kennedy Round and one-third reductions in the Tokyo Round. A similar one-third average reduction in tariffs was adopted as an Uruguay Round objective at the Montreal ministerial meeting in 1988. Participants expected that a common percentage reduction would lead to roughly comparable increases in market access on a reciprocal basis.

This underlying concept was modified substantially during the Uruguay Round, mainly at U.S. initiative. The competing concept of reciprocity envisioned a common end result in terms of access to markets, pursued on a sector-by-sector basis. For tariff reductions, the prominent zero-for-zero tariff elimination goal for selected sectors was one manifestation, as was the harmonized tariff objective for the chemicals sector. U.S. insistence on improved market access for basic telecommunications and financial services as a condition for a most-favored-nation commitment in the services agreement was a more important departure from tradition. The final result in the textile sector of linking the phaseout of import quotas to improved market access in the Asian exporting countries was yet another example. Ironically, the most important Uruguay Round result based on the traditional approach of equal percentage cuts involved farm export subsidies through the 21–36 percent reductions over six years that emerged from the Blair House Accord.

A related issue of reciprocity is the "free rider" syndrome, in which developing countries, in particular, traditionally offered more modest or even insignificant reductions in trade barriers on the grounds that full reciprocity was inimical to their development objectives. This syndrome greatly weakened in concept during the Uruguay Round years. In part, the strong export competitiveness achieved by East Asian and other newly industrialized economies belied the need for "special and differential treatment" in GATT commitments. More broadly, the open trade, market-oriented development strategy came to dominate official thinking North and South during the course of the 1980s. The NAFTA was the crowning blow against the free-rider rationale in that Mexico agreed to comprehensive free trade with the United States on an almost totally reciprocal basis even though it started with a much higher level of protection. The Uruguay Round agreement, as a result, contains a higher level of developing-country commitments than was the case in past negotiations, although there are still important differential aspects, and the overall provisions of GATT Part IV, providing special treatment for developing countries, remains in place.

The net result is that the concept of reciprocity for future negotiations within the WTO remains very much up in the air. A revised status for developing countries will depend, in important respects, on how the Uruguay Round agreement is implemented. For example, initial deliberations of WTO bodies, including dispute-settlement findings and interpretation of commitments for services and intellectual-property rights, will create significant precedents. The transitional terms for Chinese accession to the WTO will also highlight the question of comparable market access for the more advanced developing countries. In any event, more fundamental thinking about the basis for reciprocal market access within the new trade organization is in order.

4. *Risk in packaging.* A comprehensive agenda, as was the case for the Uruguay Round, leads to a point in the negotiations where the issues need to

be brought together for a package conclusion, balancing the priority interests of the various participants. A central tactical issue is how to do this
at a relatively high common denominator result while, in any event,
avoiding a general unraveling toward a minimum outcome. A successful
outcome requires both timely initiative and a degree of risk taking. Recalcitrant negotiators, under constituent pressure not to be forthcoming,
tend to hold back unless faced with some form of threat or ultimatum. A
credible ultimatum, in turn, carries risk since, if the recalcitrant parties
still say no, the threat presumably will be carried out.

Two such tactical initiatives during the Uruguay Round were of critical
importance and largely responsible for the very substantial final agreement.
The first was Arthur Dunkel's initiative in December 1991 to put forward a
comprehensive draft agreement as something of a last-chance ultimatum.
Governments were put at a tactical disadvantage since they had been unable
to bridge a number of important differences as the negotiations drifted toward
the expiration of President Bush's negotiating authority. The Dunkel Draft
contained a judicious balance of high-level commitments whereby a withdrawal of any single major component would have led almost certainly to a
broad unraveling if not a collapse of the negotiations. He presented governments, in effect, with a Pandora's box, which basically held together with one
major exception, agriculture.[2]

The second tactical initiative, by President Bush and Trade Representative
Carla Hills, dealt with the agricultural impasse and involved even greater risk.
The immediate threat of U.S. retaliation against European white wine and
other agricultural exports by the lame-duck U.S. administration was fully credible. If the Europeans were still unwilling to make binding Uruguay Round
commitments to reduce farm export subsidies, in particular, a transatlantic
trade war was almost certain, which could have destroyed the Uruguay Round
in the process. The tactic succeeded, however, and the Blair House Accord,
despite vigorous French efforts to undo it later, basically held together. A Pandora's box within a Pandora's box had been constructed, and together they
provided the framework for the final Uruguay Round agreement.

The lesson of this Uruguay Round experience for future wTO negotiations,
and international negotiations more broadly, is that able negotiators, willing
to take judicious risks as well as initiative, constitute a vital ingredient for
success. It is the tactical dimension to the broader issue of leadership.

5. *The leadership role.* A multilateral endeavor, especially one involving
   more than one hundred participants of widely varying national interests,
   requires strong leadership. The United States played that role during

nearly half a century of GATT negotiations and continued to do so throughout the Uruguay Round. The initial conceptual framework and diplomatic impulse that led to Punta came from Washington, and dominant U.S. leadership continued almost until the conclusion of the round. This was in part through self-interested habit, in part by default. A habit of assuming leadership in world trade has been deeply embedded in three generations of U.S. political leaders and trade-policy practitioners. U.S. private-sector leaders were also the only ones fully engaged in the Uruguay Round negotiating process, largely in pursuit of their particular interests but generally with a sense of global responsibility as well. The EU, in contrast, remains predominantly regional in economic outlook, while the complex process of internal decision-making can greatly inhibit strong international initiative by the Commission. French opposition to trade liberalization for agriculture and a time-tested trade negotiating posture of holding back concessions until the very end further curtailed European initiative at the Community or Union level. Japan, the only other contender for world leadership in trade, remains on the defensive about access to its market and is culturally reticent about taking strong initiatives in international trade negotiations.

The dominant U.S. leadership role weakened somewhat, however, during the final stages of the Uruguay Round, particularly through much of 1993 under the Democratic administration of President Clinton. Growing U.S. protectionist pressures to pull back from key provisions in the draft agreement and initial hesitancy on the part of the new president to take charge of trade policy slowed the political momentum for liberal trade. EU leadership under Commissioner Leon Brittan, however, took up some of the slack and became surprisingly more assertive, shifting the final Uruguay Round leadership to a more balanced U.S.-EU orientation. A stronger role by Director-General Sutherland and other senior secretariat staff also contributed to more broadly based leadership during the final phase of the negotiations.

As for the future, a central question for the WTO is how the United States will exercise its leadership role, both within the WTO and in pursuit of other regional and bilateral trade-policy objectives, A related question is to what extent a more balanced leadership will evolve, involving perhaps a measure of "cessation of sovereignty" as posed by Professor Kindleberger. Both of these questions will be pursued in the concluding chapters.

The Elements of Agreement

The final Uruguay Round agreement of December 15, 1993, consisted of 424 pages divided into twenty-eight sections.[3] It was later supplemented by country lists of tariff reductions and other market access commitments totaling more than twenty-two thousand pages. The table of contents of the December 15 agreement appears in appendix C. The summary provided here is limited to a brief description and interpretive comment for each of the eleven most important components of the agreement, followed by even briefer description of other provisions. The portions of the agreement dealing with the adoption and operation of the WTO are left for the final section of this chapter.

1. *Market access for nonagricultural goods.* The industrialized countries reduced tariffs on industrial products (excluding petroleum) by 40 percent on a trade-weighted average, covering $737 billion of total imports, while the share of imports bound at zero duty more than doubled from 20 to 44 percent.[4] Tariff bindings for this category of goods were extended from 94 percent to 99 percent of imports. Comparable tariff cuts by developing countries resulted in a 20-percent average reduction covering $305 billion, while tariff bindings were extended from 14 percent to 59 percent of imports. Average tariff levels were reduced from 6.3 percent to 3.8 percent for industrialized countries and from 15.3 percent to 12.3 percent for developing countries. Tariff reductions by industrialized countries, however, were very uneven by sector. Tariffs were eliminated for most construction and medical equipment, agricultural machinery, steel, beer, distilled spirits, pharmaceuticals, paper, toys, and furniture. Tariffs were harmonized at low rates of zero to 6.5 percent for chemicals, and reductions of 50 percent or more were achieved for segments of the electronics, wood, and nonferrous metals sectors. For textiles and apparel, tariffs were reduced by an average of only 20 percent, although the parallel phaseout of quota restrictions will have an additional strong export-stimulating effect for developing countries. This sector is discussed in greater detail below. Most tariff reductions are to be phased in over five years beginning July 1, 1995, but some will be implemented immediately and others, in sensitive sectors, are subject to phase-in periods of up to ten years.

   Comment: The tariff reductions go beyond the objective of a one-third average reduction adopted at Montreal in 1988. The zero-for-zero elimination of tariffs for eight major sectors establishes a pattern of free trade by sector, which could be pursued further in future negotiations.

2. *Agriculture.* This sector was brought for the first time within the GATT multilateral trading system through a framework of commitments covering internal support measures, export subsidies, and market access for imports. Internal support programs are to be reduced on average by 20 percent from the base level and bound against future increase. Support

programs that have no or minimal trade distorting or production effects (i.e., "green box"), as well as some other measures that meet designated criteria, will be exempted from the reductions.

Export subsidies are to be reduced by 36 percent in value and 21 percent in quantity over a six-year period, with 1991–92 as the base period. The reductions are applied to specific products or product groups, such as wheat and wheat flour, coarse grains, oilseeds, skim-milk powder, and sugar.

Market access for imports will be based on a process of "tariffication" whereby all nontariff barriers, such as variable levies, quotas, import bans, and voluntary export restraints are converted to a single fixed tariff. Existing market access will be maintained through tariff quotas and minimum access levels established where initial tariffs are very high. Tariffication of Japanese and South Korean rice imports is postponed for six years in conjunction with slightly higher initial minimum access levels. Existing and new tariffs resulting from tariffication will be reduced on average by 36 percent for industrialized countries and 24 percent for developing countries, phased in over ten years with a minimum reduction of 15 and 10 percent, respectively, for each tariff line.

Comment: The reductions in internal support measures will likely have limited impact on restraining surplus production in Europe and the United States, since such reductions had already been undertaken to a large extent by the time the agreement was concluded. Moreover, increased productivity can offset reduced government support measures. The export subsidy quantitative commitments, in contrast, will reduce existing levels of subsidized exports by about one-fifth while at the same time reserving all growth in world trade to nonsubsidized exports. The highly specific discipline of this commitment, however, raises the question of what will happen if, in particular, EU farmers continue to produce large surpluses. The tariffication–market-access framework represents fundamental change from the traditional widespread use of nontariff barriers for agriculture. It effectively ends the forty years of exclusion of most of agriculture from basic GATT rules, which began with the waiver obtained by the United States in 1955 and the subsequent implementation of the EC variable levy system. The initial tariff levels after tariffication, however, will often be extremely high, some above 100 percent, and there is no procedure to verify the new tariff levels, which may lead to excessively high "dirty tariffication." Consequently, the 36-percent average reduction will still leave many rates very high. A provision in the agreement for continuing the reform process, including further reductions in trade-distorting barriers, calls for negotiations to begin in the fifth year of implementation, but the political will to undertake substantial further reductions in agricultural trade barriers remains to be seen.

3. *Textiles and clothing.* This sector will be integrated into the GATT system over 10 years and subject to the same disciplines as other sectors. The key provisions pertain to the phaseout of existing import quotas, improved market access in all participating countries, and safeguards during the transition period.

Quotas will be removed in four stages based on the volume of imports in 1990: 16 percent immediately, 17 percent after three years, 18 percent after seven years, and the remaining 51 percent at the end of the ten-year transition period. In parallel, quotas are to be enlarged at a faster rate than in the past, which should result in increases ranging from 16 percent to more than 100 percent during the ten-year period.

Improved market access applies to all countries, industrialized and developing, in the form of tariff cuts and reduction or elimination of nontariff barriers. Many countries also agreed to comprehensive bindings of existing tariff rates. Tariff cuts, however, are relatively modest, 20 percent on average by the industrialized countries, including only 12 percent by the United States.

Safeguards that permit import quotas to avoid damaging surges of imports were more precisely specified for the transition period. The concepts of cumulative damage to industry from multiple import sources and quota circumvention through transshipment through countries not subject to quotas are clearly established.

Comment: The integration of the textiles and apparel sector into the GATT system, as for agriculture, represents a major achievement. Doubts have been raised, however, as to whether industrialized-country bilateral quotas will in fact be fully eliminated if imports threaten to grow rapidly. The agreement, in any event, is "backloaded" in that the 51 percent of import quotas left for the end of the ten-year transition will include the most import-sensitive products. The unclear degree of corresponding trade liberalization undertaken by developing countries, particularly in Asia, could become a pretext for challenging the agreement. The uncertain status of China as a member of the WTO also casts a cloud over the future trade prospects in this sector. Nevertheless, progressive liberalization during the initial years, as provided in the agreement, should reduce the continuous trade friction caused by the bilateral-quota approach over the past four decades.

4. *Services.* The General Agreement on Trade in Services (GATS) provides a framework of rules and principles for trade in services and the basis for future negotiations to reduce barriers that discriminate against foreign

service providers and deny them market access. The framework agreement includes most-favored-nation (MFN) treatment, national treatment, safeguards, transparency, dispute settlement, and the free flow of payments and transfers. These general principles are augmented by sectoral annexes dealing with financial, telecommunications, maritime, and aviation services, and movement of personnel. Disputes over GATS commitments will be settled within the WTO integrated dispute-settlement mechanism, with explicit allowance for cross retaliation.

The framework agreement is complemented by country schedules of national treatment and other market access commitments by sector. The country coverage is highest for tourism and travel services, relatively high for business, communications, engineering, and financial services, and lower for education and health services. Sector coverage is relatively complete for industrialized countries and considerably lower for most developing countries.

Provision is made for negotiations at five-year intervals to progressively broaden national treatment coverage and other market-access commitments for services as well as to provide framework provisions for areas not initially covered by the GATS, such as subsidies, government procurement, and emergency safeguard actions.

Comment: During the Uruguay Round preparatory stage through the Punta del Este conference, any binding commitments for services and their incorporation into the GATT system were widely resisted by developing countries. Thus the final outcome goes well beyond expectations. A comprehensive framework agreement brings this rapidly expanding sector of trade fully within the world trading system. Follow-up negotiations in 1995 and 1996 for inclusion of an MFN commitment by the Untied States for basic telecommunications and financial services are important because these sectors play a central role in service-driven economies. It is especially ironic that the United States held back on financial services because the most prominent early proponents for inclusion of the services sector in the multilateral trading system were the heads of such companies as American Express, AIG, and Citicorp. The sector coverage for national treatment and other market-access commitments basically constitutes a standstill on existing market access, leaving market liberalization for scheduled future negotiations, but this two-stage approach was recognized as early as the Montreal ministerial meeting in 1988. Finally, the services agreement is noteworthy in that it brings international investment policy into the WTO for this sector in a comprehensive way. National treatment for foreign providers of services involves, by definition, rights of establishment and other conditions for doing business by foreign direct investors.

5. *Intellectual-property rights.* The trade-related intellectual property rights
(TRIPs) agreement establishes strengthened standards for protection of
the full range of intellectual-property rights and the enforcement of these
standards both internally and at the border. Intellectual-property rights
covered by the agreement are patents, copyrights, trademarks, industrial
designs, trade secrets, integrated circuits, and geographical indicators. Enforcement provisions for the maintenance of standards internally and border protection against counterfeiting and piracy are subject to the WTO
dispute-settlement mechanism.

Patent protection extends twenty years from the date of application, covering patents for virtually all types of investment, and limitations are placed
on compulsory licensing. Copyright protection extends beyond literary works
to sound recordings, motion pictures, computer programs, and data bases, and
members are obligated to comply with provisions of the Berne convention. The
transition for compliance with the TRIPs agreement is one year for industrialized countries and five years for developing countries, but an extended ten-
year transition for the pharmaceutical sector applies in developing countries.

Comment: The strong and sweeping provisions of the TRIPs agreement
are even more striking, given the expectations as late as the 1988 Montreal
meeting, when India and other developing countries still strongly resisted
inclusion of trade-related intellectual-property rights in the trading system.
The integrated WTO dispute settlement mechanism, including provision for
cross retaliation of trade sanctions for violation of the TRIPs agreement, is a
critical linkage. The negotiations in this sector evolved from a predominantly
North/South orientation from 1986 to 1988 to a largely North/North orientation in the latter years of negotiation, as the United States, the EC, and Japan
grappled with the growing complexities of intellectual-property rights in
technology-intensive sectors. Considerable further negotiation toward common standards and procedures will surely take place in the future. The U.S.
pharmaceutical industry was deeply disappointed by the lengthy transition
period for its intellectual-property rights in developing countries, which could
lead to further bilateral U.S. initiatives to strengthen patent protection in this
sector, but such actions will be influenced by the degree to which developing
countries move toward compliance with the multilateral agreement.

6. *Trade-related investment measures.* The trade-related investment measures (TRIMs) agreement reinforces GATT provisions in that no such designated measures should be applied that are inconsistent with the GATT.
An illustrative list defines the initial scope of prohibited measures, specifically identifying local content, trade-balancing, and foreign-exchange
balancing requirements as falling within this prohibition. The important

category of export-performance requirements, however, is omitted from the list. Measures are prohibited whether they are mandatory conditions on investment or are required in return for an incentive/advantage. A transition for elimination of such existing TRIMs is two years for industrialized countries, five years for developing countries, and seven years for the least developed countries.

Not later than five years after the WTO takes force, there will be a review of the operation of the TRIMs agreement, at which time the WTO Council for Trade in Goods will consider whether the agreement should be complemented with additional provisions on investment and competition policies.

Comment: For this third of the three new issues proposed by the United States at Punta del Este (in addition to services and intellectual-property rights), the more modest objective was largely accomplished against widespread skeptical expectations. The issue almost dropped off the agenda at Punta and was largely neglected during the early course of the negotiations. The explicit prohibitions address some of the most flagrant trade-distorting investment measures in developing countries, and could head off a growing tendency in the United States and the EU to consider local content requirements as well. TRIMs, however, constitute only a small part of international investment policy, the one major area of international economic policy not covered by multilateral commitments. The linkage of the Uruguay Round agreement to possible future negotiations on investment and competition policies presents an opportunity to close this gap.

7. *Antidumping.* The revised antidumping agreement provides greater transparency and specification for antidumping procedures. Investigative authorities are required to provide public notice and written explanation of their actions. The agreement defines in greater detail the methodology authorities may apply in conducting antidumping investigations, including the definition of *de minimus* margins (2 percent of export price) and negligible imports (normally less than 3 percent of total imports) for purposes of terminating an investigation. Antidumping disputes will be assessed by WTO dispute-settlement panels.

Four specific provisions insisted on by the United States during the final stages of the negotiations pertained to circumvention, cumulation, determination of fair value, and standard for review. The agreement, in the end, is moot on the issue of circumvention, thus permitting the continued application of existing U.S. anticircumvention criteria, although subject to challenge by dispute panels. It authorizes the "cumulation" practice of collectively assessing injury based on imports from several countries and the disregarding of certain below-cost sales in defining fair value. The standard-of-review provision for dispute-settlement panels acknowledges that there may be more than one permissible interpretation of the agreement or facts and requires panels to defer to permissible interpretations by WTO members.

Comment: The final Uruguay Round result will not change greatly existing GATT practices for handling antidumping disputes, although procedures and some criteria are more clearly specified. The standard-of-review interpretation, for example, continues to limit the ability of dispute panels to challenge assessments by the importing countries and their application of antidumping duties. Antidumping actions will become increasingly prominent as more and more countries develop and apply laws patterned on the pro-active U.S. approach. The provision in the trade-related-investment-measures agreement that requires a review of investment and competition policies within five years thus has timely relevance since antidumping measures constitute a second-best "trade remedy" under existing circumstances of great diversity in national approaches to antitrust and other areas of competition policy.

8. *Subsidies and countervailing measures.* The agreement establishes clearer rules and stronger disciplines in the subsidies area while also making certain subsidies exempt from countervailing duty actions. Three categories, red-, amber-, and green-light subsidies, deal, respectively, with prohibited subsidies, permissible subsidies subject to countervailing duties if they cause adverse trade effects, and permissible subsidies exempt from countervailing duty actions. Export subsidies are prohibited, including de facto export subsidies and subsidies contingent on the use of local content. Adverse trade effect is defined more precisely through price effect or market share, with a presumption of "serious prejudice" in situations where the total ad valorem subsidization exceeds 5 percent or when subsidies are provided for debt relief or to cover operating losses. A special framework for developing countries provides for the gradual elimination over eight years of export and local content subsidies, but with a quick two-year phaseout for highly competitive export industries.

Green-light permissible subsidies are provided for specified government assistance for industrial research and development, regional development, and adaptation of plant and equipment to environmental requirements. Assistance is limited for "industrial research" to 75 percent of eligible costs and for "precompetitive development activity" (i.e., through the creation of the first, noncommercial prototype) to 50 percent. Government assistance for regional development is exempt from countervailing duties under certain criteria, most importantly, that the assistance not be targeted to a specific industry or group of recipients within the region. Green-light government assistance to meet environmental requirements is limited to a one-time measure for up to 20 percent of the costs of adapting existing facilities to new environmental standards.

Comment: The new agreement provides greater specificity to GATT disciplines, although important sectors of trade troubled by subsidies, such as steel and commercial aircraft production, will continue to be dealt with outside the WTO. The subsidy code is also limited to trade in goods and not services, where the U.S.-EU audiovisual impasse in the Uruguay Round carries on beyond the round. Much attention focused on the three categories of green-light permissible subsidies, and it is not clear how the technical definitions that establish the basis for exemption from countervailing duties will be interpreted in test cases. The provisions for gradual elimination of export subsidies by developing countries are vague, while in the interim developing-country exports continue to be subject to countervailing duty actions by industrialized countries.

9. *Government procurement.* The agreement on government procurement strengthens the disciplines applicable to government procurement and expands coverage to new areas of procurement. New disciplines include the requirement to inform losing bidders promptly of decisions on contract award and the provision for timely, transparent, and effective procedures for losing bidders to challenge alleged breaches in procedures as contained in the agreement. The WTO dispute-settlement mechanism is applicable to review disputes, but without authorization to assess trade retaliation.

The scope of the agreement is expanded beyond government procurement of goods to include procurement of services and construction, as well as some coverage of subcentral governments and government-owned utilities. The effective scope of the agreement has been expanded substantially and will apply annually to about $400 billion in procurement contracts, of which three-quarters are in the EU and the United States. This agreement is the only major part of the Uruguay Round package, however, that allows voluntary rather than full participation, and signatories remain essentially the industrialized grouping. The scope of the agreement is also limited by extensive lists of exceptions for key sectors such as transportation, power generation, and telecommunications.

Comment: The strengthened WTO agreement provides a framework for a further expansion of international competitive bidding for government procurement. This can be pursued through future WTO multilateral initiatives to broaden the scope of sectoral coverage and to include additional countries as signatories. It can also be pursued outside the WTO in ongoing negotiations between the United States, the EU, and Japan, and through comprehensive regional free trade agreements such as the NAFTA. Mexico, for example, agreed to fairly comprehensive commitments on government procurement in the NAFTA but did not sign the Uruguay Round agreement.

10. *Safeguards.* The safeguards provisions of GATT Article XIX are elaborated to ensure that such temporary import restrictions are transparent, temporary, degressive, and subject to review and termination. Voluntary export restraints (VERS) are also included for the first time. Injury determinations are more precisely defined and subject to a public hearing and a public report giving an analysis of the reasons for the decision. Safeguard actions are permitted for a maximum of eight years, and existing voluntary restraint agreements are to be phased out within four years. However, each country is allowed one "grandfathered" exception, which the EU used for its automotive-sector voluntary-restraint agreement with Japan. The agreement provides for suspending the automatic right of retaliation during the first three years of a safeguard measure as an incentive for countries to use the GATT procedure rather than to negotiate "voluntary" agreements outside the GATT. Restrictions need to be steadily liberalized over the period of application. With respect to the critical issue of applying restrictions on a selective basis, the agreement states that, as a general rule, restrictions shall be applied to a product "irrespective of its source," but exceptions are permitted under certain circumstances after consultations within the Committee on Safeguards.

Comment: The tightened safeguards provisions finally resolve the issue that eluded Tokyo Round negotiators and caused developing countries to boycott the signing of that agreement in 1979. One principal tradeoff is the suspension of retaliation for three years provided safeguard restrictions are implemented in accordance with the agreement. The key issue during the Tokyo and Uruguay Rounds of selective versus universal application of import restrictions was finessed through the special criteria for selectivity, and experience with the new provisions will determine how this compromise works out in practice.

11. *Sanitary and phytosanitary measures (S&P).* This agreement establishes rules and disciplines for measures taken to protect human, animal, and plant life and health in the areas of food safety and agriculture. Such measures include quarantine procedures, food processing, inspection

rules, and the establishment of pesticide tolerances. The agreement is intended to prevent the use of S&P measures as disguised barriers to trade, and requires measures to be based on scientific principles and evidence and to avoid discrimination between imported and domestic products. The agreement generally requires use of international standards, but governments are free to adopt more stringent measures based on available scientific evidence and risk assessment as provided in the agreement. Consultations related to the agreement are undertaken by a Committee on Sanitary and Phytosanitary Measures and disputes are handled by the general WTO dispute-settlement mechanism.

Comment: This highly technical part of the agricultural section of the agreement represents a significant achievement for harmonizing scientifically based standards in an area potentially subject to protectionist abuse. This area of negotiation also raised issues about the relationship between trade and environmental objectives, and environmentalist groups targeted it as possibly downgrading environmental objectives. The language in the Dunkel Draft stipulating that parties shall ensure that sanitary measures are "the least restrictive to trade" was revised to "not more trade restrictive than required" to avoid the implication of a weakened priority for high environmental standards.

Other noteworthy sections of the agreement are:

Import licensing procedures. The agreement more precisely defines automatic and nonautomatic licensing procedures, including a twenty-one-day period for license application and a maximum processing time of thirty to sixty days. New licensing procedures are subject to prior public notification.

Customs valuation. The agreement amends the existing GATT code through clarification of rights and obligations in cases of suspected fraud, sympathetic consideration for requests to retain officially established minimum value, and encouragement of developing countries to study concerns expressed about valuation of imported goods.

Preshipment inspection. Tighter disciplines are adopted for prompt and transparent preshipment inspection procedures, including those of private companies engaged by governments. A binding review procedure to resolve disputes is placed under the joint supervision of the International Chamber of Commerce and the International Federation of Inspection Agencies.

Rules of origin. A three-year work program is established to harmonize rules of origin, to be carried out by committees of the GATT and the Customs

Cooperation Council. Disciplines to be incorporated in the harmonized rules include nondiscrimination between traded and domestic goods and a maximum assessment period of 150 days.

Technical barriers to trade. The agreement provides greater specificity to the existing GATT code for standards, technical regulations, and conformity assessment procedures (e.g., registration, inspection, and laboratory accreditation). Each country has the right to determine the appropriate level of standards for life, health, and the environment, and the encouraged use of international standards does not require any downward harmonization. At the same time, the agreement seeks to ensure that product standards do not create unnecessary barriers to trade.

GATT *Articles.* This section of the agreement incorporates the results of the negotiating group that sought to improve various articles of the GATT. The most important result concerns more tightly drawn disciplines for temporary trade restrictions related to balance-of-payments problems (Article XVIII). Import quotas are limited to circumstances of a "critical balance-of-payments situation" and the need to arrest "a sharp deterioration in the external payments position." Otherwise, price-based measures such as import surcharges on an across-the-board basis are required, with specified exceptions. Other noteworthy results pertain to greater conformity of state-trading enterprises (Article XVII) and clarification of rules for the formation of customs unions and free-trade agreements (Article XXIV).

The Impact on World Income and Trade

The impact of the Uruguay Round agreement on world income and trade cannot be projected with any degree of accuracy although rough orders of magnitude can be assessed. A central methodological difficulty concerns the distinction between the "static" and "dynamic" effects of trade liberalization. Static effects involve the impact of changes in relative prices between domestically produced and imported goods—and services—when a tariff or other trade barrier is reduced.[5] The manner in which the good or service is produced is assumed to remain unchanged, stated more technically as "constant returns to scale." The dynamic effects, in contrast, stem from changes in the way goods and services are produced caused by the lowering of trade barriers or other actions to facilitate trade, and have multiple causes. A more open and predictable trading system has the dynamic effect of improving the climate for investment and technological innovation. Expanded world markets raise the rate of return for investment by lowering production costs through economies of scale and by spreading research and development costs more widely. Increased competition from imports forces firms to cut costs and accelerate technological innovation to remain competitive, as happened in the U.S. automobile industry during the 1980s. Open trade also fosters the wider exchange of technical knowledge among nations as goods and human and physical capital move more freely. Entirely new export industries are created. This overall dynamic process of structural change has been most dramatic in those developing countries that have pursued policies of open trade and more favorable conditions for foreign investment.

The central methodological difficulty for assessing the impact of trade liberalization is that the static effects from changes in relative prices are more susceptible to quantification while the dynamic effects are considered to be of far greater consequence. Economic studies tend to concentrate on the measurable static effect results, which official and media commentary highlight, ignoring general statements about the much larger dynamic effects. The net result is a gross understatement of the positive income and trade effects from trade liberalization. This tendency toward understatement is especially serious for the Uruguay Round agreement because major parts of it— including the framework agreements for services and intellectual-property rights, the trade-related investment measures, the safeguards code, and the revised dispute settlement mechanism—relate predominantly to the dynamic effects. The major extension of tariff bindings, especially in developing countries, is another part of the agreement that will foster nonquantifiable trade-creating effects from a more predictable market for exports as well as for investment.

The assessment here provides a full accounting of the static and dynamic effects, essential to a reasonable understanding of the importance of the agreement, bearing in mind that quantification of the dynamic effects, to a large extent, can be no more than an approximate order of magnitude. The impact is assessed first in terms of world income—the true gains from trade— and then for growth in trade. More detailed commentary is provided for two areas of particular interest, the impact on developing countries and on high-technology industries.

The world income effect. Several projections of the static-effect increase in world income from the Uruguay Round agreement were undertaken toward the end of the negotiations based on projected final results. The GATT and OECD secretariats produced the most widely cited. A revised estimate by the GATT secretariat based on actual results and some further development of the estimating model was released in November 1994.[6] All three were limited to the market-access provisions of the agreement—tariff reductions, phaseout of quotas, and reduced support for agriculture—and to trade in goods but not services. The estimates were based on variations of the Computable General Equilibrium (CGE) economic model, and are roughly but not fully comparable. At the end of the ten-year implementation period for Uruguay Round commitments, the projected static gains in world income were estimated to be $220 billion (preliminary GATT), $274 billion (OECD) and $184 billion (revised GATT). This represents a range from a little more than 0.5 to almost 1 percent of world income. All three projections, however, have a downward bias for two reasons. First, the models do not fully capture the price effects among sectors, particularly for manufacturing industry. And second, the estimates only relate to the market-access provisions for trade in goods and thus leave out the trade-creating effects of all other parts of the agreement. It is thus reasonable to project an approximate 0.75 to 1 percent gain in world income from these static price effects, or about $225–$300 billion per year by the year 2005.

The full dynamic effects of the Uruguay Round agreement on world income have not been projected since there is no economic model capable of doing so. The revised GATT projection, however, does estimate some of the dynamic effects related to economies of scale and imperfect competition. When these factors are included, the $184 billion projection cited above almost triples to $510 billion. This is consistent with a number of assessments of dynamic trade effects two to five times greater than the static effects.[7] It should be emphasized, however, that the $510 billion figure suffers from the same downward biases noted above for the static effects and, in addition, does not take account of the dynamic effects from new investment and technology application stimulated by all parts of the Uruguay Round agreement, which may be the most important of all. If the full dynamic effects are taken as two to three times the static effects, the overall increase rises to a range of more than 2 percent to 4 percent of world income, or roughly $700 billion to $1.2 trillion after ten years. This is clearly a very substantial gain in world income and welfare.

A breakdown of the increased gains in income by country and groups of countries is also contained in the revised GATT secretariat projection. Based on the $510 billion figure, the EU gain is $164 billion, the United States $122 billion, Japan $27 billion, China $19 billion, Canada $12 billion, and developing countries $116 billion.[8] Again adjusting for the full static and dynamic effects, these country figures would roughly double or more.

The world trade effect. Less attention has been given to projecting increases in world trade induced by the Uruguay Round agreement, but the trade increase will clearly be considerably larger, in percentage terms, than the projected increase in world income. The revised GATT estimate comparable to the $510 billion income figure projects a 23 percent increase in the volume of merchandise exports by 2005. The projected value of the increase in exports, in 1992 dollars, is $2.8 trillion globally. A breakdown includes the EU at $569 billion, the United States $448 billion, Japan $340 billion, Canada $134 billion, China $85 billion, and developing countries $906 billion. These estimates have the same downward biases as the income figures above, and the use of 1992 dollars also understates the actual dollar figures for future trade flows.

The trade growth generated by the Uruguay Round agreement has two principal implications relating to trade balances and trade dependencies. The trade-balance effect should tend toward neutrality to the extent that all participants lower trade barriers to a comparable degree. The GATT estimate of a 23 percent global increase in exports compares with country estimates of 22 percent for the United States, 19 percent for the EU, and 18 percent for Japan, while developing countries show the largest increase, 37 percent. Moreover, other factors are likely to offset the Uruguay Round effects on trade growth during the ten-year implementation period, including macro-policy and exchange-rate adjustments. The best that can be concluded for the trade-balance effect is that it will be relatively small and should be subsumed within the broader policy framework that deals with trade balance adjustment.

The trade dependency effect of the Uruguay Round agreement is, in contrast, highly significant and has two distinct aspects. First, it accelerates the trend of deepening trade dependency throughout the world (introduced in chapter 1 in terms of "global market integration"). The ratio of world exports of goods to world income was 17 percent in 1992. If world exports increase by a net 25 percent as a result of the Uruguay Round, the dependency ratio, other things being equal, would rise to 21 percent. The Uruguay Round agreement thus will have a substantial reinforcing impact on the growing trade dependency of national economies throughout the world, with all of the policy implications this implies.

The second aspect of the trade-dependency effect from the Uruguay Round agreement relates to the deepening regional orientation of the world economy (discussed as the "tripolarization of industrial development" in chapter 1). This trend will be moderated somewhat by the Uruguay Round agreement, which works to open markets on a multilateral basis, thus diluting the preferential incentives of regional free-trade agreements and other regionally oriented policies. Quantification of this effect is not feasible, but the direction of the Uruguay Round impact is clearly toward weakening regional polarization, which is generally viewed as positive.

The impact on developing countries. The Uruguay Round agreement should provide substantial net income benefits to developing countries as a group, estimated above as $116 billion or more per year. The level of benefits will vary by country, however, depending on the composition of exports and imports and on the degree of trade liberalization undertaken, and it could be negative in some cases. Imports of grains and other agricultural products could rise in price as export subsidies are reduced. The phaseout of bilateral textile quotas will enable the more competitive exporters to gain market share at the expense of the less competitive. Margins of tariff preferences extended to developing countries will be reduced as most-favored-nation rates are cut. The "least developed" grouping of countries, largely dependent on traditional commodity exports, will receive little in direct benefits from the Uruguay Round agreement, although to the extent the agreement stimulates global economic growth the volume and price of such commodity exports should rise.

Overall, however, the dynamic effects of the Uruguay Round should be of even greater benefit to developing countries than to industrialized countries. More open and secure access to export markets should encourage investment in existing and new export industries. Uruguay Round commitments with respect to trade in services and intellectual-property rights, the phaseout of trade-related investment measures, and other technical codes, should foster higher levels of investment and export-oriented growth. President Carlos Salinas de Gortari emphasized as a principal benefit of NAFTA for Mexico that it locked in the Mexican reform program as well as access to the U.S. market, thereby giving potential investors greater confidence for investing in Mexico. The dynamic effects of the Uruguay Round will produce a similar result, weaker in content but far broader in geographic scope.

The ultimate impact of the Uruguay Round on developing countries will in any event depend critically on the economic policies pursued within each developing country. The Uruguay Round agreement, to some extent, imposes policy commitments in the direction of a more open, export-oriented economic strategy, but the underlying policy orientation and political cohesion to implement it effectively remain decisive, and the degree to which these circumstances prevail varies widely among developing countries. In economic terms, a more open and predictable trading system is a necessary but not sufficient condition for enhanced economic growth. More colloquially, you can lead a horse to water, but you cannot make him drink.

The special significance for high-technology industries. Technology-intensive industries play a more and more central role in the international trading system. Trade statistics for such industries are sketchy, in part for lack of a common definition, but all indications are that it is the fastest growing sector of trade. From 1982–92, U.S. trade in "advanced technology products" grew twice as fast as total trade and accounted for 23 percent of exports and 13 percent of imports in 1992.[9] In addition, high-technology industries constitute the leading edge for defining a broadened concept of the world trading system as an integrated process of trade in goods and services, international investment, and technology transfer. Structural change in national economies throughout the world is increasingly driven by this integrated trade-investment-technology relationship.

The Uruguay Round has special significance for high-technology industries throughout almost all provisions of the agreement. The inclusion of trade in services, intellectual-property rights, and trade-related investment measures within the trading system fits precisely with the integrated nature of high-technology trade and investment, and other parts of the agreement, including standards, government procurement, and subsidies, relate largely to it. At the same time, however, the Uruguay Round agreement has left much yet to be done in areas of policy of particular relevance to high-technology trade, and the post–Uruguay Round trade agenda, as addressed in the following chapter, will likely focus heavily on the extension of commitments in these directions.

The income and trade impact of the Uruguay Round agreement on high-technology industries is the most elusive of all to project in quantitative terms yet probably the most important over the longer term. The whole process of technology-driven structural change transmitted through international trade and investment is synonymous with the preponderant dynamic effects from trade liberalization as defined here. Viewed intuitively, it represents an enormous positive-sum game, but the actual gains from trade defy measurement because they derive from such a dynamic, ever-changing set of relationships. The considerable professional literature of the 1980s about a "new trade theory" for emerging high-technology industries focused on the relatively narrow aspect of distribution of oligopoly profits under certain circumstances, largely because this particular aspect could be assimilated into the conceptual framework that trade economists use. Unfortunately, in the process, the new trade theorists tended to ignore the far greater overall gains from trade generated by an unprecedented international wave of technological innovation and application.

One distinguished economist tried to provide a more balanced perspective: "Foreign trade tends to produce an extension of productive factors over the expanding market area . . . (which) applies with special force to the developing phase of international trade, and particularly to the trade of unequally developed areas." He went on to encourage "more positive analysis than the economists have given us of the economic effects of the enormous and increasing drift of capital and labor over the world's surface."[10] Professor John Williams wrote these words in 1929 which, among other things, indicates that some aspects of the new trade theory aren't really that new. More important, his admonition lays down a marker for trade impact analysis in the post–Uruguay Round period, when the already extensive gains from high-technology trade become even more decisive to the course of the global economy.

The New Institutional Framework

The creation of the World Trade Organization (WTO) as a strengthened multilateral framework for trade and related policies provides greater predictability in trade relationships. This, in itself, will contribute further to the Uruguay Round "dynamic effects" on growth in world income and trade. The significance of the WTO, however, goes much further. Its performance will influence the evolving structure of the overall trading system and, in particular, the relative roles of multilateral commitments, regional free-trade agreements, and selective bilateral accords.

The organizational structure of the WTO is relatively simple. A ministerial conference will be held at least every two years to provide general direction to the organization. A General Council and three subsidiary councils for trade in goods, trade in services, and trade-related aspects of intellectual-property rights, plus several standing committees are charged with implementation. Decisions are made by consensus or, failing this, by a one-nation-one-vote ballot. Some voting decisions are taken by simple majority vote while other key decisions are subject to a two-thirds or three-quarters qualified majority. Unanimity is required for amendment of certain articles of the agreement.[11]

A single secretariat, headed by the director-general, supports all activities of the WTO. The secretariat functions are modeled on the GATT experience, thus involving a relatively small staff. A prominent secretariat function is implementation of the trade-policy review mechanism established at the 1988 Montreal ministerial meeting. Country reviews have proceeded on schedule in the GATT, in a relatively low-key manner, but could become a more prominent focus for trade policy discussions within the WTO. The director-general is explicitly directed to consult with the heads of the IMF and the World Bank concerning "greater coherence in global economic policy-making," but there are no specific objectives in this regard, and the existing rather perfunctory relationship among these international economic organizations is likely to continue. Indeed, it has never been clearly established how a more integrated relationship would be useful.

The most important part of the new WTO is the integrated dispute-settlement mechanism, which replaces several dispute procedures under the GATT and bridges the major components of the Uruguay Round agreement—trade in goods, trade in services, and protection of intellectual-property rights. The threat of "cross retaliation"—for example, potential sanctions on traded goods for violations of the intellectual-property rights or services agreements—is clearly established. The revised mechanism tightens procedural disciplines to ensure prompt results from dispute panels. The earlier GATT veto power, held even by the accused party, to block formation of a dispute panel or adoption of panel findings, has been dropped, and both of these steps go forward unless the Dispute Settlement Body decides otherwise. However, an appellate review procedure is available upon request by one of the parties to the dispute, and a three-member appellate panel may uphold, modify, or reverse the findings of the original dispute panel. There is no question that the new dispute-settlement procedure will be more prompt and reliable for producing results. The question is rather the extent to which WTO members, and particularly the largest members, will utilize the mechanism for important problem issues and accept panel findings. This, in turn, will be influenced by the perceived degree of competence and nonpolitical orientation of the dispute process.

The charter for the WTO is, in fact, a minicharter compared to the articles of agreement for other international organizations. The detailed procedures for dispute settlement were under negotiation throughout the Tokyo and Uruguay Rounds and could have gone forward with or without a new trade organization. The Canadian initiative to create the new organization, late in the negotiations in 1990, principally focused on securing a strong dispute-settlement mechanism to restrain unilateral actions by larger countries, particularly the United States. Two other tactical objectives of the WTO initiative were to integrate commitments for trade in goods, trade in services, and intellectual-property rights, which had been resisted by some developing countries, and to force all Uruguay Round participants to ratify almost the entire agreement as a "single undertaking" in order to become members of the WTO. The latter result contrasts sharply with the Kennedy and Tokyo Round agreements, wherein most developing countries drew back from significant commitments at the end of the day.

Looking ahead, the central question about the WTO is whether it will be fully utilized as the central forum for trade-policy deliberations and dispute resolution. The scope of its substantive mandate is formidable in terms of national political as well as economic interests. The WTO should, on this basis alone, become *primus inter pares* in its relationship with the international financial institutions. The systemic difference between the international financial institutions and the WTO, however, is that the former have a preeminent mandate, with smaller groupings feeding into its multilateral bodies. The WTO, in contrast, is challenged in its trade mandate by a broadening network of regional free-trade groupings and selective bilateral trade relationships, and it is not clear to what extent the WTO will become central to the overall structure of trade relationships. Three aspects of WTO performance will likely weigh significantly in the balance during the initial years of its operations:

1. *Efficient management.* All WTO bodies, like their GATT predecessors, are plenary, which became more and more unwieldy as GATT membership grew from 84 in 1980 to 117 when the Uruguay Round was concluded. Such plenary bodies do not generally lend themselves to efficient operational management or serious policy discussion. Attempts to form a small executive body, including proposals put forward during the Uruguay Round within the FOGS group, were unsuccessful, and the smaller GATT members remain strongly opposed to the concept. The international financial institutions, the OECD, and other international bodies have their executive committees or informal select groups, and if the WTO does not do likewise, serious trade deliberation could well continue to take place elsewhere, such as through Quad, G-7, and OECD mechanisms, without participation of the WTO secretariat or the majority of its members.

2. *Secretariat initiative.* GATT tradition had been to place tight restraints on secretariat functions and initiatives, forcefully implemented through budget limitations. The WTO secretariat numbers 350, compared to 2,100 for the OECD, 2,500 for the International Monetary Fund, and 7,100 for the World Bank. The secretariat role increased during the course of the Uruguay Round, initially in preparing basic analytic work for the negotiating groups and then by assuming a more central leadership role during the final months of negotiation. The trade-policy review mechanism enhances secretariat responsibility for assessing member-country trade policies. But for charting the future trade agenda and getting out front on new issues, the WTO secretariat cannot compare with World Bank secretariat work with respect to developing countries and the OECD work program for industrialized-country interests. The WTO constraints are part

tradition, part budget, and part the unwieldy plenary structure of its bodies.

3. *Decision-making.* The WTO charter has reaffirmed the primacy of one-nation-one-vote just as the outlook for existing nation-state mandates is becoming less clear. Former states such as the Soviet Union, Yugoslavia, and Czechoslovakia have broken up into smaller states, some with unclear prospects for survival. In the other direction, the EU and, to a lesser extent, North America, have merged economic sovereignties in important aspects related to the WTO mandate. The imbalance between participation in world trade and legal status, including voting rights, within the WTO are stark. Fifty percent of GATT member countries in 1994 accounted for only 1 percent and 75 percent of the members for only 8 percent of world exports. The EU has fifteen votes, which could increase to twenty or more by the end of the decade, even though it is represented by a single representative in WTO bodies, compared to one vote each for the United States and Japan. Other principal international organizations have weighted or selective decision-making. The UN Security Council has a select membership with veto power for five permanent members. The international financial institutions utilize weighted majority voting throughout. The GATT has traditionally operated on the basis of consensus, but it is not clear whether the WTO will continue to do so as membership by smaller developing countries continues to grow. The entry of China and Russia may also change the political setting for decision-making.

)(

The Uruguay Round agreement, in conclusion, is a major achievement in broadening and deepening the multilateral framework for world trade. The substantive commitments extend the mandate into important new areas, especially trade in services and intellectual-property rights. The reduction in trade barriers and enhanced predictability of member-country trade policies will generate substantial growth in world income and trade. The creation of the WTO strengthens the institutional basis for the extended multilateral mandate, although organizational challenges remain to be tested. The overall result will have a major influence on the evolving orientation of the world trading system during the decade ahead, and in particular on the balance between its multilateral and regional free-trade dimensions. The Uruguay Round agreement will also affect the longer-term post–cold war world political order, which will have closely linked economic and political underpinnings.

NINE

A Trade Agenda for the 1990s

A trade agenda for the remainder of the 1990s was already taking shape at the conclusion of the Uruguay Round, just as an earlier agenda had at the end of the Tokyo Round in 1979, and at a faster pace. There were follow-up issues left unresolved in the Uruguay Round agreement. Outstanding problems related to financial, basic-telecommunications, and maritime services were to be negotiated by June 1996. The draft multilateral agreement for commercial aircraft, linked to the subsidies code, was abandoned in the final days of the Uruguay Round, as were the attempted agreement on government intervention in the steel sector and the U.S.-EU negotiations on audiovisual services. All of these issues are likely to be reengaged. The Uruguay Round agreement also explicitly calls for negotiations within five years to further service-sector and agricultural-trade liberalization and to consider WTO commitments in the areas of investment and competition policies. Finally, the ministers at Marrakesh established an agenda for discussing trade and environmental policies within the World Trade Organization, and noted a number of other issues for possible future deliberations there as well.

The full trade agenda for the 1990s, however, will address an even broader range of issues and will extend beyond the multilateral WTO framework. The process begun in the Uruguay Round to expand the mandate of the world trading system beyond trade policy in the narrow sense will inevitably continue. The meaning of the world trading system, in economic terms, is broadening to encompass an integrated set of trade, investment, and technology issues. The social-sector areas of environmental and labor policies are now inscribed on the agenda as trade-related, at least at the regional level, and the political objectives of respect for human rights and democratization have become involved in certain trade relationships as well.

The framework of the trading system to accommodate this widening agenda has also become more complex. It evolved during the 1980s into what came to be described as a three-track structure: a multilateral foundation of commitments within the WTO, a broadening set of regional free trade agreements, and selective bilateral accords. This three-track construct continues to be the appropriate framework for addressing a trade agenda for the remainder of the 1990s, although the relative importance and forward momentum of the individual tracks are likely to change, depending, to a considerable extent, on trade policies pursued by the major economic powers. The multilateral track has been greatly bolstered by the Uruguay Round agreement. Regional free trade continues to have immediate momentum in Europe, the Americas, and the Asia-Pacific region, although the longer term outlook is less certain. The bilateral track has the least clear prospect. There is presumptive reason to predict a relative decline in bilateralism as a result of the Uruguay Round, but the course of U.S. trade policy, as in the 1980s, will be decisive.

The operative question underlying this three-track structure is whether the individual tracks are being pursued in a mutually reinforcing way toward broad policy objectives, or whether they are working at cross purposes. Many examples can be cited from the 1980s of both convergent and divergent track results. The clearest case of a mutually reinforcing three-track strategy involved protection of intellectual-property rights. A multilateral framework of commitments was pursued in the Uruguay Round while the United States, under Special Section 301, pressed bilaterally with selected key countries, especially in East Asia, to strengthen national standards and their enforcement. At the regional level, Mexico, as a party to the NAFTA negotiations, adopted a model new law for the protection of intellectual-property rights. A good example in the other direction of divergent tracks was strong U.S. initiative in the Uruguay Round to prohibit content and other performance requirements in the trade-related investment measures (TRIMs) negotiations, while insisting on similar content requirements within NAFTA in order for foreign investors to benefit from regional free trade, and, at the bilateral level, pressing Japanese automobile transplants in the United States to increase U.S. content.

The following trade agenda is presented in terms of a three-track strategy, highlighting the mutually reinforcing opportunities as well as potential conflicts among the tracks. The agenda is principally predictive in terms of the most likely course of events, but normative comments are inserted at appropriate points, particularly in the concluding section. There is first the need to define the broader objectives toward which the three tracks are or should be converging. Such definition indeed deserves more serious discussion than it has thus far received. Over the short to medium term, however, which encompasses the remainder of the 1990s and then some, there is relatively broad consensus on four general objectives:

1. *Progressive lowering of trade barriers.* This simply continues the trade lib-

eralization carried forth over the past half century. It also constitutes policy reinforcement to the process of deepening trade dependency among national economies introduced in chapter 1 as "Global Market Integration." The pace of liberalization will be uneven, proceeding faster within free-trade arrangements than at the multilateral level, and in some developing countries fastest through unilateral reduction in trade barriers. There will also be sectoral exceptions, at least to a degree. Defense industries, for example, have always been protected to achieve a given level of self-sufficiency in weapons production. More important and controversial exception pertains to high-technology industries. The overall direction, however, even including high-technology industries, will likely continue to be toward progressively lower barriers to international trade and investment.

2. *Broadening the mandate of the trading system.* This objective will also continue a process begun during the 1980s, when the multilateral GATT mandate expanded to include trade in services and intellectual-property rights, while regional free-trade arrangements moved even further to include foreign investment, transportation, environmental, and labor policies. This objective is likewise unclear as to scope and pace, with regional or even bilateral initiatives more likely to be at the leading edge.

3. *Strengthening the rules and harmonizing the regulations.* This is a wide-ranging and, in some respects, highly technical area of policy. It includes much of the Uruguay Round agreement and its follow-on, as well as much of what is happening at the regional free-trade level within the EU and the NAFTA. The objective is challenged at the bilateral level, however, through special market-access arrangements, such as the EU automobile restrictions against Japan and, more broadly, U.S. attempts to obtain sector-by-sector quantitative targets for trade with Japan and perhaps other countries. Such managed trade approaches are fundamentally at odds with a rules-based trading system.

4. *More prompt and equitable dispute settlement.* This objective presented a contrast during the 1980s between the strengthened dispute-settlement mechanisms negotiated in the Uruguay Round and at the regional level within NAFTA, and a tendency toward ad hoc, bilateral dispute resolution outside formal frameworks. The period ahead is likely to see a focus on the growing number of antidumping and subsidy–countervailing-duty disputes which, in fact, bring together aspects of all four objectives presented here.

This general statement of short- to medium-term objectives is next elabo-

213

rated from the perspective of each of the three tracks, followed by a brief commentary about priorities. The ultimate question—where should the three tracks converge over the longer term?—is left for the concluding chapter.

The Multilateral Track

The multilateral track for the remainder of the 1990s will center largely on the initial performance of the newly established WTO. The immediate challenge is to establish the credibility of the organization through implementation of the comprehensive Uruguay Round agreement. Interpretation of commitments within the services and intellectual-property rights agreements will have an important bearing on attitudes about the WTO. The credibility of the revised safeguards mechanism will depend on the prompt phasing out of "voluntary" bilateral quota arrangements, as provided for in the agreement, and on the processing of any new temporary restrictions for reasons of market disruption within the revised WTO mechanism. The agricultural and textile sectors will need rigorous surveillance as inevitable political pressures build to weaken implementation. The integrated dispute-settlement mechanism cuts across almost all areas of the agreement, and the new mechanism will be observed critically, both for disputes referred to it and for those that governments choose to deal with elsewhere. Finally, the organizational issues raised earlier—effective management, secretariat initiative, and decision-making—will influence the general assessment of the initial years of WTO performance.

The WTO will also have to develop, parallel to Uruguay Round implementation, a work program—ultimately a negotiating agenda—to address identified problem areas and to further the process of multilateral trade liberalization. There will be three principal categories to consider: old-business issues left by the Uruguay Round agreement for follow-up negotiation; new social-sector issues, particularly the trade-policy relationship to environmental policy and labor practices; and a set of issues referred to here as the conditions of competition for high-technology industries.

Old-business follow-up. Specific problem issues include improved market access for basic telecommunications, financial, and audiovisual services, and government support for the commercial aircraft and steel sectors. Broader areas for future negotiation involve scheduled initiatives to improve market access for trade in services and to further liberalization of agricultural trade. The oldest business of the GATT, with continual follow-up, is the reduction and elimination of tariffs. In this area, except for a few politically sensitive sectors, tariffs are now sufficiently low that zero-for-zero tariff elimination can be pursued more broadly the next time around. The elimination of tariffs in the majority of industrial sectors, at least by the industrialized countries, would not only produce direct trade benefits but send a strong symbolic message for open trade and provide a cooperative bridge among regional free-trade groupings.

New social-sector issues. The United States is pressing to bring environmental and labor standards within the WTO mandate in a major, integrated way, and these two areas are likely to be at least as controversial as were trade in services and intellectual-property rights during the early 1980s. There are also important differences, however, between the trade/environment and the trade/labor policy interfaces.

The trade/environment relationship has already been developed to a considerable degree within the GATT, and the Marrakesh ministerial decision established an initial WTO work program. A number of technical issues are well engaged. The central unresolved issues pertain to the possible use of trade sanctions for environmental purposes. There is broad acceptance of the need for some form of sanction procedure once a multilateral environmental accord on standards is in place, for example, the trade policy response to violations of the agreement on ozone depletion. Developing countries, however, whose environmental standards in general are lower than those of industrialized countries, are extremely wary of being threatened with trade sanctions if they do not strengthen standards. The most difficult issue, which pits the United States against everyone else, is the unilateral imposition of trade sanctions against a production process in the exporting country that does not meet the environmental standards in the importing country.

The trade/labor-standards issue has a longer history, dating back to the unratified ITO charter of the late 1940s. It was pursued by the United States for inclusion on the Uruguay Round agenda. The Clinton administration is more determined than was the Reagan administration to achieve results, but resistance runs deep in many other countries as well as on the Republican side of the U.S. Congress. Whereas there is broad recognition that something has to be done about the international trade/environment interface, labor practices are primarily political issues at the national level. There is general condemnation of slave-, prison-, and child-labor practices, but the broader issues of union activities, workplace safety and health regulations and minimum wage laws, are not generally viewed as appropriate targets for trade-policy actions. Unlike environmental policy, labor policy also has a major international organization base of its own, the International Labor Organization (ILO).

Both the environmental and labor-policy linkages to the trading system

215

will be pursued during the 1990s at both the multilateral and regional levels. Actions within the multilateral WTO will likely be more limited in scope. At the regional level, these areas of policy are largely harmonized within the EU, while the NAFTA has related provisions plus side agreements, which may be extended to any additional free-trade agreements in the Western Hemisphere. Environmental issues are also on the Asia-Pacific agenda within the APEC.

Conditions of competition for high-technology industries. This may not become the official term of reference, but it is an accurate rendering of the cluster of issues affecting trade, investment, and technology transfer, particularly for technology-intensive industries. Most were the subject of Uruguay Round negotiation but with generally limited results: public procurement, technical standards, trade-related investment measures, intellectual-property rights for computer and related services, market access for telecommunications services, and government subsidies. The Uruguay Round trade-related investment measures agreement calls for a review of possible WTO commitments in the areas of competition and investment policies, which could be broadened to include most of the foregoing issues.

"High-tech industry" was proposed by the United States in 1981 as a priority area for multilateral negotiation, but it was dropped at Punta del Este in 1986 because it could not be defined clearly in terms of negotiating objectives. This definitional problem remains, but the issues loom much larger than they did a decade ago. There are various specific negotiating agendas that could be developed. An integrated sectoral approach for the telecommunications sector, with a view toward open and reciprocal market access, would be one logical starting point in view of the central position of this sector as the infrastructure for applied-information-technology goods and services. Recommendations for international technology cooperation have been developed in the OECD, and this issue could be brought within the WTO with a view to more open participation in government-supported R&D programs. The inclusion of a comprehensive agreement on international investment within the WTO would fill the one major gap in multilateral economic institutions. Underlying this entire set of substantive issues is the conceptual issue of reciprocity, which no longer fits the traditional model of equal percentage cuts in trade barriers, as applied to tariffs. The alternative concept of reasonably comparable market access at the end of the negotiation is a more appropriate approach.

A noteworthy institutional aspect of the high-technology industry grouping of issues is the relationship between the WTO and the OECD. The OECD responds to a more closely aligned set of interests among the advanced industrialized countries and has a more flexible committee structure to develop new issues, as it did for trade in services in the late 1970s. The OECD was already working on most of the high technology-related issues noted above in the late 1980s, and is picking up the pace in the post–Uruguay Round period. This presents an opportunity for mutual reinforcement between the two organizations, but also a situation of some institutional rivalry. The OECD has in the past been out front in developing new issues in analytic and policy terms, which may be the best way for the overall process to move ahead during the 1990s as well. The WTO nevertheless faces a challenge if it wishes to play the central role in developing new trade and related issues for its more broadly based constituency.

These are the key elements of what will likely constitute the multilateral track agenda for the remainder of the decade. Other issues will undoubtedly emerge, and a process of setting priorities will have to be engaged. There is finally the question of whether the issues will be pursued individually within the WTO or brought together within a new "round." Some issues, such as market access for basic telecommunications and financial services, have a specified early deadline linked to the U.S. MFN commitment in the Uruguay Round. They should move ahead on a fast track for this reason. The trade/environmental policy relationship is also under pressure to move forward promptly and may have the elements of an internally balanced package. For all of the rest, time will tell, but the diversified interests of WTO members creates an undertow momentum toward yet another comprehensive round for the 1990s, with an inspired name, to be completed by the year 2000 or shortly beyond.

The Regional Track

The regional track, which evolved decisively during the 1980s, consists of comprehensive free-trade arrangements among neighboring countries who usually have disproportionately high trade and investment interdependencies and, to varying degrees, share cultural and political roots. The adjective *comprehensive* is key in that it indicates agreements that go beyond the elimination of border impediments to trade—as stipulated in Article XXIV of the GATT—and can include such policy areas as investment, transportation, financial services, intellectual-property rights, competition, public procurement, environmental standards, and government support programs for agriculture and regional development. Such regional groupings have constituted the leading edge for integration of various trade-related policies and the general broadening of the policy scope of the world trading system.

The most important and advanced groupings in this context are, of course, the EU and the NAFTA. Other regional free trade agreements involve Australia/New Zealand, the Association of Southeast Asian Nations (ASEAN), and the Mercosur (Argentina, Brazil, Paraguay, and Uruguay), although the latter two are still at the early stages of eliminating border restrictions. In 1992 internal trade within the European free trade grouping, which included EU and EFTA members, and the NAFTA accounted for 38 percent of world trade, and a broadening of these and other regional free-trade groupings during the 1990s should raise this figure to the range of 40–50 percent.

The broadening and deepening of regional free-trade groupings will almost certainly continue over the remainder of the decade. The regional track, however, is a dynamic interactive process with no obvious state of equilibrium in sight. Charting the policy course therefore requires a higher degree of longer-term strategizing than is the case for progressive trade liberalization at the multilateral level. Next regional steps in Europe, the Americas, and the Asia Pacific region, for example, will elicit responses elsewhere, while the policy scope of regional commitments can set the stage for further commitments between the regional groupings or within the WTO. In any event, prospects are favorable for comprehensive regional free trade to grow in relative as well as absolute importance during remainder of the 1990s and beyond.

The EU has broadened its geographic scope to include most EFTA countries in 1994, and the Czech Republic, Hungary, Poland, and Slovakia will likely join by decade's end or soon thereafter. Others in Eastern and Southeastern Europe are increasingly drawn toward a dominant trade and investment relationship with the EU. Dedication to democratic government and individual rights—liberal democracy—constitutes the essential political dimension for EU membership. The extent and time frame for further Union membership is not clear, but the longer-term momentum is to polarize around and be drawn into the advanced industrialized EU economy. Slovenia and the Baltic republics are possible next-tier candidates. Turkey, Malta, Cyprus, and other Balkan countries are interested parties. Full or associate membership for Ukraine and Russia are more distant prospects with major political as well as economic implications.

The scope of policy commitments among EU members also will continue to deepen. The EC-92 market unification program requires further important decisions—concerning public procurement, for example—while steps toward monetary union will create pressures for convergence of member-state macro-policies. Environmental, labor, and other social policies will likely be harmonized further, while increased membership will intensify the need for stronger decision-making powers at the EU level, including a greater role for the European Parliament.

U.S. initiative to broaden the regional NAFTA should also continue. The ultimate objective is free trade among all nations of the hemisphere, although the route to be followed is not yet clear. Chile is next in line for full membership, and there is urgency for transitional if not full-member status for smaller Caribbean Basin countries overwhelmingly dependent on the North American market. A newly democratic Cuba could move quickly to NAFTA membership. For others in South America, the process is uncertain, with the economic and political course of Brazil a central factor. A step-by-step functional approach, establishing hemispheric agreements in such areas as investment policy, intellectual-property rights, and financial services has practical appeal.

Political cohesion based on democratic government and market-driven economies is critical for prospects in the Western Hemisphere as it is for the prospects of the European regional grouping. The NAFTA precedents covering environmental standards and labor practices add an important yet controversial social dimension to the regional relationship. The almost total absence of preferential treatment for Mexico as a developing country in the NAFTA also represents a fundamental change from the special and differential treatment North/South orientation of the GATT multilateral trading system over the past decades.

The regional trade-policy dimension for East Asia, the third highly industrialized region, is in a state of post–Uruguay Round flux. In November 1994, members of APEC—including East Asia, North America, and Chile—agreed in principle to regional free trade by 2020, with an earlier target date of 2010 for industrialized members. The "blueprint" for achieving this objective has not yet been developed, however, and there is understandable skepticism that national trading systems as diverse as those of the Untied States, Japan, South Korea, Indonesia, and China can be brought together within a common free-trade arrangement. A critical question is whether the blueprint will be consistent with GATT Article XXIV, which limits adverse impact on nonmembers or will permit more discretionary elements of "conditional MFN." In any event, drawing together trans-Pacific trading patterns will create a new dynamic relative to Europe. It could facilitate evolution of the current tripolar regional orientation of the world economy into a bipolar Europe/Asia Pacific setting.

The alternatives to an Asia-Pacific policy framework for East Asians need also be considered in view of the lengthy time frame and the political uncertainty of the APEC free-trade objective. Discussion of some form of East Asian economic grouping as a counterweight to the European and North America free-trade arrangements gathered momentum during the late 1980s and crystallized when Prime Minister Mahathir Mohamad of Malaysia called for an East Asian Economic Caucus in 1990. The caucus concept remains vague, and historic political rivalries among Japan, Korea, China, and Southeast Asian nations constitute a barrier to far-reaching economic policy commitments. Nevertheless, steadily rising trade and investment dependencies within East Asia and a shared vision of economic dominance in the next century could rekindle regional ambitions if the APEC objective should falter.

Other regions of the world, including South Asia, the Middle East, Africa, and the former Soviet Union—which together constitute a declining share of about one quarter of world trade—risk marginalization if free-trade agreements in the three advanced industrialized regions come to dominate the world trading system. A maximum Uruguay Round agreement was thus clearly in their interest, although this was not always well perceived. A further strengthening of the multilateral framework should likewise be their preferred trade strategy for the remainder of the 1990s. Another interest would be to encourage, through whatever available means, a relationship among the industrialized groupings that is open and cooperative rather than conflictive.

The overall course of the regional track is thus uncertain even over the coming five to ten years. Extended free-trade agreements in Europe and the Western Hemisphere will shift the balance between multilateral and regional trade relationships further toward the latter, while the realization of an Asia-Pacific free-trade agreement could alter the global structure of the trading system dramatically. A logical next step to avoid drift toward a bipolar European/Asian Pacific orientation would be to revive earlier proposals for a North Atlantic free-trade agreement (the original claimants to the NAFTA acronym) or an even broader arrangement among all industrialized and newly industrialized countries.

Ultimately nations must ask: are evolving regional trade groupings "building blocks" toward a more open global trading system or inwardly directed protectionist "blocs"? The distinction can be difficult to assess, but strict adherence to GATT Article XXIV is the minimum condition to avoid the protectionist bloc outcome. A further strengthening of Article XXIV provisions would be a useful priority objective for the WTO agenda.

The Bilateral Track

Selective bilateral trade agreements are of two distinct varieties. The first is unambiguous protectionism in the form of import quotas or "voluntary" restrictions on exports. These have generally been negotiated outside the GATT multilateral framework, although in some instances, most prominently the Multifiber Arrangement for textiles and apparel, with explicit GATT recognition. They can be highly specified public agreements or informal "grey area" arrangements. Such bilateral restrictions proliferated during the late 1970s and early 1980s, particularly against East Asian exporters, and their elimination became a central Uruguay Round negotiating objective for developing countries in the safeguards and textile sector negotiating groups.

The second category of bilateral agreements emanated from U.S. initiatives under Section 301 and from a series of bilateral negotiations with Japan to open targeted export markets where access was judged inadequate. This process became more structured and far more prominent with the Omnibus Trade Act of 1988. If market opening results were not forthcoming, U.S. trade sanctions were stipulated, although such sanctions were rarely implemented. The United States claims that Section 301 and related bilateral initiatives were intended to open markets on a nondiscriminatory basis, which was generally but not always the case.[1]

Although these various actions are usually referred to as bilateral, they are essentially unilateral to the extent that the initiating country is pressing its demands, under some form of threatened sanction, on an unwilling trading partner. This is distinct from the mutual interests pursued in the GATT multilateral rounds or in the creation of a regional free-trade agreement.

In light of the Uruguay Round agreement, the outlook for the bilateral track during the remainder of the 1990s is for a greatly reduced scope of bilateralism in certain important sectors, but with a continuing emphasis on the bilateral approach in other areas, particularly by the United States. The Uruguay Round agreement provides for the phaseout of textile quotas and the conversion of agricultural quotas to MFN tariffs, thus eliminating the two most prominent sectors in which bilateral quotas have long taken precedence over MFN tariff commitments. The revised Article XIX safeguards procedures call for early termination of other bilateral quota restrictions and the application of much tighter criteria for any new country-specific restrictions. Similarly, revised criteria for balance-of-payments–related restrictions under Article XVIII should reduce bilateral import quotas by developing countries.

The Uruguay Round agreement should also constrain U.S. actions under Section 301, although how this will play out in practice remains to be seen. The United States has agreed to exhaust its rights under the revised and streamlined WTO dispute-settlement procedure before having recourse to unilateral actions, but what these rights are for intellectual property and trade in services, in particular, will only become clear as the Uruguay Round agreement is applied by members and interpreted by wto dispute panels. In this context, constructive and truly bilateral negotiations in parallel with wto review would be helpful in establishing a credible framework for the new dimensions of multilateral commitments contained in the Uruguay Round agreement.

Beyond these important sectors, wherein bilateral actions should be greatly curtailed compared with the 1980s, several other lines of policy could become more prominent and largely determine the role of bilateralism in the post–Uruguay Round period. In each case the course of U.S. policy will be decisive.

The linkage of trade policy to environmental standards and labor practices is one such area where domestic political interests in the United States have created pressures for an activist unilateral approach abroad. Such initiatives are not entirely new. The tuna/dolphin dispute with Mexico is a precedent in the environmental field, while labor practices have been an issue of U.S. bilateral negotiation with developing countries over eligibility for generalized tariff preferences (GSP) and trade benefits under the Caribbean Basin Initiative. These issues could become more prominent in the post-Uruguay Round period, although this is subject to internal partisan debate, with Democrats generally in favor and Republicans opposed. The United States is also isolated in bringing unilateral pressures to bear in these politically sensitive areas and would have to weigh the broader foreign policy costs of such actions.

Other forms of bilateralism come together most prominently in the U.S.-Japan relationship. Sectoral targets for bilateral trade became the initial centerpiece of the Clinton administration trade strategy vis-à-vis Japan in 1993. Such quantitative targets are conceptually in conflict with the wto approach of market-based rules for trade and tend to discriminate against third-country trading interests. Some form of quantitative monitoring might be appropriate in exceptional cases, but a general trade framework based on quantitative targets rather than market forces, especially between the two largest trading nations, would seriously undermine the wto multilateral trading system. Proposals for overall bilateral trade-balance targets, resurgent in the United States in the early 1990s in the face of extremely large trade deficits with Japan and China, constitute an even more sweeping repudiation of the wto. Chronic trade imbalances should rather be dealt with in terms of a multilateral adjustment process with emphasis on macro-policy and exchange-rate actions.

Yet another important category of bilateral trade negotiations, also centered on the U.S.-Japan relationship, concerns improved market access based on rules and regulations rather than quantitative targets. Such actions are more compatible with the objectives of the wto multilateral system, and the results are more apt to be nondiscriminatory in that improved access to the Japanese or other targeted markets would apply equally to all trading partners. This was the case for much of the U.S.-Japan bilateral negotiations during the 1980s and early 1990s, including actions involving reduced barriers for Japanese beef and other imports, a more open distribution system, and more competitive public procurement procedures for construction contracts. Japanese political reform and economic restructuring caused by the bursting financial bubble of the late 1980s create broader mutual interests for further U.S.-Japan initiatives in this direction. In effect, the objective is convergence of the Japanese economy with the more market-oriented U.S. economy and with the free-market norms and commitments of the WTO. This is not only multilateral-bilateral "convergent track" trade strategy but the linchpin convergence for the troubled bilateral trading relationship between the two largest and most advanced industrialized nations.

The U.S.-China trade relationship will also continue to have an important bilateral dimension, even when China finally becomes a member of the WTO. The fundamental differences in trading systems and the lopsided trade balance—in the order of 4-1 in favor of China in 1994—create strong political pressures in the United States for a targeted bilateral approach. At the same time, the substantial mutual gains from trade and investment between the largest and the soon-to-be third or fourth largest trading nations should be an incentive for the two governments to develop a more balanced and satisfactory trade-policy relationship. The transition of China from a predominantly centrally planned economy to a market economy in conformance with WTO norms could be supported by a more creative and pro-active bilateral approach by both parties, yet another example of multilateral/bilateral track convergence.

The bilateral track, in sum, is an aggregate of disparate trade actions—trade expanding as well as inhibiting—with varying impact on the broader system of multilateral rules and regional free trade groupings. The Uruguay Round agreement should reduce bilateralism of a trade-restricting character, but in new areas of trade-related policies and in U.S. initiatives to open selective markets on a more comparable basis with conditions in the U.S. market, the bilateral track remains important. Indeed, the considerable results of U.S. bilateralism during the 1980s have nurtured a strong internal constituency, particularly in the U.S. Congress, to continue this path in the future. The guiding principle, however, should be that bilateral market opening or standard setting constitute a last resort when the multilateral approach alone is inadequate. Such initiatives should be clearly justified as to purpose and effect.

Finally, such bilateralism—which is for the most part unilateralism—carries a political cost for the initiator, usually the United States, which will likely become higher in the years ahead.

High-Tech Economic Nationalism/Regionalism

The foregoing synopsis of the prospective trade agenda for the remainder of the 1990s examines the multilateral, regional free-trade, and selective bilateral tracks, including noteworthy interactions among the tracks. It is a strongly pro-liberal trade projection of a trading system that continues to evolve in concert with the four broad objectives stated at the outset: a progressive lowering of trade barriers, a broadening of the trade system policy mandate, strengthened rules and regulations, and more equitable dispute-settlement procedures. The basis for this assessment rests heavily on the decisive four-week period from November 17 to December 15, 1993, when first the U.S. Congress defeated the blatantly protectionist drive against the NAFTA and then the Uruguay Round was concluded with a very high level of achievement. In the liberal trade glow of these extraordinary events, it appears extremely unlikely that nations will reverse the course for the trading system over the short to medium term. The bicycle theory has a new lease on life as the post–Uruguay Round agenda shapes up, and it will be facilitated by a somewhat downhill bicycle path that permits some coasting.

This does not mean that difficult and threatening trade issues will not arise. To the contrary, they will, and several of the most important potential challenges can be identified. Implementation of the Uruguay Round commitments in the agriculture and textiles sectors—the two traditional albatrosses for the GATT—is one such challenge. In particular, a buildup of EU farm surpluses could trigger a renewed crisis in agricultural trade. Another challenge is WTO participation for China and Russia. It is anomalous that two of the five permanent members of the UN Security Council are not full members of the WTO, and yet WTO membership, especially for the still predominantly state-controlled Chinese economy, presents major problems of assimilation with the market-based trade organization. Yet another challenge is the political divisiveness stemming from initiatives to link trade with environmental standards and labor practices.

The most threatening and overarching challenge to the world trading system, however, concerns the relationship among the advanced industrialized countries in their policies to nurture and support technology-intensive industries. The challenge essentially pits the momentum—mainly private-sector driven—toward a progressively more open, globalizing economy against what can be called high-tech economic nationalism/regionalism. The latter concept, in simplest terms, is a national or regional (EU, NAFTA) goal of higher self-sufficiency and more rapid technology development in such industries, induced by various forms of government support, so as to be more advanced than other industrialized powers and thus more competitive on world markets. In systemic terms, the national or regional track would turn inward and become protectionist for high-technology industries, placing it on a sharply divergent course from that of multilateral trade liberalization.

The debate of the 1980s over government support for technology-intensive industries continues into the 1990s with heavy political content. A critical dimension, often lost in the heat of trade-policy debate, is that broad agreement exists on the need to stimulate new-technology development for mutual benefit. Intellectual-property rights, government-sponsored basic research, and tax incentives for technology development have long been in general use and are compatible with WTO commitments. Rather, the issue is where to draw the line in other areas of policy that impact on commercial competition and in what direction existing lines should be moved.

The Uruguay Round places some constraints on government support for high-technology industries, and other issues are ripe for inclusion on the multilateral track agenda of the WTO. The principal issues, moreover, are engaged at the regional and bilateral levels as well, and how they are addressed on all three tracks during the decade ahead will shape both the challenge and the outcome for high-tech economic nationalism/regionalism.

The most important of these technology-related policy areas is investment policy, which extends beyond the relationship among industrialized countries and is critical to economic relationships at all levels of development. Multinational corporations account for one-third of world trade. Trade and investment are ever more closely linked, and in the process become the principal conveyors of new technologies across borders. The logic is for international investment policy to be incorporated within the WTO at the multilateral level. Investment policy is also a shining example for a final reprise for the three-track concept. More than one hundred bilateral investment treaties have been adopted over the past three decades, establishing broad acceptance of basic principles and commitments. Chapter 11 of the NAFTA contains a model investment agreement between industrialized and developing countries that can be utilized in broader regional terms within the Western Hemisphere and the APEC. A reasonable multilateral goal by decade's end would be incorporation of such investment provisions within the WTO, thereby making it a World Trade and Investment Organization, or WTIO.

The broadening scope of policy commitments within the world trade—or trade and investment—system, as outlined here in terms of a trade agenda for the remainder of the 1990s, has profound political as well as economic implications. International constraints on national economic sovereignty have direct political consequences while the progressive deepening of inter-dependencies among national economies entails indirect political and secu-rity dependencies as well. This political/economic relationship is more stark in the case of comprehensive regional free trade than it is for multilateral trade-policy commitments up to this point. A nation would be ill-advised to enter into comprehensive free trade with a politically hostile or unstable neighbor. This political/economic relationship, in fact, is fundamental to the question of where the evolving three-track trading system is or should be heading over the long term. Where, in particular, are the multilateral WTO and the more deeply integrated regional free-trade groupings ultimately head-ing? Are they converging toward some form of fully integrated world eco-nomic order, and if so, what will it consist of? It is vital to at least try to answer this architectonic question.

TEN

The Brave New World Economic Order

Aldous Huxley wrote *Brave New World* in 1931, but in a foreword to a new edition fifteen years later, he explained that the most serious defect of the story was that the principal protagonist—the Savage—"is offered only two alternatives: an insane life in Utopia, or the life of a primitive in an Indian village." He goes on to say that if he were to rewrite the book "as an older, other person," he would offer a third alternative, and he provides two tantalizing clues as to what it would be based on: First, "it is conceivable that we may have enough sense, if not to stop fighting altogether, at least to behave as rationally as did our eighteenth century ancestors . . . determined at all costs to keep the world intact, a going concern." And second, "only a large-scale popular movement toward decentralization and self-help can arrest the present tendency toward statism." Huxley quickly went on, however, to note that there was no sign that such a movement would take place and ended with a brooding commentary about the just-lowered iron curtain, the imminent spread of totalitarian government, and the prospect of nuclear holocaust.[1]

The search for a third alternative goes to the heart of the current debate about the new world order that will emerge from the debris of the iron curtain and the grievous toll of totalitarianism that is the hallmark of the twentieth century. The Utopian and Primitive alternatives can be reformulated into current terms of U.N.-based internationalism versus far-from-primitive warfare with weapons of mass destruction. The unrealism and negative consequences of either extreme remain as compelling today as they did for the Huxley vision a half century ago. We need to elaborate a third alternative.

This study is about the world trading system, which will play a central role in the quest for such a third alternative. The system writ large beyond trade in goods and services to include international investment, new technology development, competition policy, environmental standards, and labor practices intrudes on many prime areas of national sovereignty. The trade relationship is progressively deepening as national economies become more dependent on imported goods, services, and capital, and as national companies operate on a more global scale. The structure of the system has also been evolving, most importantly through a growing emphasis on regional free-trade

227

groupings with ever more closely integrated national economic sovereignties. All of these developments progressed decisively during the Uruguay Round period of 1981–94, creating the foundation for what can be called a new world economic order. It is not, however, a definitive or stable order, and it will continue to evolve. The normative question here, in this conclusion, is thus addressed toward what long-term paradigm—or third alternative, in economic terms—should the current trading system be directed?

The starting point for elaborating a new-economic-order paradigm is, conveniently, the two clues provided by Huxley: the rational behavior of our eighteenth-century ancestors and movement away from statism to decentralization and self-help. The enlightened eighteenth-century advocates of reason and scientific method—John Locke, the French *philosophes,* and the American founding fathers—concluded that the best way "to keep the world intact, a going concern" was through democratic government and respect for individual initiative and private property. It was a first formulation of the latter-day "triumph of economic liberalism and liberal democracy" that transpired during the 1980s. The call to move away from statism was a further elaboration of this same theme in the context of post–World War II Europe. It, too, became a central issue of debate during the 1980s and is continuing on through the 1990s.

The Industrialized Democracies

These ideological underpinnings lead directly to a first approximation for the central goal of a new world economic order, namely the progressive deepening and broadening of the grouping of market-oriented democracies to the point where they constitute most if not all of the world political order. A critical qualification to this formulation is that durable market-oriented democracies need to be based on a sustained path of industrial development and modernization. This puts the limited current grouping of industrialized democracies—roughly congruent with membership in the OECD—at the forefront of the process, with particular responsibility to provide leadership and other support through example as well as resource contributions. The most telling role-model example, in political terms, is that industrialized democracies are least likely to go to war with one another, the minimum condition for keeping the world intact. The ultimate goal can thus be more narrowly formulated as a broadening and deepening of the grouping of industrialized democracies.

Even such a general formulation of long-term objective sheds considerable light on how the trading system is evolving and why, based on two causal linkages. First, more open international trade and investment produces more rapid economic growth and modernization, particularly in less developed countries. This causality has been demonstrated in numerous empirical studies and could be even more powerful than indicated in such studies since the most dynamic growth effects of free trade, as described earlier, defy economic analysis.[2] The open trade/growth effect was the most important consequence of the Uruguay Round agreement as it will be for further trade liberalization within the WTO during the remainder of the 1990s and beyond. Graduation from developing to newly industrialized country status for major trading nations in East Asia and Latin America is a critical stage toward the goal of a broadened group of industrialized democracies.

The second causal relationship underlying the evolving world order as elaborated here is that market-oriented industrialization and modernization nurture democratization. This linkage is less clearly established although observation of wide-ranging recent developments strongly supports it. Democratization within newly-industrialized South Korea and Taiwan is most evident and pressures toward political pluralism if not full democratic government are building in almost all of the more advanced developing countries. The record in lower-income countries is less clear, but the dominant assessment even for authoritarian regimes such as China, Vietnam, and Cuba is that market-oriented economic reforms strengthen the forces for democratic political reform as well.

The application of this second linkage of free trade to democratization within the evolving trading system is less clearly established and subject to some conflict. It is most clearly integrated at the regional level within the EU and NAFTA relationships. A democratic political structure is an integral part of the EU. The NAFTA, including its likely extension elsewhere in the Western Hemisphere, is based on shared democratic objectives as expressed in the Organization of American States. Democratization and respect for human rights in Mexico became part of the U.S. debate over ratification of NAFTA, which included a general assessment that comprehensive free trade would support the process of democratic reform within Mexico.

The free-trade–democratization relationship has been far more muted within the multilateral GATT in view of the considerable number of members with nondemocratic governments. At the bilateral level, the United States has been somewhat contradictory in its policies relating open trade with democratization. Official statements support the causal relationship, and yet a trade embargo against Cuba has been maintained as a means of fostering democratization and suspension of normal MFN trade relations with China was threatened, until May 1994, in an attempt to speed political reform.

The central focus for articulating the critical free-trade–democratization dimension to the international economic order should be the advanced industrialized country grouping, as represented institutionally by the OECD and, at highest level, the annual G-7 economic summit meetings. OECD ministerial-level declarations, in fact, have tended in the early 1990s to give less emphasis to the shared political objectives of the "industrialized democracies" than they did during the height of the cold war, and this could be rectified. The G-7 summits should emphasize that the leaders represent not just the major industrialized economic powers but the mature and deeply rooted democracies as well.

One broad line of policy that could consequently be developed within the G-7–OECD framework would be a more consistent and effective strategy for utilizing trade liberalization in support of democratization. Unilateral embargoes are generally counterproductive in this sense while universal embargoes need to be limited to the most reprehensible political behavior, such as apartheid in South Africa and genocide by Serbians against Bosnian Muslims. Otherwise, normal commercial relations should be maintained as a longer-term vehicle supportive of democratic reform, while sanctions to achieve short-term political objectives should be pursued through other means.

These are the general lines of rationale and policy in support of the long-term goal of deepening and broadening the industrialized democracy grouping. The two directional qualifiers *deepening* and *broadening,* however, require closer consideration.

How Deep?

This is the more elusive but less important of the two qualifiers. The depth of economic policy integration among nations becomes increasingly political as it progresses beyond the elimination of border restrictions to trade. Full economic and monetary union involves a merging of fundamental aspects of national sovereignty and requires an essentially political decision-making mechanism at the supranational level. The EU—with a customs union, wide-ranging common agricultural, regional, and social policies, the EC-92 market unification program, and plans for monetary union—is far advanced toward this stage of merged sovereignty. The NAFTA involves a considerably lower level of commitment, and the WTO a still lower level, although after the Uruguay Round the overall process is significantly more advanced at all levels than it was in 1980.

The path toward deeper economic policy integration can also have a complex technical dimension. Monetary union, for example, in addition to curtailed national sovereignty for monetary and related macro-economic policies, has consequences deriving from empirical relationships, including relative trade and investment dependencies and the degree of capital and labor mobility across member-state borders. Empirical analysis of an "optimum currency area," however, defies conclusive evaluation, and final judgments become largely political. Why the EU and not U.S.-Canada?

It is simply not possible to project or even predicate an optimum path of deepening economic integration among the current grouping of industrialized democracies or on a broader multilateral basis. It is possible, however, to provide four guidelines which, together, are adequate for keeping the overall process on course toward the long-term goal:

First, it is the direction that counts, and that should be, on balance, preponderantly toward a higher degree of policy integration at all three levels. This is the basic concept underlying the three-convergent-tracks trade strategy.

Second, the operational agenda should emphasize those specific policy objectives where there are the most self-evident mutual gains from trade and where national or regional policies are in the most threatening conflict. For the 1990s, a multilateral agreement for international investment is the prime example of the former category while competition/antidumping policy is the most likely candidate in the latter. Indeed, the trade agenda for the 1990s contained in the previous chapter was derived largely on this basis.

Third, the regional track of comprehensive free trade will generally constitute the leading edge for further deepening of economic-policy integration. This characteristic has been highlighted at various points for specific areas of policy. The political will for the EU and the NAFTA to move forward at a faster pace is based heavily on their shared democratic values and supporting institutions.

And fourth, the tripolar regional economic orientation of the industrialized democracies—in Western Europe, North America, and East Asia—which intensified during the 1970s and 1980s, should not be considered immutable. The variation most seriously debated in the early 1990s is a looser Asia-Pacific free trade relationship that would draw North America and East Asia closer together and transform the tripolar relationship, to some extent, into a bipolar Asia-Pacific–European relationship. More definitive moves toward comprehensive free trade—between the United States and Japan or NAFTA and the EU, for example—or jointly among all of the industrialized democracies appeared unrealistic from the vantage of the early 1990s. However, recent experience demonstrates that the "objective conditions" of history, to use the now-benign Marxist term, can change very quickly.

How Broad?

This is the vital, make-or-break question for the long-term economic order as developed here. What will be the pace and scope for extending the grouping of industrialized democracies over the coming several decades? Unless a major broadening takes place in more or less this time frame, the momentum of the industrialized democracy grouping will likely be overtaken by some alternative wave of history.

In 1991 the OECD countries accounted for 77 percent of world income, 71 percent of world exports of goods, and 16 percent of world population. All projections into the early twenty-first century show these figures declining substantially. One projection of world trade, for example, shows the share of total trade held by China and nine other "emerging markets" increasing from 13 percent in 1991 to 26 percent in 2010 while the corresponding share for the United States drops from 20 percent to 16 percent.[3] Population growth is substantially higher throughout the developing world while negative—that is, in absolute decline—in some industrialized countries such as Italy and Germany. More than 90 percent of babies born in the 1990s are in non-OECD countries, which projects to a decline in the OECD share of world population to only 12 percent in 2020.

A relatively specific scenario for broadening the industrialized democracy grouping is therefore fundamental to the overall credibility of the paradigm. Table 10.1 presents the prospects for such broadening in terms of additional countries or groups of countries, with cumulative figures for share of world population and other economic indicators. The selection is based on the likelihood of nations to make the transition and on the relative size of their potential influence on the global figures. The listing is not all-inclusive, and some obvious yet smaller candidates are excluded, but the overall orders of magnitude are clearly established.

The first extension of scope from OECD (24) to OECD (30), line 1 to line 2, is largely accomplished. Mexico joined the OECD in 1994 and the Czech Republic, Hungary, Poland, Slovakia, and South Korea should follow shortly. All six have achieved or are close to achieving industrial-democracy status, albeit on shaky foundations.

Lines 3 and 4 extend the grouping southward in the Western Hemisphere and eastward in Europe to include Russia and other European members of the former Soviet Union. Momentum in the Americas is based on extension of the NAFTA or other forms of free trade throughout the hemisphere, and political commitments, particularly within the Organization of American

TABLE 10.1: Cumulative Indicators for Projected Industrialized Democracies (percent of world total, 1991)

	Population	GDP	Exports	Foreign Direct Investment
1. OECD (24)	16	77	71	96
2. OECD (30)[a]	19	80	75	96+
3. Line 2 plus other Western Hemisphere	25	84	79	96+
4. Line 3 plus Russia, Ukraine, Belarus, Baltic Republics	30	87	80	96+
5. Line 4 plus ASEAN	35	89	85	96+
6. Line 5 plus India	50	90	85	96+
7. Line 6 plus China	72	92	87	96+

Sources:Population: *Statistical Abstract of the United States* (Washinton, D.C.: U.S. Census Bureau, 1992); *World Tables* (Washington, D.C.: World Bank, 1994). GDP *International Financial Statistics Yearbook* (Washington, D.C.: IMF, 1994). Exports: *International Trade: Statistics* (Geneva: GATT, 1993). FDI: *World Investment Report* (New York: UN, 1994).

States, to support democratic governments. Major steps forward are likely by the end of the decade. Russia and the other former Soviet republics are committed to market-oriented economic restructuring and democratic political reforms. The course of such change is troubled and unclear, however, and while important decisions will be confronted during the remainder of the 1990s, the definitive resolution of the politico-economic orientation of the new Russia will likely stretch into the next century.

Lines 5 through 7 relate to Asia, where most of the world's population lives, and to the ASEAN, India, and China in particular. Members of the ASEAN—Brunei, Indonesia, Malaysia, the Philippines, Singapore, and Thailand—with a population of about 350 million, constitute a pivotal subregion in the global process of change. In economic terms, they are rapidly industrializing countries, have adopted a regional free-trade program of their own, and are active participants in APEC and the WTO. Only the Philippines, however, has a fully democratic political system, and it is unclear how the open-trade–industrialization–democratization causal linkages will play out. Some key transitional steps will likely occur during the remainder of the 1990s, and the longer-term direction of political change will constitute an important test for the rapidly industrializing Southeast Asia region. India has a firmly established democratic political system but a largely disappointing economic record troubled by a highly statist bureaucracy and intractable ethnic conflicts. A shift in economic policy in the early 1990s toward open trade and a more competitive private sector is producing positive results, including a growing inflow of foreign direct investment. Newly industrialized status, in the East Asian sense of the term, however, remains a relatively long-term prospect for India. China, finally, is of central importance for the evolving economic order in view of its size, extraordinary growth in industrial production and exports, and central location in Asia. The inevitable political transition during the latter 1990s sets the stage for the most important test case of all for the open-trade–industrialization–democratization causal relationships, although again a definitive outcome will extend well beyond the year 2000.

These are the broad dimensions affecting the prospective broadening of the industrialized democracy grouping. The extension of the current OECD grouping southward in the Western Hemisphere and eastward in Europe (including Russia), still only encompasses 31 percent of the global population.[4] The objective of including the majority of world population thus depends on the future course of Asia, with the listed countries in table 10.1 raising the cumulative population share to 72 percent. For the other economic indicators listed—global share of GDP, exports, and foreign direct investment—the extended OECD (30) grouping already accounts for 75–96 percent of the totals, and these figures move substantially higher as other countries are added.

The broadening of the industrialized democracy grouping is the critical factor for realizing the new economic order developed here. Some important transitional stages for key countries or regions will occur during the remainder of the 1990s, but definitive resolution of the future politico-economic course for the largest potential entrants—including Russia, India, and China—will extend well into the next century. The post-Uruguay Round trading system and the likely trade agenda for the decade ahead, as presented in chapter 9, are generally supportive of the process of transition to industrialized democracy status, and will play an important role toward achieving the proposed paradigm. The adequacy of the broader post–cold war international order to this end, including the leadership role of the current industrial democracies within it, goes beyond this work although some related commentary is provided in the concluding section.

How Long Is Long Term?

This chapter assesses the direction of the world economic order over the long term, which requires some definition of the term *long term*. The term, in fact, is relative. Astrophysicists have a long-term horizon of eight to twenty billion years, anthropologists of six million years, and social scientists of the six thousand years since the dawn of organized society. The international trading system will evolve within an even more compressed time frame because of the accelerating rate of change for almost all political, social, and economic benchmarks.

In any event, the practical definition of long term for purposes of this study is taken to be as long as the systemic model being addressed and the behavioral relationships that drive it remain relevant. The current trading system is one of nation-states whose economies are driven primarily by private sectors and who are open to trade within a complex, three-track international system. These basic relationships can change substantially over time while the systemic model retains relevance. For example, the current characteristics and configuration of nation-states may evolve into something quite different. The political basis for an international system of trade commitments could also take on various reforms. There is already serious analysis of the change in behavior of national private enterprises as they become increasingly multinational in their interests. The long-term definition adopted here would encompass all such dimensions of change and would remain applicable through the evolutionary process of a deepening and broadening of the industrialized democracy grouping. This long-term time frame will nevertheless be of relatively short duration by historical standards. An approximate order of time for the critical phase of the evolving international trading system is likely to be a matter of decades rather than centuries, perhaps best specified as sixty years—to maintain the order of sixes and to reach the middle of the coming century.

Beyond the long term on this basis is beyond the scope of this study and is left to more creative futurologists. There is one recent phenomenon of extraordinary long-term global implications, however, which requires some comment, not only because it will be the principal bridge between "long term" here defined and "beyond the long term," but because it already is central to the world trading system and will become even more so in the period immediately ahead. It is the unprecedented wave of technological innovation that is beginning to sweep the globe.

This phenomenon has been addressed at various points during the account of the Uruguay Round. The United States first raised high-tech trade as a priority negotiating objective in 1981, and the final Uruguay Round agreement has many provisions related to technology development and technology-intensive industries. The trade agenda outlined for the 1990s similarly focuses on how the burgeoning technology-investment-trade relationship can be brought more fully within a cooperative international framework of rules and market-access commitments.

The significance of this truly revolutionary change for the long-term evolution of the world economic and political orders, however, is far more profound. There is already a widespread fallout on private- and public-sector behavior that goes beyond near term policy debate and influences the longer-term direction of the global economic system. The so-called information technology revolution, as of the early 1990s, has three distinct characteristics, each highly relevant to projecting the course of the international trading system over the coming decades and beyond:

1. *It is only beginning.* The explosion of new technology during the 1970s and 1980s has centered on ever-more-powerful semiconductors and computers, communications networks, and new materials to house them. The application of the new technologies lags far behind capability.

2. *In technical terms, it will have a pervasive global effect, with some quantum changes of unpredictable impact.* All sectors will be transformed—agriculture, manufacturing, and services—both in the social manner and the economic form of production, within and across borders. Technological breakthroughs in energy and biotechnology are examples of likely areas where transforming quantum change is likely. As a consequence, the nation-state and the private company, as we know them, could undergo fundamental change.

3. *In human terms, it is already producing a dynamic new behavior pattern.* The utopian New Soviet Man never materialized, but the New High-tech Economic Person is already among us and exercising a growing influence. These new economic persons have a common educational grounding across national borders based on scientific inquiry and the rule of reason. They have an optimistic disposition, working within the enormous positive sum game environment of new technology development and application, and are negatively disposed to economic nationalism that holds back technological change. At the international level, they communicate freely with each other despite widely differing cultural backgrounds and provide the expertise and leadership for the economic globalism under way. They are engineers, scientists, economists, business-school graduates, and technicians nurtured on computers and jointly able to create amazing new technology-intensive enterprises oriented toward international trade and investment. They are the traders in a brave new economic world, and their eighteenth-century forefathers would be very proud of them.

How Beauteous is Mankind?

The industrialized democracy paradigm presented here is not original. In the summer of 1989, when the Soviet Bloc was in process of disintegration, Francis Fukuyama wrote "The End of History?" in which he argued that liberal democracy may constitute the "end point of mankind's ideological evolution" and the "final form of human government" and as such the "end of history."[5] Economic liberalism was closely associated with the global trend toward political freedom. The related contribution of this work is to elaborate this proposition with respect to the central role of the international trading system and, in particular, to document the highly relevant transition that took place in the system during the Uruguay Round period. That transition established the terms of reference for an even more decisive period ahead.

The Fukuyama article and a subsequent book-length exposition on the same subject elicited considerable commentary and skepticism. Initial euphoria about a new world order following the collapse of Soviet communism has been followed by a series of sobering realities. The Gulf War. Ethnic conflict in the former Soviet Union and Yugoslavia. Clan and tribal warfare in parts of Africa. The threat of nuclear proliferation to renegade states such as North Korea and Iran. A downward cycle of poverty, environmental destruction, and social disintegration in some of the poorest countries. Defiant communist dictatorships in China and Vietnam.

Conditions within and among the industrialized democracies have also been troubled. Unemployment, crime, and rising social costs for an aging population frustrate governments from Europe to North America to Japan. Structural adjustment to new technology application causes anxiety in the work force while trade conflict breeds new forms of beggar-thy-neighbor economic nationalism (or regionalism).

The judgment of much expert opinion tends toward pessimism, and classic realpolitik can appear more realistic than a world order of friendly and cooperative democracies. During 1992, the last long year of Uruguay Round impasse, three widely-read books in the United States bore the subtitles, *Trade Conflict in High Technology Industries, The Coming Economic Battle among Japan, Europe, and America,* and *America, Japan, Germany, and the Struggle for Supremacy* (emphasis added). Two of the authors received senior economic positions in the Clinton administration the following year, and the third became a valued adviser to it.[6] This pessimistic momentum is fueled by unemployed "cold war warriors" who are redirecting their formidable intellectual firepower from military strategy to trade and economic issues with habitual insistence on defining relationships in terms of adversaries, conflict, and power manipulation. Geopolitics has simply been transformed into "geoeconomics," defined by one outspoken author as "equivalent of the defended frontiers and fortified lines of war and old-style world politics."[7]

The ultimate world-order question is whether a system of broadening cooperation among industrialized democracies is a feasible long-term objective, and should receive corresponding priority in the conduct of foreign policy or whether old-style power politics should be reasserted on a new post–cold war configuration of nations. The assessment derived here from the extraordinary events of the 1980s, and from fundamental changes in international economic relationships in particular, is optimistic, anticipating the cooperative path among a progressively larger group of industrialized democracies. It is nevertheless a contingent assessment. An underlying theme of this study is that the future of the global political order is largely—if not preponderantly—dependent on how the evolving world trading system is managed. The efforts of the 1980s and early 1990s deserve relatively high marks for trade cooperation in view of the successful Uruguay Round, despite protracted delays, and related actions at the regional and bilateral levels. The course ahead, however, is clouded. Immediate crisis management for security problems in various corners of the world—from Bosnia to North Korea to the Middle East—can be all-consuming for the industrialized powers, while extremely important yet longer-term political-economic relationships with the ASEAN countries and India, for example, are mostly ignored. Narrowly based trade interests can be pursued in ways that undermine broader interests, as has often been the case between the United States and Japan. Future leadership for open trade remains unsettled as the United States appears hesitant to continue its long-standing dominant role as a leader for open trade, and as no alternate basis for leadership is apparent.

We are entering a new world order with the international trading system a leading edge for defining its content, but how new and different will it really be? If we are not at the end of history, are we not at least at an essentially new and more hopeful stage? The original formulation of the response to the question of hope for a brave new world came, of course, from the Stratford Bard, and his message was not reassuring. The beguiling yet worldly innocent Miranda gained lasting fame through her ode to human goodness, concluding, "How beauteous mankind is! O brave new world, that has such people in it." Her father, Prospero, however, cut short such unbridled optimism with four piercing words: "'Tis new to thee."[8] *The Tempest* was one of Shakespeare's last plays, and it is believed that he wrote it as a summing up, speaking himself as Prospero. The response to Miranda leaves little doubt as to his view of history.

The world has come a long way, however, from the troubled times of Elizabethan England. Shakespeare lived in the shadow of the War of Roses and the reign of Henry the VIII, an era of extraordinary lows in human behavior, and he had no good grounds to project otherwise for the future. The age of reason was still two centuries into the future, the hard lessons learned from twentieth-century hot and cold wars were absent, and the prospect of enormously beneficial technological change was unthinkable. Economic liberalism and liberal democracy have not yet fully triumphed, but to rational people, to traders even more so than to diplomats, they constitute the only feasible basis for keeping the world intact and for making it more just and prosperous as well. There is indeed hope for a brave new world economic order. Miranda lives!

Appendix A
Chronology of Events

April 1979	Conclusion of the Tokyo Round; developing countries boycott signing ceremony over failure to reach agreement on safeguards.
June 1981	U.S. Trade Representative William Brock, at OECD ministerial meeting, calls for action program "to address the trade issues of the future."
November 24–29, 1982	GATT ministerial meeting fails to agree on new multilateral trade initiative and ends in discord; a two-year interim work program is most tenuous with respect to trade in services.
June 1983	The United States calls for a new GATT round at Williamsburg G-7 summit meeting, but others only agree "to continue consultations."
September 1984	President Ronald Reagan, at the annual meeting of the IMF and the World Bank, calls on other nations: "Support with us a new, expanded round of trade liberalization." Others do not support him.
May 1985	G-7 summit leaders at Bonn call for new round "as soon as possible."
September 1985	President Reagan announces a tough new trade policy "to negotiate the elimination of unfair trade practices abroad," including greater use of Section 301 authority.
November 1985	GATT members agree to establish a preparatory committee to develop a negotiating agenda for a new round to be adopted in September 1986.
September 15–20, 1986	Puna del Este GATT ministerial conference agrees to launch the Uruguay Round with a four-year deadline for completion.
July 1987	Single European Act takes force to implement the EC-92 market unification program.
January 1988	The United States and Canada conclude a free trade agreement.

August 1988	President Reagan signs the Omnibus Trade and Competitiveness Act giving him authority to negotiate the Uruguay Round under fast-track authority, and, at the same time, strengthening his authority for unilateral actions under new "special" and "super" 301 authorities.
December 5–9, 1988	Montreal GATT ministerial midterm review. Some initial results, but U.S.-EC impasse on agriculture dominates.
June 1989	Austria applies for full EC membership, followed by other EFTA countries.
November 1989	Ministerial meeting in Canberra establishes the Asia Pacific Economic Cooperation (APEC) intergovernmental mechanism.
April 1990	President Carlos Salinas de Gortari of Mexico seeks a free-trade agreement with the United States, leading to the NAFTA.
June 1990	President George Bush calls for free trade throughout the Western Hemisphere in his Enterprise for the Americas Initiative.
December 2, 1990	First all-German elections in more than half a century give Chancellor Helmut Kohl a resounding victory.
December 3–7, 1990	Brussels GATT ministerial meeting fails to conclude the Uruguay Round over the continuing U.S.-EC impasse on agriculture.
May 1991	U.S. Congress extends fast-track authority for the Uruguay Round and NAFTA negotiations.
December 20, 1991	GATT Director-General Arthur Dunkel puts forward his "Draft Final Act."
November 4, 1992	George Bush loses presidential election to Bill Clinton.
November 20, 1992	U.S.-EC Blair House Accord reached, breaking agricultural impasse.
June 1993	U.S. Congress again renews fast-track authority.
July 1993	G-7 summit meeting in Tokyo achieves breakthrough on market access for the industrial sector.
November 17, 1993	President Clinton wins surprising victory for NAFTA.
December 15, 1993	Final Uruguay Round agreement reached in Geneva.
April 15, 1994	Ministers sign final Uruguay Round agreement at Marrakesh, Morocco.

December 1994   U.S. Congress approves implementing legislation for
                       the Uruguay Round agreement, which is signed by
                       President Clinton.

January 1, 1995   The new World Trade Organization comes into
                       being.

Appendix B
Punta del Este Ministerial Declaration, adopted September 20, 1986

Ministers, meeting on the occasion of the Special Session of CONTRACTING PARTIES at Punta del Este, have decided to launch Multilateral Trade Negotiations (The Uruguay Round). To this end, they have adopted the following Declaration. The multilateral trade negotiations (MTN) will be open to the participation of countries as indicated in Parts I and II of this Declaration. A Trade Negotiations Committee (TNC) is established to carry out the negotiations. The Trade Negotiations Committee shall hold its first meeting not later than 31 October 1986. It shall meet as appropriate at Ministerial level. The Multilateral Trade Negotiations will be concluded within four years.

PART I
Negotiations On Trade in Goods

The CONTRACTING PARTIES meeting at Ministerial level

DETERMINED to halt and reverse protectionism and to remove distortions to trade

DETERMINED also to preserve the basic principles and to further the objectives of the GATT

DETERMINED also to develop a more open, viable and durable multilateral trading system

CONVINCED that such action would promote growth and development

MINDFUL of the negative effects of prolonged financial and monetary instability in the world economy, the indebtedness of a large number of less-developed contracting parties, and considering the linkage between trade, money, finance and development

DECIDE to enter into Multilateral Trade Negotiations on trade in goods within the framework and under the aegis of the General Agreement on Tariffs and Trade.

A. Objectives

Negotiations shall aim to:
   (i) bring about further liberalization and expansion of world trade to the benefit of all countries, especially less-developed contracting parties, including

the improvement of access to markets by the reduction and elimination of tariffs, quantitative restrictions and other non-tariff measures and obstacles;

(ii) strengthen the role of GATT, improve the multilateral trading system based on the principles and rules of the GATT and bring about a wider coverage of world trade under agreed, effective and enforceable multilateral disciplines;

(iii) increase the responsiveness of the GATT system to the evolving international economic environment, through facilitating necessary structural adjustment, enhancing the relationship of the GATT with the relevant international organizations and taking account of changes in trade patterns and prospects, including the growing importance of trade in high-technology products, serious difficulties in commodity markets and the importance of an improved trading environment providing, *inter alia,* for the ability of indebted countries to meet their financial obligations;

(iv) foster concurrent co-operative action at the national and international levels to strengthen the interrelationship between trade policies and other economic policies affecting growth and development, and to contribute towards continued, effective and determined efforts to improve the functioning of the international monetary system and the flow of financial and real investment resources to developing countries.

B. General Principles Governing Negotiations

(i) Negotiations shall be conducted in a transparent manner, and consistent with the objectives and commitments agreed in this Declaration and with the principles of the General Agreement in order to ensure mutual advantage and increased benefits to all participants.

(ii) The launching, the conduct and the implementation of the outcome of the negotiations shall be treated as parts of a single undertaking. However, agreements reached at an early stage may be implemented on a provisional or a definitive basis by agreement prior to the formal conclusion of the negotiations. Early agreements shall be taken into account in assessing the overall balance of the negotiations.

(iii) Balanced concessions should be sought within broad trading areas and subjects to be negotiated in order to avoid unwarranted cross-sectoral demands.

(iv) CONTRACTING PARTIES agree that the principle of differential and more favourable treatment embodied in Part IV and other relevant provisions of the General Agreement and in the Decision of the CONTRACTING PARTIES of 28 November 1979 on Differential and More Favourable Treatment, Reciprocity and Fuller Participation of Developing Countries applies to the negotiations. In the implementation of standstill and rollback, particular care should be given to avoiding disruptive effects on the trade less-developed contracting parties.

(v) The developed countries do not expect reciprocity for commitments made by them in trade negotiations to reduce or remove tariffs and other barriers to the trade of developing countries, i.e. the developed countries do not expect the developing countries, in the course of trade negotiations, to make contributions which are inconsistent with their individual development, financial and trade needs. Developed contracting parties shall therefore not seek, neither shall less-developed contracting parties be required to make, concessions that are inconsistent with the latter's development, financial and trade needs.

(vi) Less-developed contracting parties expect that their capacity to make contributions or negotiated concessions or take other mutually agreed action under the provisions and procedures of the General Agreement would improve with the progressive development of their economies and improvement in their trade situation and they would accordingly expect to participate more fully in the framework of rights and obligations under the General Agreement.

(vii) Special attention shall be given to the particular situation and problems of the least-developed countries and to the need to encourage positive measures to facilitate expansion of their trading opportunities. Expeditious implementation of the relevant provisions of the 1982 Ministerial Declaration concerning the least-developed countries shall also be given appropriate attention.

C. Standstill and Rollback

Commencing immediately and continuing until the formal completion of the negotiations, each participant agrees to apply the following commitments:

Standstill

(i) not to take any trade restrictive or distorting measure inconsistent with the provisions of the General Agreement or the Instruments negotiated within the framework of GATT or under its auspices;

(ii) not to take any trade restrictive or distorting measure in the legitimate exercise of its GATT rights, that would go beyond that which is necessary to remedy specific situations, as provided for in the General Agreement and the Instruments referred to in (i) above;

(iii) not to take any trade measures in such a manner as to improve its negotiating positions.

Rollback

(i) that all trade restrictive or distorting measures inconsistent with the provisions of the General Agreement or Instruments negotiated within the framework of GATT or under its auspices, shall be phased out or brought into conformity within an agreed timeframe not later than by the date of the formal completion of the negotiations, taking into account multilateral agreements, undertakings, and understandings, including strengthened rules and disciplines, reached in pursuance of the objectives of the negotiations;

(ii) there shall be progressive implementation of this commitment on an equitable basis in consultations among participants concerned, including all affected participants. This commitment shall take account of the concerns expressed by any participant about measures directly affecting its trade interests;

(iii) there shall be no GATT concessions requested for the elimination of these measures.

Surveillance of standstill and rollback

Each participant agrees that the implementation of these commitments on standstill and rollback shall be subject to multilateral surveillance so as to ensure that these commitments are being met. The Trade Negotiations Committee will decide on the appropriate mechanisms to carry out the surveillance, including periodic reviews and evaluations. Any participant may bring to the attention of the appropriate surveillance mechanism any actions or omissions it believes to be relevant to the fulfillment of these commitments. These notifications should be addressed to the GATT secretariat which may also provide further relevant information.

D. Subjects for Negotiations
Tariffs

Negotiations shall aim, by appropriate methods, to reduce or, as appropriate, eliminate tariffs including the reduction or elimination of high tariffs and tariff escalation. Emphasis shall be given to the expansion of the scope of tariff concessions among all participants.

Non-tariff measures

Negotiations shall aim to reduce or eliminate non-tariff measures including quantitative restrictions, without prejudice to any action to be taken in fulfillment of the rollback commitments.

Tropical products

Negotiations shall aim at the fullest liberalization of trade in tropical products, including in their processed and semi-processed forms and shall cover both tariff and all non-tariff measures affecting trade in these products.

CONTRACTING PARTIES recognize the importance of trade in tropical products to a large number of less-developed contracting parties and agree that negotiations in this area shall receive special attention, including the timing of the negotiations and the implementation of the results as provided for in B(ii).

Natural resource-based products

Negotiations shall aim to achieve the fullest liberalization of trade in natural resource-based products, including in their processed and semi-processed forms. The negotiations shall aim to reduce or eliminate tariff and non-tariff measures, including tariff escalation.

Textiles and clothing

Negotiations in the area of textiles and clothing shall aim to formulate modalities that would permit the eventual integration of this sector into GATT on the basis of strengthened GATT rules and disciplines, thereby also contributing to the objective of further liberalization of trade.

Agriculture

CONTRACTING PARTIES agree that there is an urgent need to bring more discipline and predictability to world agricultural trade by correcting and pre-

247

venting restrictions and distortions including those related to structural surpluses so as to reduce the uncertainty, imbalances, and instability in world
agricultural markets.

Negotiations shall aim to achieve greater liberalization of trade in agriculture
and bring all measures affecting import access and export competition under
strengthened and more operationally effective GATT rules and disciplines, taking
into account the general principles governing the negotiations, by:

 (i) improving market access through, *inter alia,* the reduction of import bar-
     riers;
 (ii) improving the competitive environment by increasing discipline on the use
      of all direct and indirect subsidies and other measures affecting directly or
      indirectly agricultural trade, including the phased reduction of their nega-
      tive effects and dealing with their causes;
 (iii) minimizing the adverse effects that sanitary and phytosanitary regulations
       and barriers can have on trade in agriculture, taking into account the rele-
       vant international agreements.

In order to achieve the above objectives, the negotiating group having primary responsibility for all aspects of agriculture will use the Recommendations
adopted by the CONTRACTING PARTIES at their Fortieth Session, which were developed in accordance with the GATT 1982 Ministerial Programme and take account of the approaches suggested in the work of the committee on Trade in
Agriculture without prejudice to other alternatives that might achieve the objectives of the negotiations.

GATT Articles

Participants shall review existing GATT Articles, provisions and disciplines as
requested by interested contracting parties, and, as appropriate, undertake negotiations.

Safeguards

 (i) A comprehensive agreement on safeguards is of particular importance to
     the strengthening of the GATT system and to progress in the MTNs.
 (ii) The agreement on safeguards:
 — shall be based on the basic principles of the General Agreement;
 — shall contain, *inter alia,* the following elements: transparency, coverage, objective criteria for action including the concept of serious injury or threat
 thereof, temporary nature, degressivity and structural adjustment, compensation and retaliation, notifications, consultation, multilateral surveillance and
 dispute settlement; and
 — shall clarify and reinforce the disciplines of the General Agreement and
 should apply to all contracting parties.

MTN Agreements and Arrangements

Negotiations shall aim to improve, clarify, or expand, as appropriate,
agreements and arrangements negotiated in the Tokyo Round of Multilateral Negotiations.

Subsidies and countervailing measures

Negotiations on subsidies and countervailing measures shall be based on a review of Articles VI and XVI and the MTN agreement on subsidies and countervailing measures with the objective of improving GATT disciplines relating to all subsidies and countervailing measures that affect international trade. A negotiating group will be established to deal with these issues.

Dispute settlement

In order to ensure prompt and effective resolution of disputes to the benefit of all contracting parties, negotiations shall aim to improve and strengthen the rules and the procedures of the dispute settlement process, while recognizing the contribution that would be made by more effective and enforceable GATT rules and disciplines. Negotiations shall include the development of adequate arrangements for overseeing and monitoring of the procedures that would facilitate compliance with adopted recommendations.

Trade-related aspects of intellectual property rights, including trade in counterfeit goods

In order to reduce the distortions and impediments to international trade, and taking into account the need to promote effective and adequate protection of intellectual property rights, and to ensure that measures and procedures to enforce intellectual property rights do not themselves become barriers to legitimate trade, the negotiations shall aim to clarify GATT provisions and elaborate as appropriate new rules and disciplines.

Negotiations shall aim to develop a multilateral framework of principles, rules and disciplines dealing with international trade in counterfeit goods, taking into account work already undertaken in the GATT.

These negotiations shall be without prejudice to other complementary initiatives that may be taken in the World Intellectual Property Organization and elsewhere to deal with these matters.

Trade-related investment measures

Following an examination of the operation of GATT Articles related to the trade restrictive and distorting effects of investment measures, negotiations should elaborate, as appropriate, further provisions that may be necessary to avoid such adverse effects on trade.

E. Functioning of the GATT System

Negotiations shall aim to develop understandings and arrangements:
(i) to enhance the surveillance in the GATT to enable regular monitoring of trade policies and practices of contracting parties and their impact on the functioning of the multilateral trading system;
(ii) to improve the overall effectiveness and decision-making of the GATT as an institution, including, *inter alia,* through involvement of Ministers;
(iii) to increase the contribution of the GATT to achieving greater coherence in global economic policy-making through strengthening its relationship with

other international organizations responsible for monetary and financial matters.

F. Participation

(a) Negotiations will be open to:
  (1) all contracting parties,
  (2) countries having acceded provisionally,
  (3) countries applying the GATT on a *de facto* basis having announced, not later than 30 April 1987, their intention to accede to the GATT and to participate in the negotiations,
  (4) countries that have already informed the CONTRACTING PARTIES, at a regular meeting of the Council of Representatives, of their intention to negotiate the terms of their membership as a contracting party, and
  (5) developing countries that have, by 30 April 1987, initiated procedures for accession to the GATT, with the intention of negotiating the terms of their accession during the course of the negotiations.
(b) Participation in negotiations relating to the amendment or application of GATT provisions or the negotiation of new provisions will, however, be open only to contracting parties.

G. Organization of the Negotiations

A Group of Negotiations on Goods (GNG) is established to carry out the programme of negotiations contained in this Part of the Declaration. The GNG shall, *inter alia*;
  (i) elaborate and put into effect detailed trade negotiating plans prior to 19 December 1986;
  (ii) designate the appropriate mechanism for surveillance of commitments to standstill and rollback;
  (iii) establish negotiating groups as required. Because of the interrelationship of some issues and taking fully into account the general principles governing the negotiations as stated in B(iii) above it is recognized that aspects of one issue may be discussed in more than one negotiating group. Therefore each negotiating group should as required take into account relevant aspects emerging in other groups;
  (iv) also decide upon inclusion of additional subject matters in the negotiations;
  (v) co-ordinate the work of the negotiating groups and supervise the progress of the negotiations. As a guideline not more than two negotiating groups should meet at the same time;
  (vi) the GNG shall report to the Trade Negotiations Committee.

In order to ensure effective application of differential and more favourable treatment the GNG shall, before the formal completion of the negotiations, conduct an evaluation of the results attained therein in terms of the Objectives and the General Principles Governing Negotiations as set out in the Declaration, taking into account all issues of interest to less-developed contracting parties.

Part II
Negotiations on Trade in Services

Ministers, also decided, as part of the Multilateral Trade Negotiations, to launch negotiations on trade in services.

Negotiations in this area shall aim to establish a multilateral framework of principles and rules for trade in services, including elaboration of possible disciplines for individual sectors, with a view to expansion of such trade under conditions of transparency and progressive liberalization and as a means of promoting economic growth of all trading partners and the development of developing countries. Such framework shall respect the policy objectives of national laws and regulations applying to services and shall take into account the work of relevant international organizations.

GATT procedures and practices shall apply to these negotiations. A Group on Negotiations on Services is established to deal with these matters. Participation in the negotiations under this Part of the Declaration will be open to the same countries as under Part I. GATT secretariat support will be provided, with technical support from other organizations as decided by the Group on Negotiations on Services.

The Group on Negotiations on Services shall report to the Trade Negotiations Committee.

IMPLEMENTATION OF RESULTS UNDER PARTS I AND II

When the results of the Multilateral Trade Negotiations in all areas have been established, Ministers meeting also on the occasion of a Special Session of CONTRACTING PARTIES shall decide regarding the international implementation of the respective results.

Appendix C
Final Uruguay Round Agreement, Table of Contents

Appendix D
Marrakesh Ministerial Decision on
Trade and Environment, April 14, 1994

Ministers, meeting on the occasion of signing the Final Act embodying the results of the Uruguay Round of Multilateral Trade Negotiations at Marrakesh on
15 April 1994,

Recalling the preamble of the Agreement establishing the World Trade Organization (WTO), which states that members' "relations in the field of trade and economic endeavour shall be conducted with a view to raising standards of living,
ensuring full employment and a large and steadily growing volume of real income and effective demand, and expanding the production of and trade in goods
and services, while allowing for the optimal use of the world's resources in accordance with the objective of sustainable development, seeking both to protect and
preserve the environment and to enhance the means for doing so in a manner
consistent with their respective needs and concerns at different levels of economic development."

Noting:
• the Rio Declaration on Environment and Development, Agenda 21, and its
  follow-up in GATT, as reflected in the statement of the Chairman of the Council
  of Representatives to the CONTRACTING PARTIES at their 48th Session on December 1992, as well as the work of the Group on Environmental Measures and International Trade, the Committee on Trade and Development, and the Council
  of Representatives;
• the work programme envisaged in the Decision on Trade in Services and the Environment; and
• the relevant provisions of the Agreement on Trade-Related Aspects of Intellectual Property Rights,

Considering that there should not be, nor need be, any policy contradiction between upholding and safeguarding an open, non-discriminatory and equitable
multilateral trading system on the one hand, and acting for the protection of the
environment, and the promotion of sustainable development on the other,

Desiring to coordinate the policies in the field of trade and environment, and
this without exceeding the competence of the multilateral trading system, which
is limited to trade policies and those trade-related aspects of environmental policies which may result in significant trade effects for its members,

Decide

- to direct the first meeting of the General Council of the WTO to establish a Committee on Trade and Environment open to all members of the WTO to report to the first biennial meeting of the Ministerial Conference after the entry into force of the WTO when the work and terms of reference of the Committee will be reviewed, in the light of recommendations of the Committee,
- that the TNC Decision of 15 December 1993 which reads, in part, as follows:

"(a) to identify the relationship between trade measures and environmental measures, in order to promote sustainable development;

(b) to make appropriate recommendations on whether any modifications of the provisions of the multilateral trading system are required, compatible with the open, equitable and non-discriminatory nature of the system, as regards, in particular:

- the need for rules to enhance positive interaction between trade and environmental measures, for the promotion of sustainable development, with special consideration to the needs of developing countries, in particular those of the least developed among them; and
- the avoidance of protectionist trade measures, and the adherence to effective multilateral disciplines to ensure responsiveness of the multilateral trading system to environmental objectives set forth in Agenda 21 and the Rio Declaration, in particular Principle 12; and
- surveillance of trade measures used for environmental purposes, of trade-related aspects of environmental measures which have significant trade effects, and of effective implementation of the multilateral disciplines governing those measures;"

constitutes, along with the preambular language above, the terms of reference of the Committee on Trade and Environment,

- that, within these terms of reference, and with the aim of making international trade and environmental policies mutually supportive, the Committee will initially address the following matters, in relation to which any relevant issue may be raised:
- the relationship between the provisions of the multilateral trading system and trade measures for environmental purposes, including those pursuant to multilateral environmental agreements;
- the relationship between environmental policies relevant to trade and environmental measures with significant trade effects and the provisions of the multilateral trading system;
- the relationship between the provisions of the multilateral trading system and;
    (a)charges and taxes for environmental purposes
    (b) requirements for environmental purposes relating to products, including standards and technical regulations, packaging, labelling and recycling;
- the provisions of the multilateral trading system with respect to the transparency of trade measures used for environmental purposes and environmental measures and requirements which have significant trade effects;
- the relationship between the dispute settlement mechanisms in the multilateral trading system and those found in multilateral environmental agreements;
- the effect of environmental measures on market access, especially in relation to

developing countries, in particular to the least developed among them, and environmental benefits of removing trade restrictions and distortions;
- the issue of exports of domestically prohibited goods,
- that the Committee on Trade and Environment will consider the work programme envisaged in the Decision on Trade in Services and the Environment and the relevant provisions of the Agreement on Trade-Related Aspects of Intellectual Property Rights as an integral part of its work, within the above terms of reference,
- that, pending the first meeting of the General Council of the WTO, the work of the Committee on Trade and Environment should be carried out by a Sub-Committee of the Preparatory Committee of the World Trade Organization (PCWTO), open to all members of the PCWTO,
- to invite the Sub-Committee of the Preparatory Committee, and the Committee on Trade and Environment when it is established, to provide input to the relevant bodies in respect of appropriate arrangements for relations with inter-governmental and non-governmental organizations referred to in Article V of the WTO.

Notes

Prologue

1. During his weekly radio talk on September 13, 1986.
2. *New York Times,* September 7, 1986.
3. The English text is contained in GATT archives, Geneva, MIN(86)/2, September 15, 1986.
4. GATT, MIN(86)/ST/39, September 17, 1986.
5. See *New York Times,* September 19, 1986, and the *Times* (London), September 24, 1986.
6. From his opening speech, contained in GATT, MIN (86)/ST/33, September 17, 1986.
7. Diane Yu, ed., *Punta: An Oral History of the 1986* GATT *Ministerial Meeting in Punta del Este, Uruguay* (U.S. Trade Representative Archives, Washington, D. C., 1987), p. 68. This volume consists of interviews by Ms. Yu with twenty-nine members of the U.S. delegation to the Punta meeting. Another primary source account of the Punta meeting by the Australian Permanent Representative to the GATT appears in Alan Oxley, *The Challenge of Free Trade* (New York: St. Martin's Press, 1990), pp. xiii–xvi, 141–44.
8. *New York Times,* September 15, 1986. The fact that only one member of Congress attended the conference was itself a message of congressional disaffection with the GATT.
9. The speech was given on September 10, 1986. The text is contained in Yu, *Punta.*
10. Yu, *Punta,* p. 82.
11. *Times* (London), September 24, 1986.
12. *Financial Times,* September 22, 1986; *New York Times,* September 25, 1986.
13. *New York Times,* September 22, 1986.
14. Ibid.
15. The sensible diplomat was Warren Lavorel, then the U.S. deputy chief of mission to the GATT and later U.S. Uruguay Round coordinator, with the rank of ambassador, in the office of the U.S. trade representative. In 1993, he was appointed deputy-director general of the GATT.

Chapter 1

1. John Hagedoorn and Jos Schakenraad, "Leading Companies and Networks of Strategic Alliances of Technologies," *Research Policy* 21 (1992): 163–90.

2. For example, see Ernest H. Preeg, *Economic Blocs and U.S. Foreign Policy* (Washington, D.C.: National Planning Association, 1974). It concludes: "The trend toward economic tripolarization among the industrialized countries will continue. Steadily deepening economic interdependence . . . will create irresistible pressures for the governments involved to coordinate objectives and policies more closely on a regional basis. Moreover, the policies affected will broaden well beyond narrowly defined economic issues to social, environmental and, ultimately, some political objectives" (p. 185). Not a bad projection for the North American Free Trade Agreement twenty years later.

3. The term *bloc* can have negative connotations, but it is used here for any arrangement that has a broad scope of preferential market access for trade among members.

4. *New York Times,* October 23, 1981.

5. Ibid., October 22, 1981.

6. *Washington Post,* May 26, 1991. This article also notes that "new world order" appeared more than forty times in presidential statements in the eight months following the August 1990 Iraqi invasion of Kuwait.

7. Charles P. Kindleberger, *The World in Depression: 1929–1939,* rev. ed. (Berkeley and Los Angeles: University of California Press, 1986), 289, 291, 304. In addition to maintaining an open market for imports, the stabilizing goals involve short- and long-term financial support, relatively stable exchange rates, and coordination of macroeconomic policies. The Kindleberger book was widely cited during the late 1980s as the U.S. leadership role in the international economy was increasingly questioned.

8. Winston S. Churchill, *A History of the English-Speaking Peoples* (New York: Dorset Press, 1956), 1:viii. During the final months of the Uruguay Round (see chapter 7), critical and forceful leadership was provided by EC Commissioner Leon Brittan, U.S. Trade Representative Mickey Kantor, and Director-General Peter Sutherland of the GATT, all products of the English-speaking world.

Chapter 2

1. GATT press release, Geneva, April 12, 1979.

2. *Financial Times,* May 3, 1979.

3. *New York Times,* April 13, 1979; *Journal de Genève,* April 16, 1979; *Economist,* April 21, 1979; *Frankfurter Allgemeine Zeitung,* April 17, 1979, reprinted in English in the *German Tribune,* April 29, 1979. Translations to English, unless otherwise specified, are by the author.

4. *New York Times,* May 11, 1979.

5. A "Reagan for President" press release of January 31, 1980, calls for "a new and vital era of North American cooperation—a North American Accord—through a developing closeness among Canada, Mexico, and the U.S." Privately, Reagan spoke of a North American free-trade arrangement, but his advisers convinced him to use more veiled language in public statements.

6. Photocopy, May 10, 1982.

7. *Financial Times,* October 28, 1982.

8. Ibid.

9. Respectively, the *Economist,* December 4, 1982; the *Washington Post,* December 2, 1982; and the *Guardian,* November 30, 1982.

10. *Le Monde,* November 28–29, 1982.

11. *New York Times,* November 30, 1982. The EC head of delegation at Geneva was Commissioner Wilhelm Haferkamp, although he is not mentioned by name in the reference.

12. *Christian Science Monitor,* December 6, 1982.

13. Attributed to Geza Feketekuty in *U.S. Export Weekly,* December 7, 1982. Feketekuty was the U.S. official who traveled from the 1981 OECD ministerial to Geneva for the meeting with Arthur Dunkel, and he was principal adviser to the U.S. trade representative for the new issues. He later became chairman of the OECD Trade Committee.

14. GATT, Spec(82)/87, November 1982.

15. OECD, *Report by the High Level Group on Trade and Related Problems* (Paris: OECD, 1982).

16. The Feketekuty book contains a detailed history of the campaign to make services a trade issue, which is drawn on in this account (*International Trade in Services: An Overview and Blueprint for Negotiations* [Washington, D.C.: AEI, 1988], pp. 295–322).

17. Sections 102, 135, and 121 of the Trade Act of 1974, respectively.

18. The first comprehensive analysis published by the GATT secretariat was contained in GATT *International Trade 88–89* (Geneva, 1990), 1:23–43, which explains the basis for their statistical presentations.

19. The growth rate for services is overstated to some extent because trade in services has historically been underreported. As reporting broadened in more recent years the calculated growth rate increased as a result.

20. See GATT *International Trade 88–89,* 1:29, and Bernard Hoekman and Guy Karsenty, "Trade Structure, Economic Development and International Transactions in Services," 30 pages, photocopy dated November 16, 1990. Hoekman was the member of the GATT secretariat most expert in data analysis for trade in services.

Chapter 3

1. Michel Albert and James Ball, *Toward European Economic Recovery in the 1980s* (Westport, Conn.: Praeger, 1984), pp. 141–42.

2. *New York Times,* April 10, 1983.

3. Ibid., April 20, 1983; Ronald D. Palmer and Thomas J. Reckford, *Building ASEAN: 20 Years of Southeast Asian Competition* (Washington, D.C.: CSIS, 1987), p. 133.

4. Professor Paul Krugman, a leading economist in the strategic-trade-policy debate, concluded, "It is possible then, both to believe that comparative advantage is an incomplete model of trade and to believe that free trade is nevertheless the right policy" ("Is Free Trade Passé?" *Economic Perspectives,* fall 1987, p. 143).

5. During a televised news conference, September 17, 1985.

6. From a speech at the White House to business and congressional leaders, September 22, 1985.

7. GATT document L/5647, May 4, 1984.

8. *Trade Policies for a Better Future: Proposals for Action* (Geneva: GATT, March 1985). The other members of the panel were Bill Bradley (United States), Pehr Gyllenhammar (Sweden), Guy Ladrett de Lacharriere (France), Indraprasad Patel (India), Mario Henrique Simonsen (Brazil), and Sumitro Djojohadikusomo (Indonesia). The report was financed privately to get around Brazilian and Indian opposition, but a publications glitch, in which "GATT" was inadvertently stamped on the cover, caused Dunkel to cancel planned public promotional activities so as to avoid conflict with developing-country representatives.

9. For example, at the Quad meeting at the Cheeka Lodge, Islamorada, Florida, in February 1984, the United States presented a ten-page paper, "USTR Concept Paper on New Multilateral Trade Negotiations." It included detailed discussion of a possible agenda and procedures for launching a new round, beginning with the statement, "There are a number of reasons why it is timely to consider a new multilateral negotiation." The other Quad ministers, however, were not yet prepared to respond positively to the U.S. initiative.

10. *New York Times,* September 26, 1984.

11. Ibid., April 12, 1985.

12. Ibid., May 4, 1985.

13. Ibid., May 3, 1985.

14. *Financial Times,* December 3, 1984.

15. GATT document, Prep. Com (86) SR/3, April 1986, p. 10.

16. GATT document, Prep. Com (86) SR/4, April 1986, p. 18.

17. For two insider accounts of this critical phase of informal negotiations, see Charles Blum's commentary in Yu, *Punta,* pp. 23–27; and Alan Oxley, *The Challenge of Free Trade* (New York: St. Martin's Press, 1990), pp. 137–40.

18. *News of the Uruguay Round,* October 1986, p. 6. This series, by the Information and Media Relations Division of the GATT, had twenty-three issues during 1987–88.

19. U.S. International Trade Commission, *Foreign Protection of Intellectual Property Rights and the Effect on U.S. Industry and Trade,* publication 2065, Washington, D. C., February 1988.

20. The GATT also refers explicitly to intellectual-property rights in Articles XII and XVIII, which prevent members from applying import restrictions for balance-of-payments reasons to prevent compliance with intellectual-property procedures.

21. Office of the U.S. Trade Representative, *Statement on the Protection of U.S. Intellectual Property Rights Abroad,* April 7, 1986, p. 4.

22. The United States first made a statement in March 1987 on deficiencies in the existing protection of intellectual-property rights, and then presented the detailed proposal in October. They are contained in GATT, MTN.GNG/NG 11/W/2, April 3, 1987; and MTN.GNG/NG 11/W/14, October 20, 1987.

23. The statement was issued by the Trilateral Secretariat in Washington. The citation is from p. 8.

24. GATT, MTN.GNG/NG 11/W/30, October 31, 1988, p. 3.

25. GATT, MTN.GNG/NG 11/W/37, July 10, 1989, pp. 1, 20.

26. One suggested origin for the twenty-year period for patent protection, which may be apocryphal, was the length of time required for an apprentice to become a master carpenter in seventeenth-century England.

27. Ibid., p. 3.

28. There is some relevant professional literature of broad analytic content, especially concerning the circumstances in developing countries, for example, Alan V. Deardorff, "Should Patent Protection Be Extended to All Developing Countries?" *World Economy,* spring 1993, pp. 497–507. There is little from economists, however, concerning how to measure the level and distribution of the welfare effects from protecting intellectual-property rights. In fact, the subject of government policies to stimulate new technology development and application goes beyond intellectual-property rights to include tax credits for R&D, publicly funded research, subsidies for private research, preferential public procurement, and relaxation of antitrust laws. This entire subject is worthy of far more professional attention at both the national and international levels.

29. Bruce Wilson, the assistant trade representative for the United States, commented, "We envisaged at the outset that it would be a fairly simple negotiating model primarily north-south in nature. It hasn't worked out that way. . . . Between April of '89 and June 1990 . . . we really got into the realization that we were going to have a very tough north-north negotiation." From *Waiting for the* GATT: *Intellectual Property and International Trade in the 1990s,* Proceedings of a Symposium presented by the *Economist,* March 11, 1991, pp. 16–17.

Chapter 4

1. A Surveillance Body was also established to oversee the standstill and rollback commitments in the ministerial declaration. It met regularly during the course of the Uruguay Round but accomplished almost nothing.

2. A listing of all official meetings of the negotiating groups, with a summary of subjects discussed, is contained in the GATT series, *News of the Uruguay Round,* hereafter *NUR.*

3. France had also linked agreement on an Uruguay Round timetable to the agricultural dispute over Spanish accession to the Community. Compromise agreements in Geneva and Brussels were reached simultaneously in late January 1987. See the *New York Times,* January 29, 1987.

4. An internal U.S. government review in 1987 uncovered only one passing reference to the definition of a developing country, during a discussion within the GATT balance-of-payments committee, which referred to GDP per-capita income and the share of manufactured goods in total exports as criteria.

5. References to the interagency group are based on the author's participation as chairman of the group.

6. The speech was delivered before the American Enterprise Institute in Washington, D.C.

7. In the early 1980s, the United States prepared a detailed presentation of the issue of countertrade with centrally planned economies for discussion by the G-18. There was no substantive response by other members, which dampened

U.S. interest in trying to use this GATT body as a forum for discussing new and complex trade-policy issues.

8. See, for example, Shailendra J. Anjaria, "Balance of Payments and Related Issues in the Uruguay Round of Trade Negotiations," *World Bank Economic Review,* September 1987, pp. 669–88.

9. For a fuller discussion of this debate, see Robert E. Hudec, "Dispute Settlement," in *Completing the Uruguay Round,* ed. Jeffrey Schott (Washington, D.C.: Institute for International Economics, 1990) pp. 180–204.

10. A detailed yet readable summary of the provisions of the 1988 trade act is *The Omnibus Trade and Competitiveness Act of 1988: A Straightforward Guide to Its Impact on U.S. and Foreign Business.* (Washington, D.C.: U.S. Chamber of Commerce, 1988).

11. For a discussion of a possible U.S.-Japan agreement from the 1988 vantage, see Ernest H. Preeg, "Next, a Free-Trade Pact with Japan?" *Wall Street Journal,* August 12, 1988.

12. The speech was delivered on February 8, 1988, before the National Cotton Council of America in Memphis, Tennessee.

13. A three "convergent" track strategy is elaborated in Ernest H. Preeg, *The American Challenge in World Trade: U.S. Interests in the GATT Multilateral Trading System* (Washington, D.C.: CSIS, May 1989), chaps. 4–7. A "three-pronged strategy," including multilateral, regional and bilateral market-opening initiatives, was first presented officially by Trade Representative Carla Hills in an address before the Japan National Press Club in Tokyo, October 13, 1989.

14. See Paolo Cecchini, *The European Challenge 1992: The Benefits of a Single Market* (Hants, England: Wildwood House, 1988), chaps. 9, 10.

15. The speech was delivered before the Institute for International Economics in Washington D.C.

16. *New York Times,* October 20, 1988.

17. See the *Wall Street Journal,* August 20, 1990. The article recounts developments since 1987.

18. *NUR,* no. 28, May 26, 1989. Earlier press reports contained higher figures of $25–30 billion, but this is the definitive level.

19. *Le Figaro,* December 1, 1988.

20. All plenary speech texts cited are from copies distributed at the conference.

21. The quote is from Mr. Conable's opening plenary speech.

22. *Le Monde,* December 8, 1988.

23. *Journal of Commerce,* December 12, 1988.

24. *New York Times,* December 9, 1988.

25. Ibid., December 10, 1988.

26. Respectively, the *International Herald Tribune,* December 10, 1988; the *Washington Post,* December 15, 1988; *Le Monde,* December 10, 1988; the *New York Times,* December 12, 1988; *Journal de Genève,* December 10, 1988; the *Journal of Commerce,* December 12, 1988; and *Le Monde,* December 14, 1988. The final phrase about egoisms is attributed to Charles de Gaulle.

27. Before the Senate Finance Committee, January 27, 1989, publication 101–52, p. 9.

28. December 19, 1988.

29. The Thurow statement was circulated in copier form. For reactions, see the *Journal of Commerce,* January 30, 1989.

30. The complete text of the *Mid-Term Review Agreements* runs forty-one pages and is contained in *NUR,* no. 27, April 24, 1989.

31. The language in the September 1986 Punta del Este declaration, while somewhat ambiguous, appeared to link a multilateral framework of principles to an "elaboration of possible disciplines for individual sectors, with a view to expansion of such trade . . . and progressive liberalization." See appendix B.

32. For a fuller account of GATT provisions for agriculture, see Dale Hathaway, *Agriculture and the GATT: Rewriting the Rules* (Washington, D.C.: Institute for International Economics, 1987), pp. 103–111.

33. See Ernest H. Preeg, *Traders and Diplomats: An Analysis of the Kennedy Round of Negotiations Under the General Agreement on Tariffs and Trade* (Washington, D.C.: Brookings Institution, 1970), especially chap. 9. Agreement was reached on a range of world wheat prices, which soon broke down under market pressures, and a joint food aid commitment of 4.5 million tons per year for three years.

34. There was a direct clash in third-country markets for exports of frozen poultry. It was contained during the 1970s through negotiated market sharing arrangements.

35. Members of the agricultural committees were prominent and vocal at the Montreal ministerial meeting in December 1988, attended by a large contingent of congressional advisers.

36. Proposals along these lines, put forward at about the same time as the United States announced its free trade objective, were contained in Hathaway, *Agriculture and the GATT,* pp. 140–53.

37. By 1991, however, EC Agricultural Commissioner Ray MacSharry was advocating just such a restructuring of the CAP away from price supports and toward income supports.

38. See Kym Anderson and Rod Tyers, "How Developing Countries Could Gain from Agricultural Trade Liberalization in the Uruguay Round," in *Agricultural Trade Liberalization,* ed. Ian Golding and Odin Knudsen (Paris: OECD, 1990), pp. 41–54. They cite projections indicating that complete liberalization would shift the food self-sufficiency of developing countries from 95 to 104 percent. The welfare impact projected if only OECD countries liberalized is slightly negative for developing countries, from $2–13 billion per year, because the phaseout of export subsidies would lead to some increase in world prices. However, if developing countries also liberalized agricultural trade, they would become "substantial net gainers" (p. 53).

Chapter 5

1. *NUR,* no. 30, August 3, 1989.

2. *NUR,* no. 29, July 7, 1989.

3. The figures are quoted in the *New York Times,* June 28, 1989. The sector consists of trade in both textiles and apparel, but is also referred to, for short, as the textile sector.

4. More precisely, the American proposal would initially establish a global

quota for imports not covered by existing bilateral quotas, and would allow unspecified growth; bilateral quotas would then be shifted into the global quota over a transitional period.

5. Amendment of GATT Article XVIII would be more difficult since it would require ratification by two-thirds of member governments. Thus the interpretive declaration was chosen as a more practical vehicle for negotiation.

6. Views differed within the World Bank as to whether to encourage developing countries to adopt antidumping codes as a flexible measure for dealing with import surges, but it was advocated in some instances. This caused consternation in the GATT secretariat, a miniproblem of noncoherence in international decision-making. During 1980–85, there were no antidumping actions by developing countries, while in 1988 there were forty-seven, somewhat more than the forty each by the United States and the EC. See Patrick A. Messerlin, "Antidumping," in *Completing the Uruguay Round,* ed. Jeffrey J. Schott (Washington, D.C.: Institute for International Economics, 1990), p. 111.

7. This was a reversal from the Kennedy Round of 1963–67, when the United States pressed for 50 percent across-the-board cuts as the best way to achieve maximum results.

8. The initial Swiss proposal actually called for an open-ended, ad hoc ministerial group, but Director-General Dunkel summarized the issue at the July 1990 TNC meeting as a "small" group. See GATT, MTN.NG14 W/41 May 17, 1990, for the Swiss proposal and *NUR,* no. 39, July 30, 1990, for the Dunkel summary.

9. As illustrative of the differing views, India maintained that imperfections in developing-country markets, including underdeveloped infrastructures, poor marketing, and high cost of imports, can make offsetting subsidies necessary and legal under GATT, "even if they are limited to exports and are specific to certain sectors." When the United States challenged Japanese practices related to "industrial targeting," Japan maintained this subject was not covered by the negotiating group's mandate. See *NUR,* no. 33, January 11, 1990, and *NUR,* no. 38, July 16, 1990.

10. *NUR,* no. 30, August 3, 1989.

11. The procedural choice between "top down" and "bottom up" probably would have had little effect on governments' specific, commitments in the services agreement, but the U.S. private-sector advisory committee was adamant in its stand for "top down." It hoped that this option would result in broader coverage by developing countries in particular. This put great pressure on the U.S. delegation because the service-sector coalition provided critical private-sector support for the overall Uruguay Round negotiation.

12. GATT observer status was usually granted in the context of actual or imminent negotiations for full membership. Clearly, the Soviet Union was not in a position to undertake such negotiations, and the decision in May 1990 to grant observer status was thus special and unusual treatment.

13. The discussion here is limited to the trading system, but analogous situations of less than universal participation exist in the international financial and development fields as well.

14. The speech was given in the East Room of the White House and was distributed as a White House press release.

15. The quote is from Lim Keng, Malaysian minister of industries (*Far Eastern Economic Review,* January 31, 1991, p. 32).

16. Initial membership consisted of the United States, Canada, Japan, South Korea, Australia, New Zealand, and the six ASEAN countries. For an assessment of the Canberra meeting and the prospects of APEC from the vantage of 1990, see Ernest H. Preeg, "Rationale, Objectives, and Modalities," in *Asia Pacific Economic Cooperation: The Challenge Ahead,* ed. Richard L. Grant, et al. (Washington, D.C.: CSIS, 1990), 13–35.

17. The Economic Strategy Institute in Washington conducted the study. The administration disagreed, based on a separate analysis by the Australian Centre for International Economics. See the *Journal of Commerce,* October 24, 1990.

18. Quoted in the *Journal of Commerce,* March 13, 1990.

19. The initial proposal by Minister Crosbie, accompanied by media background material, was issued as a press release in Geneva on April 11, 1990; Minister Crosbie amplified his thinking in "My Plan for a World Trade Organization," *International Economy,* June/July 1990, pp. 40–43.

20. John H. Jackson, *Restructuring the GATT System* (London: Royal Institute of International Affairs, 1990). The book was the product of a public-private-sector study group sponsored by Chatham House. It began deliberations in mid-1989 and thus provided seminal thinking for later official discussions. Jackson also circulated a memorandum to a few "Interested Persons," dated April 30, 1990, with a five-page summary of his proposal for a WTO.

21. Reported in the *Financial Times,* October 2, 1990. Foreign Minister Reinaldo Figueredo of Venezuela announced the proposal. The other countries supporting it were Argentina, Brazil, Egypt, India, Indonesia, Jamaica, Malaysia, Mexico, Nigeria, Peru, Senegal, Yugoslavia, and Zimbabwe.

22. A report of the EC response appears in *Inside U.S. Trade,* June 29, 1990.

23. Ibid.

24. The text of de Zeeuw's report appears in *Inside U.S. Trade,* July 6, 1990.

25. *Financial Times,* July 20, 1990.

26. A French delegate persuaded the GATT secretariat director for agriculture, who also happened to be French, to have the translator change the French version from "a means" to "one of several means." It was clumsy on the part of the French because it was bound to be challenged by others, as it was in the concluding session of the TNC. It also damaged the credibility of the secretariat since the director-general, when he found out about it after the fact, did not reverse his director's impropriety but let the French version stand on the grounds that the English text was definitive.

27. Distributed as an informal press release, July 26, 1990.

28. The Dunkel statement, in this and succeeding quotes, appears in *NUR,* no. 39, July 30, 1990.

29. Hugo Paeman, speaking at a briefing on July 24, 1990.

30. The authorities were less successful in deflecting environmental activists who distributed leaflets critical of the GATT trading system under the heading GATTastrophe. See the topical addendum to chap. 6.

31. The all-German elections had been scheduled the previous July with no apparent regard for the fact that the date fell a day before the GATT ministerial.

Later consideration of postponing the GATT ministerial until January proved impractical because, among other reasons, adequate hotel space would not be available in Brussels.

32. The Andriessen and Ruggiero quotes are from the *Journal of Commerce,* November 16, 1990.

33. This early edition of the *Financial Times* was corrected in later editions, but too late to benefit breakfast readers in Brussels. American journalists took advantage of the transatlantic time difference and filed the correct story.

34. They would have been better off to maintain the low profile they had assumed up to that point. By spring 1991, South Korea had officially acknowledged the need to be forthcoming in agriculture while the Japanese continued to drop hints that ultimately they would liberalize rice imports to some extent.

35. *NUR,* no. 44, December 12, 1990.

36. Antidumping, subsidies, and trade-related investment measures are parts of the ultimate Uruguay Round agreement that were likely to have been dropped or treated minimally in a hurried conclusion after Brussels. The services agreement would have been less complete and most market-access commitments would have been left for post-Uruguay Round negotiations. Tariff reductions would have been much smaller and the creation of a World Trade Organization, at most, agreed in principle for later, uncertain negotiation.

37. *Wall Street Journal,* December 10, 1990.

38. *Journal of Commerce,* December 18, 1990.

39. December 8, 1990.

40. *Financial Times,* December 7, 1990.

41. *New York Times,* December 4, 1990.

42. *International Herald Tribune,* December 1–2, 1990. The Americans quoted were Michael Aho of the Council on Foreign Relations and Robert Hormats of Goldman Sachs International.

43. Richard N. Gardner, *Sterling-Dollar Diplomacy* (Oxford: Oxford University Press, 1956), p. 349.

44. A 1955 attempt to establish an Organization for Trade Cooperation, a scaled down ITO, also failed to get congressional approval. In 1965, Part IV of the GATT was added, which dealt with developing-country participation.

45. The original formulation of a GATT-Plus initiative dates from 1976. It appears in a study by the Atlantic Council, GATT *Plus: A Proposal for Trade Reform* (New York: Praeger, 1976).

46. There were differences of view within the secretariat as to how to launch the new mechanism, and Director-General Dunkel began cautiously, avoiding pointed criticism. This changed with the review of the European Community trade policy in April 1991, which sharply criticized the Community's highly discriminatory practices. The report received widespread press coverage and drew an official response from Brussels labeling it "unbalanced."

47. Gary Clyde Hufbauer, *The Free Trade Debate,* (New York: Priority Press for the Twentieth Century Fund, 1989), p. 154. The Task Force split in its recommendation. Seven members supported the call for such an OECD free-trade initiative while the other five espoused general objectives related to bilateral managed trade. Nobody looked to the GATT as the principal focus for post-Uruguay Round negotiations.

48. The hearing was held on April 18, 1991.

49. There were several proposals in the United States for such a bilateral trade balance approach, mostly related to Japan. Among the more noteworthy were the Gephardt amendment to the 1988 trade act, which was later revised into Section Super 301; an article in *Foreign Affairs,* summer 1988, by former secretaries of state Henry Kissinger and Cyrus Vance; and a report by the private-sector Advisory Committee on Trade Policy and Negotiations (ACTPN), *Analysis of the U.S.-Japan Trade Problem,* 1988.

50. American Society of International Law, Proceedings of the 86th Annual Meeting, Washington, D.C., April 1-4, 1992, p. 87.

Chapter 6

1. Significantly, Japan and South Korea also gave tacit agreement to the negotiating platform, including its explicit, binding commitment on market access, since both would later backtrack on any commitment to liberalize their rice markets. In the end, they did accept some market access for rice.

2. Statement by the AFL-CIO Executive Council on U.S.-Mexico Free Trade Agreement, February 20, 1991, Bal Harbour, Florida.

3. Press release, March 27, 1991, from the office of the house majority leader.

4. From an op-ed piece, "Don't Jump the Fast Track," *Wall Street Journal,* April 25, 1991.

5. The party vote on fast track in the Senate was Democrats 23 for and 32 against, Republicans 38 for and 6 against. In the House the vote was Democrats 92 for and 173 against, Republicans 142 for and 20 against.

6. Before the Senate Foreign Relations Committee, April 11, 1991. This lengthy, tightly reasoned presentation of the rationale for a NAFTA was generally considered the definitive statement of administration policy on the subject.

7. *Journal of Commerce,* July 18, 1991.

8. The low U.S. priority on tariff cuts at the time of the Punta meeting was based on the fact that tariffs were on average already very low, at least in the industrialized countries, and that changes in relative prices from exchange rate adjustments, which had swung widely since the early 1980s, would far outweigh the relative price effects of tariff reductions. This complacent attitude continued until 1990, when private-sector interests became more vocal.

9. From a speech in Bombay by Commerce Ministry official Anwarul Hoda, as reported in the *Journal of Commerce,* August 30, 1991. Hoda would later become a deputy director-general in the GATT secretariat.

10. Other "disciplines" under negotiation in the Uruguay Round included commitments to undertake a structural adjustment program and to consult with interested third parties beforehand, neither of which was part of the EC-Japan accord. The EC-Japan accord was accommodated in the final Uruguay Round agreement on safeguards by allowing each participant one exception to the agreed provisions.

11. The fast-track procedure provided for a ninety-day consultative period before the agreement was formally submitted to the Congress and then for up to sixty legislative days for the Congress to take its final vote. The presidential nominating conventions in July and August would reduce the number of legislative days in those months.

12. *Journal of Commerce,* August 19, 1991, quoting a statement of Mrs. Hills of July 31.

13. *Journal of Commerce,* September 23, 1991.

14. A blocking majority for EC voting on these agricultural issues would consist of two large countries and one small country or one large country and three small countries.

15. *Financial Times,* September 17, 1991.

16. *Journal of Commerce,* October 16, 1991.

17. *Economist,* October 19, 1991.

18. *Financial Times,* November 11, 1991.

19. Ibid., December 12, 1991.

20. *Journal of Commerce,* December 20, 1991. The quote is from ATMI Executive Vice President Carlos Moore.

21. Office of the U.S. Trade Representative, press release, December 18, 1991.

22. Statement by Arthur Dunkel, chairman of the Trade Negotiations Committee, Geneva, December 20, 1991.

23. For an account of the Eric Wyndham White package deal in the Kennedy Round, see Ernest H. Preeg *Traders and Diplomats: An Analysis of the Kennedy Round of Negotiations under the General Agreement on Tariffs and Trade* (Washington, D.C.: Brookings Institution, 1970), pp. 189–95.

24. Dunkel Draft Final Act, p. L-15, December 20, 1991.

25. Statement by Arthur Dunkel, chairman of the Trade Negotiations Committee, Geneva, December 20, 1991.

26. *Financial Times,* December 19, 1991.

27. Office of the U.S. Trade Representative, press release, December 20, 1991.

28. *Washington Post,* December 24, 1991.

29. From a speech by George Bush on January 13, 1992, before the American Farm Bureau Association in Kansas City.

30. *Financial Times,* January 16, 1992.

31. *Wall Street Journal,* July 8, 1992.

32. *Financial Times,* October 24, 1992.

33. *Wall Street Journal,* November 6, 1992.

34. Ibid., November 5, 1992.

35. Ibid., November 6, 1992.

36. *Journal of Commerce,* November 17, 1992.

37. *Economist,* November 14, 1992, p. 51.

38. Associated Press, November 20, 1992.

39. In several conversations with the Bush trade negotiators, the Clinton transition team conveyed a message: if the negotiations can be concluded, do it.

40. *Journal of Commerce,* March 9, 1993.

41. "Environment and the General Agreement on Tariffs and Trade (GATT)," briefing packet provided by the International Division of the National Wildlife Federation, Washington, D. C., dated November 15, 1990.

42. *Journal of Commerce,* June 4, 1991.

43. *Financial Times,* September 18, 1991.

44. *Financial Times,* September 18, 1991.

45. "Trade and the Environment" (GATT press release, Geneva), February 12, 1992.

46. *Wall Street Journal,* February 12, 1992.

47. UN Conference on Environment and Development, Agenda 21, Chap. 2, Rio de Janeiro, June 3–14, 1992.

48. For a summary of earlier meetings of the group, see *Trade and the Environment,* no. 001, the GATT, April 1, 1993. The text of the chairman's report of December 3, 1992, is included.

49. See *Inside U.S. Trade,* special report, October 15, 1993. The quote is from p. S-3.

Chapter 7

1. *Journal of Commerce,* January 20 and 28, 1993.

2. Ibid., January 29, 1993.

3. Ibid., February 1, 1993.

4. See Laura D'Andrea Tyson, *Who's Bashing Whom? Trade Conflict in High-Technology Industries* (Washington, D.C.: Institute for International Economics, 1992), pp. 2, 5, 258.

5. See *Washington Post,* September 15, 1993. The statement was made when former presidents Bush, Carter, and Ford met with President Clinton to support NAFTA.

6. See Ernest H. Preeg, *Washington Quarterly,* "Who's Benefiting Whom? A Trade Agenda for High-Technology Industries," pp. 17–33, for an analysis of these trade developments in high-technology industries.

7. See Tyson, *Who's Bashing Whom?* p. 1.

8. See the *Economist,* February 20, 1993, p. 29.

9. *Journal of Commerce,* March 16, 1993.

10. U.S.I.A., Foreign Media Reaction, special report, April 1, 1993.

11. *Financial Times,* July 2, 1993.

12. A specific criticism held that Dunkel avoided negotiating changes in his draft text during 1992 for fear it would unravel when considerable further work was clearly needed. However, in view of the continued U.S.-EC impasse over agriculture through the fall of 1992 and the increasing likelihood of President Bush's election defeat, Dunkel's hesitancy had some justification.

13. See *New York Times* and *Financial Times,* July 8, 1993.

14. *Journal of Commerce,* July 15, 1993.

15. An unpublished, firsthand account of the final negotiating period—which is drawn on throughout this and the following section of the chapter—is by GATT Deputy Director-General Warren Lavorel, entitled "Endgame" and written shortly after December 15.

16. GATT press release, July, 1993.

17. *Journal of Commerce,* June 30, 1993. The quote refers to the upcoming Tokyo summit meeting but had broader implications for the post-Tokyo negotiations.

18. See *Executive News Service,* April 6, 1993, and *Journal of Commerce,* May 14, 1993.

19. *Journal of Commerce,* June 11, 1993.

20. *New York Times* and *Wall Street Journal,* August 30, 1993. The quote is based on a Kohl interview published in *Die Zeit am Sontag,* August 29, 1993.

21. *Journal of Commerce,* September 22, 1993.

22. *Washington Post,* September 22, 1993; Office of the U.S. Trade Representative, press release, September 21, 1993.

23. The commitment appears in a November 16 letter to Chairman John Spratt (D-S.C.) of the Textile Caucus and nine other House members.

24. The House Democratic vote on NAFTA was 156–102 against, the Republican vote 132–43 in favor, and one independent voted against. The Senate Democratic vote was 28–27 against, the Republican vote 34–10 in favor.

25. At the Seattle conference Secretary of State Warren Christopher was more direct: "I think that it will not be lost on European leaders that . . . the countries of the Asia Pacific are working together toward trade liberalization." If Europe fails to move the Uruguay Round negotiations forward, he said, APEC may well "turn to other measures to achieve more open trading." Quoted in the *Wall Street Journal,* November 19, 1993.

26. See the *Financial Times,* November 22, 25, 26, 1993, and the *New York Times,* December 2, 1993, for the various quotes. Craig Whitney describes the Kohl/Mitterand relationship in the *New York Times,* December 14, 1993. He includes the key point: "The Germans made it clear to the United States that in talks officially being conducted by European Community negotiators they could not be asked to choose between their relationship with the French and their relationship with the Americans . . . nor did the Clinton Administration ask the Germans to pass tough messages to Paris."

27. The shift in the base period also helped U.S. oilseed exporters by permitting a higher level of U.S. export subsidies, particularly well received since U.S. oilseed exports to the European market had not fared well under the Blair House Accord. However, higher U.S. export subsidies for oilseeds would adversely affect Brazil and other third-country exporters, and they rightly complained that the bilateral U.S.-EU deal was in this respect at their expense.

28. *Wall Street Journal,* December 16, 1993.

29. *Financial Times,* December 10, 1993.

30. *Journal of Commerce,* December 16, 1993. There was also agreement to continue negotiations up to April 15, 1994, to improve market-access commitments in the textiles sector by India and other exporting countries, but nothing was forthcoming until much later.

31. The United States never had a clear position on "green light" subsidies, though it tried to minimize them. The Dunkel Draft had included such permitted subsidies for regional policies and R&D (at the 50 and 25 percent levels) while excluding earlier proposals for environmental and structural-adjustment related subsidies. When the United States belatedly proposed increasing the percentages on R&D to 75 and 50 percent, however, developing countries insisted on inclusion of environmentally based subsidies as well, and in the end they prevailed (see note 34 below).

32. Accounts of this last day of U.S.-EU negotiations appear in the *Financial Times,* the *Washington Post,* and the *Wall Street Journal,* all December 15, 1993, and the *New York Times,* December 16, 1993.

33. Although the WTO was the last issue formally negotiated in the Uruguay Round, one important loose end remained in contention through the afternoon

of December 15, and is related to a touching anecdote. With agreement on the WTO in the morning of December 15, the eight "survivors"—the only senior negotiators who had been at Punta del Este and were still engaged at the conclusion—met for lunch. They were Anwarul Hoda (India) and Warren Lavorel (United States), by then both in the GATT secretariat, country delegates Michael Cartland (Hong Kong), Pierre Louis Girard (Switzerland), Felipe Jaramillo (Colombia) Julio Lacarte-Muro (Uruguay), and Christer Manhusen (Sweden)—who each had been away for part of the negotiations—and EU veteran negotiator Paul Tran, the only resident delegate from start until finish. Before the lunch began, however, Hoda and Lavorel were called back to Sutherland's office to confront the final minicrisis. The EU had withdrawn some previous market-access offers on leather goods, beef, and oranges, and in response Brazil, Uruguay, and other Latin American nations threatened to withdraw from the overall final agreement. Peter Sutherland, through phone calls to Brussels and Latin America capitals, finally convinced the EU to restore sufficient offers to satisfy the Latin Americans.

34. The United States, responding to strong pressure by the Intel company, including a call from its chairman to President Clinton, wanted a last-minute change to exempt computer chips from the compulsory licensing provisions of the IPR agreement. To obtain this, the United States had to agree to a Canadian request for a revision concerning subsidies by provincial governments and to developing-country requests to exempt certain environmentally based subsidies from countervailing duties.

35. *Washington Post,* December 16, 1993.

36. The media-reaction assessment is based on selected U.S. press coverage and a survey of about 170 reports from other countries contained in *USIA Media Reaction,* December 15, 16, 22, 1993. All of the non-U.S. quotes are taken as translated in the USIA source.

37. The only parts of the overall agreement that were open to selective application and therefore not a condition for WTO membership were the government procurement agreement, the international dairy arrangement, and the arrangement regarding bovine meat.

38. From the *Washington Post,* December 16, one of several sources.

39. The December 15, 1993, agreement set the date for WTO entry into force as "not later than July 1, 1995," and participants later agreed upon January 1, 1995.

40. The language on appropriate recommendations comes from a TNC decision of December 15, 1993, as noted in the Marrakesh ministerial decision.

41. The full listing was presented by Chairman Bonilla as follows: "Ministers representing a number of participating delegations stressed the importance they attach to their requests for an examination of the relationship between the trading system and internationally recognized labor standards, the relationship between immigration policies and international trade, trade and competition policy, including rules on export financing and restrictive business practices, trade and investment, regionalism, the integration between trade policies and policies relating to financial monetary matters, including debt, commodity markets, international trade and company law, the establishment of a mechanism for compensation for the erosion of preferences, the link between trade, development, politi-

cal stability and the alleviation of poverty, and unilateral or extraterritorial trade measures" (GATT, MTN.TNC/MIN (94) 6, April 15, 1994).

42. *Focus: Gatt Newsletter,* no. 107, special issue, "The WTO is Born," May 1994, p. 47.

43. See the *Washington Post,* April 7, 1994. The quotation is attributed to Aalyan Singh, a leader of the Hindu-Nationalist Bhartya Janata Party (BJP).

44. *Journal of Commerce,* January 3, 1995.

Chapter 8

1. A "concession" in this traditional GATT bargaining context means a reduction in import barriers and thus greater competition for domestic producers. Free-trade theorists are quick to point out that such reductions in trade barriers are in fact benefits to the consumer, but in the political context of trade negotiations the particular interests of producers and related labor, in exporting and import-competing industries, far outweigh the general interests of the consumer or the economy at large. This critical reality underlies the concept of reciprocal reductions in trade barriers within GATT rounds, pursued by politically hard-headed free traders.

2. Aside from agriculture, the important area of negotiation where the Dunkel Draft was significantly weakened was the antidumping agreement, the focus of extreme U.S. pressure during the final weeks of negotiation. In most other areas the final text was stronger than the Dunkel Draft.

3. A far more detailed assessment of the agreement appears in Jeffrey J. Schott *The Uruguay Round: An Assessment,* with Johanna W. Buurman (Washington, D.C.: Institute for International Economics, 1994), which was of great benefit in drafting this section. Schott assigns grades to each of the major sectors of the agreement, including an overall grade of B+, based on the most feasible and desirable outcome as earlier prescribed by him in mid-1990 in anticipation of the scheduled conclusion of the negotiation at Brussels in December. The comments made in chapter 8 here, however, assess the results more in terms of expectations at the 1986 Punta del Este meeting, where the objectives were adopted by ministers. From this perspective, the final results almost all score better than from the mid-1990 Schott benchmark—which would justify an even higher overall grade.

4. These and subsequent figures on market access are from *NUR,* April 12, 1994, "Increases in Market Access Resulting from the Uruguay Round," and Anwarul Hoda, "Trade Liberalization," in *The New World Trading System: Readings* (Paris: OECD, 1994), pp. 41–56.

5. The phrase "a reduction in trade barriers" is used loosely and is meant to include all "trade-distorting measures" such as export subsidies.

6. "Economywide Effects of the Uruguay Round," GATT Background Paper, December 3, 1993; *Assessing the Effects of the Uruguay Round* (Paris: OECD, October 1993); and *The Results of the Uruguay Round of Multilateral Trade Negotiations* (Geneva: GATT, November 1994). The figures in the latter document are drawn from estimates made by three economists in the GATT secretariat, which are explained in detail in a paper by the three, Joseph F. Francois, Bradley McDonald,

274

and Häkan Nordström, "The Uruguay Round: A Global General Equilibrium Assessment," November 4, 1994 (revised).

7. An assessment of the Tokyo Round tariff reductions suggested "a figure five times as large as static welfare gains" (William R. Cline et al., *Trade Negotiations in the Tokyo Round* [Washington, D.C.: Brookings Institution, 1978], p. 79). A study of the effects of EC-92 implies dynamic effects in the order of three to four times the static effects (Richard Baldwin, "The Growth Effects of 1992," *Economic Policy*, October 1989, pp. 248–81). A 1993 report prepared for the Office of the U.S. Trade Representative by DRI/McGraw Hill, "Impacts of Trade Liberalization under the Uruguay Round," produced a combined static and dynamic income gain of 4.5 percent. The U.S. International Trade Commission concluded, "the long-run dynamic effects of trade liberalization may be two to three times the static estimates" (*Potential Impact on the U.S. Economy and Industries of the* GATT *Uruguay Round Agreements,* USITC publication 2790, June 1994, vol. 1, p. I-13). For a survey of recent literature, see *The Dynamic Effects of Trade Liberalization: A Survey,* USITC publication 2608, February 1993.

8. The $116 billion figure includes some former communist countries "in transition," but they account for less than a tenth of the total.

9. These figures are from Ernest H. Preeg, "Who's Benefitting Whom? A Trade Agenda for High Technology Industries," *The Washington Quarterly,* Fall 1993, pp. 17–33.

10. John H. Williams, "The Theory of International Trade Reconsidered," originally published in *Economic Journal* 39 (June 1929) and reprinted in *Postwar Monetary Plans and Other Essays* (New York: Alfred A. Knopf, 1947), in which these quotations appear on pp. 152–53.

11. For example, a two-thirds majority is required to propose amendments to the Uruguay Round agreement, but acceptance of such amendments for key parts of the agreement requires a unanimous vote. Interpretation of, or waiver from, parts of the agreement requires a three-fourths majority. Procedural, budget, and other routine decisions are taken by simple majority if a consensus is not reached.

Chapter 9

1. Strengthened standards for intellectual-property rights as well as improved access to the Japanese market for certain categories of imports are examples of nondiscriminatory market-opening. More recent Japanese quantitative commitments in the automotive and cellular phone sectors were directly linked to U.S. companies. For a full account of the Section 301 experience, see Thomas O. Bayard and Kimberly Ann Elliott, *Reciprocity and Retaliation in U.S. Trade Policy* (Washington, D.C.: Institute for International Economics, 1994).

Chapter 10

1. Classic Editions (New York: Bantam, 1946), pp. vii–xiv.

2. A summary of empirical studies supporting the relation between trade and growth appears in the GATT secretariat background paper, "The Growth Effects of the Uruguay Round," December 3, 1993, pp. 14–15.

3. *Washington Post,* March 20, 1994, p. A34.

4. The population percentages for 1991 overstate somewhat the future share held by the projected groupings of industrialized democracies since population growth is higher in poorer countries.

5. Francis Fukuyama, "The End of History?" *National Interest,* summer 1989, p. 4. He elaborated his arguments in a follow-up book, *The End of History and the Last Man* (New York: Free Press, 1992).

6. Jeffrey E. Garten, *A Cold Peace: America, Japan, Germany, and the Struggle for Supremacy* (New York: Twentieth Century Fund, 1992); Lester Thurow, *Head to Head: The Coming Economic Battle among Japan, Europe, and America* (New York: William Morrow, 1992); and Laura D'Andrea Tyson, *Who's Bashing Whom? Trade Conflict in High-Technology Industries* (Washington, D.C.: Institute for International Economics, 1992). Tyson was named chair of the President's Council of Economic Advisers, and Garten became undersecretary of the Department of Commerce.

7. Edward N. Luttwak, *The Endangered American Dream: How to Stop the United States from Becoming a Third-World Country and How to Win the Geoeconomic Struggle for Industrial Supremacy* (New York: Simon & Schuster, 1993), p. 36.

8. Act V, scene 1.

Index

Ad-Hoc Working Group on Trade and Environmentally Sustainable Development, 147

AFL-CIO, 129, 130, 131, 154, 181

Aggregate Measure of Support (AMS), 133–34

Agricultural Adjustment Act of 1933 (U.S.), 93

agricultural products: bananas, 180; dairy products, 26, 93; decline in exports of, 13, 14; disposing of EC grain surplus, 167; grain, 68–69, 93, 94–95; Japanese ban on rice imports, 111, 168–69; Korean ban on rice imports, 168–69, 177; ministerial meeting of 1982 on, 35; as not covered by GATT, 11; oilseeds, 137, 143–45, 163, 189, 272n.27; wheat, 93, 167; white wine, 143, 189

agricultural subsidies (farm subsidies): Brussels ministerial conference on, 118, 119–20; de Zeeuw report on, 115; Dunkel Draft on, 140; EC on, 1, 7–8, 26, 60, 82, 84, 92, 93–99, 111, 114–15, 118, 119–20, 137–38; European grain subsidies, 93, 94–95; ministerial meeting of 1982 on, 35; at Montreal midterm conference, 84, 85, 92; negotiating committee profile on, 114–15; at Punta del Este meeting, 4, 60; Reagan on, 1, 7; at Tokyo Round, 28, 93; U.S. on, 1, 4, 7–8, 26, 60, 82, 84, 92, 93–99, 111, 114–15, 118, 119–20, 137–38; Zero 2000 proposal, 86–87, 96, 97, 127–28

agriculture, 93–99, 127–52; Aggregate Measure of Support, 133–34; Andriessen, 87, 118, 121, 144; Blair House Accord on, 143–47, 155, 159, 163–64, 165–67, 189, 242; Brussels ministerial conference on, 118, 119–20, 127–28; change in EC policy at Strasbourg, 128; chemical fertilizer use, 150; de Zeeuw report on, 115; Dunkel Draft on, 140, 141; Franco-German confrontation on, 135–36; French opposition to farm sector liberalization, 22, 60, 70, 98, 155, 190; GATT committee agreement on, 51–52; green box, 137, 140, 142, 192; at G-7 Munich summit, 141; Kohl on EC farm policy, 136; at Montreal ministerial meeting, 86–88, 91–92; negotiating committee profile on, 114–15; at Punta del Este, 4, 7–8, 60, 247–48; revolutionary EC proposals of January 1991, 127; sanitary and phytosanitary measures, 147–48, 171, 199–200; total world cost of farm supports, 94; Uruguay Round final agreement on, 191–93; U.S. Zero 2000 proposal for, 86–87, 96, 97, 127–28. *See also* agricultural products; agricultural subsidies; Cairns group; Common Agricultural Policy; MacSharry, Ray

Aho, Michael, 268n.44

aircraft, 167, 171, 198, 211

American Textile Manufacturers Institute, 138

AMS (Aggregate Measure of Support), 133–34

Amstutz, Daniel, 87, 96

Anderson, Kym, 265n.38

Andriessen, Frans, 87, 118, 121, 144

Anell, Lars, 69, 104, 132